TRAVELER'S ECUADOR COMPANION

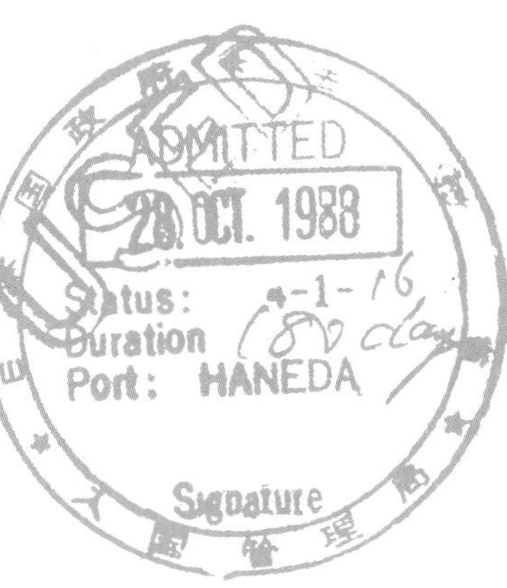

The 1998–1999 Traveler's Companions
ARGENTINA • AUSTRALIA • BALI • CALIFORNIA • CANADA • CHINA • COSTA RICA • CUBA • EASTERN CANADA • ECUADOR • FLORIDA • HAWAII • HONG KONG • INDIA • INDONESIA • JAPAN • KENYA • MALAYSIA & SINGAPORE • MEDITERRANEAN FRANCE • MEXICO • NEPAL • NEW ENGLAND • NEW ZEALAND • PERU • PHILIPPINES • PORTUGAL • RUSSIA • SPAIN • THAILAND • TURKEY • VENEZUELA • VIETNAM, LAOS AND CAMBODIA • WESTERN CANADA

Traveler's Ecuador Companion
First Published 1998
The Globe Pequot Press
6 Business Park Road, P.O. Box 833
Old Saybrook, CT 06475-0833
www.globe.pequot.com

ISBN: 0-7627-0251-6

By arrangement with Kümmerly+Frey AG, Switzerland

Created, edited and produced by
Allan Amsel Publishing, 53, rue Beaudouin
27700 Les Andelys, France. E-mail: Allan.Amsel@wanadoo.fr
Editor in Chief: Allan Amsel
Editor: Fiona Nichols
Original design concept: Hon Bing-wah
Picture editor and designer: Matt Bargell

ACKNOWLEDGEMENTS
The author thanks all those who have helped with this book in various ways, especially Francisco Mallinson, Victor Eastman and Alexander Linford.

Printed by Samwha Printing Co. Ltd., Seoul, Korea

TRAVELER'S ECUADOR COMPANION

by Derek Davies

Photographed by Robert Holmes

Kümmerly+Frey

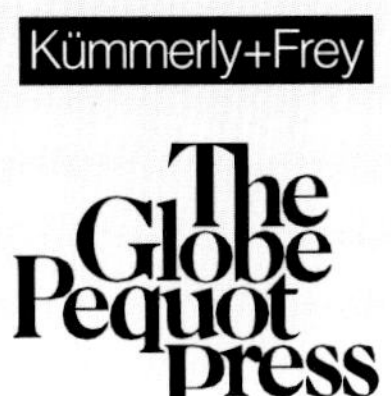

Contents

TRAVELER'S ECUADOR COMPANION

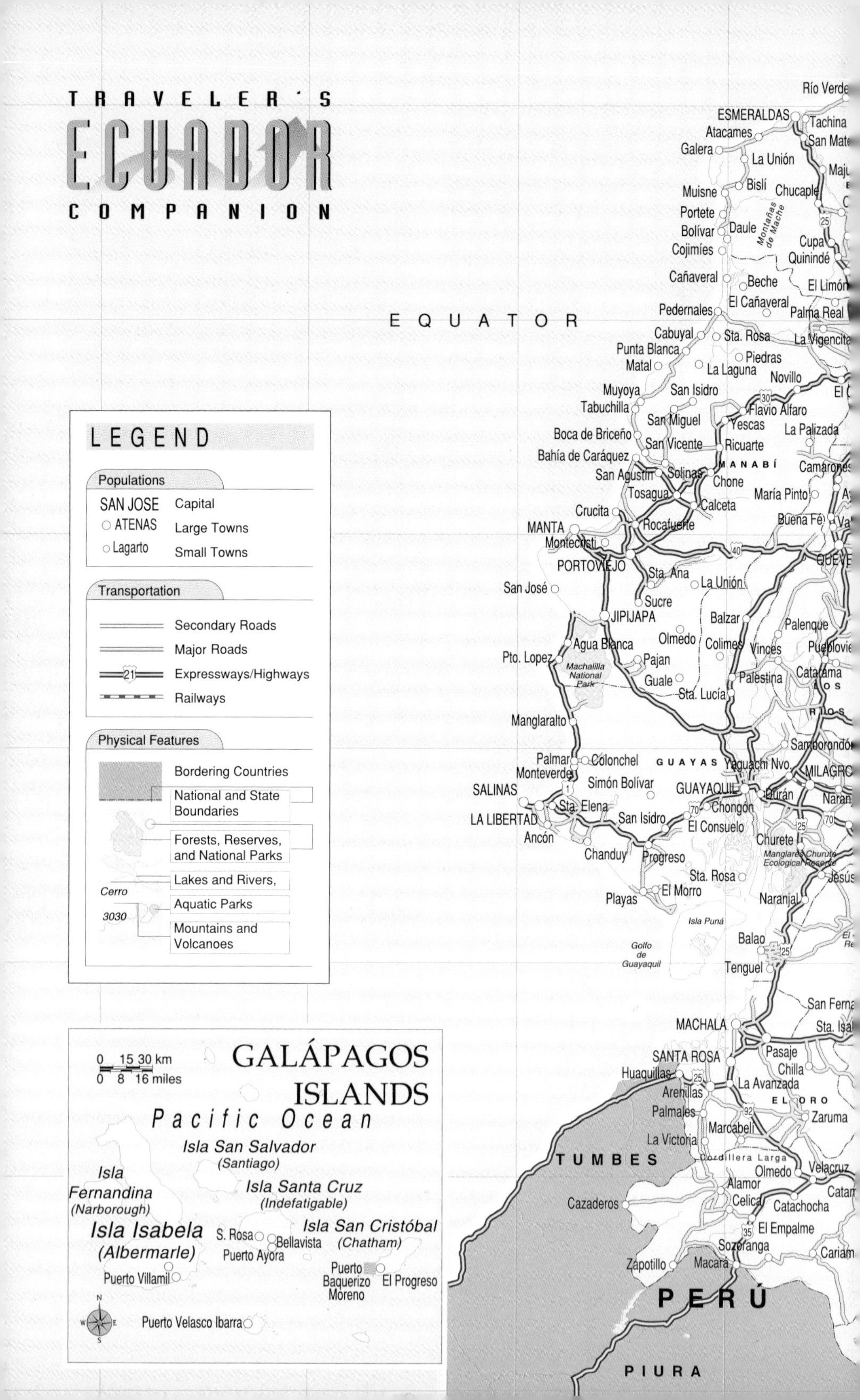

EQUATOR

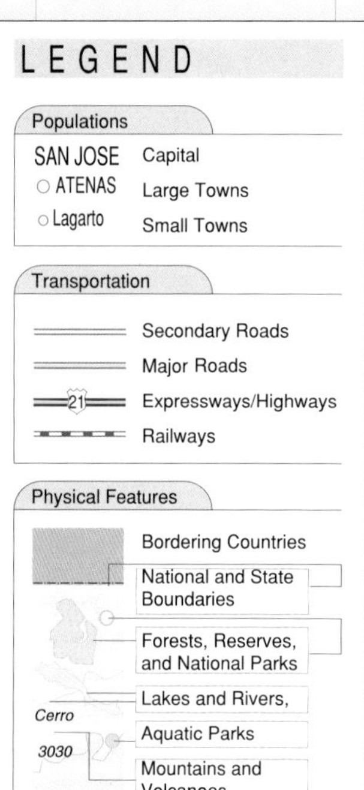

GALÁPAGOS ISLANDS

0 15 30 km
0 8 16 miles
Pacific Ocean
Isla San Salvador (Santiago)
Isla Fernandina (Narborough)
Isla Santa Cruz (Indefatigable)
Isla Isabela (Albermarle)
Isla San Cristóbal (Chatham)
S. Rosa
Bellavista
Puerto Ayora
Puerto Villamil
Puerto Baquerizo Moreno
El Progreso
Puerto Velasco Ibarra

Río Verde
ESMERALDAS
Tachina
Atacames
San Mate
Galera
La Unión
Muisne
Bislí
Chucaple
Portete
Montañas de Mache
Bolívar
Daule
Cupa
Cojimíes
Quinindé
Cañaveral
Beche
El Limón
Pedernales
El Cañaveral
Palma Real
Cabuyal
Sta. Rosa
La Vigencita
Punta Blanca
Piedras
Matal
La Laguna
Novillo
Muyoya
San Isidro
30
Tabuchilla
Flavio Alfaro
San Miguel
Yescas
La Palizada
Boca de Briceño
San Vicente
Ricuarte
Bahía de Caráquez
MANABÍ
Camarones
San Agustín
Solinas
Chone
Tosagua
María Pinto
Calceta
Crucita
Buena Fé
MANTA
Rocafuerte
Montecristi
40
PORTOVIEJO
QUEVE
Sta. Ana
San José
La Unión
Sucre
JIPIJAPA
Balzar
Palenque
Olmedo
Colimes
Vinces
Pueblovie
Agua Blanca
Pto. Lopez
Pajan
Machalilla National Park
Guale
Palestina
Catarama
Sta. Lucía
LOS RÍOS
Manglaralto
Samborondón
Palmar
Colonchel
GUAYAS
Yaguachi Nvo.
MILAGRO
Monteverde
Simón Bolívar
SALINAS
1
GUAYAQUIL
Durán
Naran
Sta. Elena
70
Chongón
LA LIBERTAD
San Isidro
El Consuelo
25
70
Ancón
Churete
Chanduy
Progreso
Manglares Churute Ecological Reserve
Sta. Rosa
Jesús
El Morro
Playas
Naranjal
Isla Puná
Golfo de Guayaquil
Balao
25
Tenguel
San Ferna
MACHALA
Sta. Isa
Pasaje
SANTA ROSA
Chilla
Huaquillas
25
La Avanzada
Arenillas
EL ORO
Palmales
92
Zaruma
Marcabelí
La Victoria
TUMBES
Cordillera Larga
Olmedo
Velacruz
Alamor
Catam
Cazaderos
Celica
Catachocha
El Empalme
35
Sozoranga
Cariam
Zapotillo
Macará
PERÚ
PIURA

NARIÑO
COLOMBIA
El Viento
Mataje
San Lorenzo
Tobar Donoso
Cayapas Mataje National Park
Awa Indian Preserve
Carondelet
Urbina
Alto Tambo
Maldonado
TULCÁN
Lita
San Miguel
Guadaul
CHARCHI
Cotocachi-Cayapas Ecological Reserve
El Ángel
San Gabriel
Cahuasquí
Mira
Bolívar
El Rosario
Apuela
Pimampiro
IMBABURA
IBARRA
PUTUMAYO
La Bonita
Buenavista
La Barquilla
Pto. Colón
San Miguel
Selva Alegre
Otavalo
Peguchi
Chespi
Olmedo
Cayambe-Coca Ecological Reserve
Santa Cecilia
Lago Agrio
Montepa
Sansahuario
La Delicia
Puluahua Geobotanical Reserve
Puéllaro
Ayora
Lumbaquí
SUCUMBÍOS
Centinela
La Armenia
Otón
Cangahui
Cuyabeno Wildlife Reserve
El Palmar
PICHINCHA
Nono
Ascázubi
Manual Galindo
Tarapoa
Pto. Bolívar
COLORADOS
QUITO
Zaruquí
San Cristóbal
Río Guajalito Reserve
Pifo
El Chaco
Sumaco Galeros National Park
Cuyabeno
Limoncocha Biological Reserve
S. Juan
Sangolquí
El Paraíso
Zábalo
Terere
Alóag
Pasochoa Forest Res.
Baeza
San José de Payamino
Coca
Aloasí
Machachi
Antisana Ecological Reserve
Sumaco
Garzacocha
Pava Isla
Zancudo
Calupiña
Sumaco Forest Reserve
Pto. Colón
Sinchi Chicta
Sigchos
Cotopaxi National Park
El Progresso
Las Palmas
NAPO
Ancayacu
Isinliví
Narupa
Avila
Bellavista
Tiputini
Mulaló
Boliche Nat. Rec. Area
Pto. San Miguel
Guaytacama
Cord. Galeras
Sarayacu
Humoyacu
Ballesteros
LATACUNGA
Yasuni National Park
Pilaló
Pujilí
Tena
Campana Cocha
PILLARO
Pto. Napo
Llanganates National Park
Huaorani Reserve
Piatua
Durán
Tihuano
Reparado
Mihuanoyacu
AMBATO
Río Negro
Sta. Clara
Cochaquinga
Quero
Pelileo
San Antonio
TUNGURAHUA
Chimborazo Fauna Reserve
Puyo
Villano
Conanaco
El Altar
Chino Playa
Guaranda
Guano
RIOBAMBA
Bolívar
Primavera
Cajabamba
Chambo
Sarayaquillu
PASTAZA
La Esperanza
Conambo
Balaura
Guayusa
Sangay
Sangay National Park
Guamote
Chuitayo
Shiona
Balsaura
LORETO
CHIMBORAZO
Chiguaza
Montalvo
Sta. Rosa
Palmira
Río Tigre
Alausí
PERÚ
Chunchi
Macas
Río Corrientes
MORONA
Zhud
Sucúa
SANTIAGO
Cañar
(Santiago de) Méndez
Cushimi
Azogues
Patuca
Paute
CUENCA
Morona
Indanza
Sígsig
Cordillera Boliche
0 20 40 60 80 km
0 10 20 30 40 50 miles
Banderas
Oña
Gualaquiza
UNITED STATES OF AMERICA
MEXICO
CUBA
JAMAICA
HONDURAS
COSTA RICA
NICARAGUA
COSTA RICA
VENEZUELA
PANAMA
COLOMBIA
GALAPAGOS
ECUADOR
BRAZIL
PERU
BOLIVIA
CHILE
ARGENTINA
Los Encuentros
ZAMORA
Guayzimi
Zamora
CHINCHIPE
Podocarpus National Park
N
W
E
S
Valladolic
AMAZONAS
PERÚ

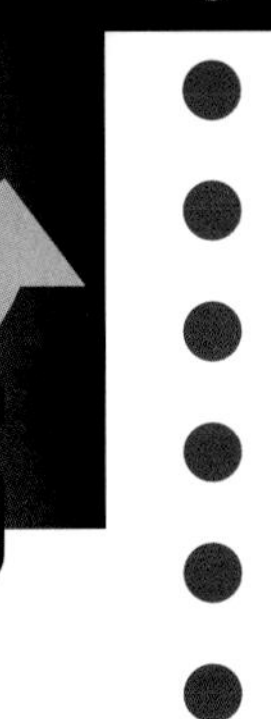

Going for Gold

THE SPANISH CONQUISTADORS OF THE SIXTEENTH CENTURY WERE OBSESSED WITH DISCOVERING THE SOURCE OF INCA GOLD when they arrived in South America. Though they never located an El Dorado, City of Gold, they found plenty of gold ornaments and jewelry made by the indigenous peoples.

Some of that gold was sent back to Spain and some of it was used to gild the interiors of Ecuador's fine churches. To admire these magnificently ornate and gilded churches for yourself, go to the Old City in Quito. At the sublime **La Compañía de Jesús**, surely one of the most beautiful churches in South America, little wealth was spared in covering the elegant columns, impressive altars and soaring ceilings with gold. The effect is so sumptuous as to be quite breathtaking. Similarly, the altar, roof and choir of the colossal **Iglesia de San Francisco**, Quito's oldest church, are richly decorated with baroque carvings and gold leaf.

For fine examples of pre-Columbian gold ornaments (made in times before Christopher Columbus's voyages to the New World at the end of the fifteenth century), visit the excellent **Museo Nacional del Banco Central del Ecuador** (see QUITO MUSEUMS, page 73). The extraordinary ceremonial gold mask from the Tolita culture, which the bank uses as a logo, is on display along with an entire salon of gold objects. You will see how techniques for working gold and platinum used by the ancient coastal cultures of Ecuador were astoundingly advanced for their times.

Hacienda Living

UNTIL QUITE RECENTLY THE PATRÓN OF HACIENDA PINSAQUÍ USED TO ENJOY RIDING ABOUT ON HIS WHITE STALLION INSIDE HIS GRAND MANSION. It was the kind of traveler's tale you heard long before you finally met the patriarch himself.

Gold from ancient artifacts, like this mask ABOVE now in the Casa de La Cultura, was melted down and used in churches such as El Sagrario LEFT in Quito.

Señor Pedro Freile would greet guests in the living room, on horseback, and ride down the stairway to the bodega bar to join them for an *aperitivo*. There he would have a tot or two in the saddle, rather in the style of a red-coated huntsman gathered with his hounds before setting off for the hunt.

Sadly, the white stallion died and now Sr. Freile is training his successor, an Arab chestnut, in the same tradition of hospitality.

One suspects there are many more stories like this about the habits of the landed gentry of Ecuador. The grand Ecuadorian haciendas were built, after all, for good living. Now many have become hotels and some of the old families are learning the tricks of the tourist trade.

Hacienda Pinsaquí dates back some 200 years. It brings to mind other palaces, such as those in northern India, princely homes where furniture and food, servants and *señores* all have that old-world charm. In the same area north of Quito, the exquisite **Hacienda Cusín** has been refurbished by its owner to a standard fit to be photographed by glossy New York lifestyle magazines. Its stable of horses is particularly well looked after.

Hacienda Guachala (also known as the Hostería Guachala), the oldest hacienda in Ecuador, has elegance but more atmosphere. It's the perfect place to film a period piece movie such is its gorgeous colonial architecture. It takes little to stimulate the imagination: You are almost there with those Spanish conquistadors as they saddle up and sally forth into the sierra.

The former monastery of **Hacienda San Agustín de Callo** offers a different atmosphere. This hostelry has a reputation as a hotel run more like a private house party, albeit a rather flamboyant one. Parts of the walls date back to the days of the Incas, and embrace stones that were once part of a temple.

Hacienda stays, which can be arranged by any travel agent specializing in Ecuador, are highly recommended for those who enjoy the pleasures of fine food, gardens, horse riding, walking and good country living (see THE HACIENDA LIFESTYLE, page 91).

Volcanic Experiences

ECUADOR HAS SOME OF THE TALLEST AND MOST ACTIVE VOLCANOES IN THE WORLD. On a clear day, traveling along the spine of the country, known as the "Avenue of Volcanoes," you will glimpse several of their lofty, snow-capped peaks.

With an almost perfectly symmetrical cone, the beautiful **Volcán Cotopaxi**, at a height of 5,897 m (19,655 ft), is the second tallest mountain in Ecuador after Mt. Chimborazu and considered to be the tallest continuously active volcano in the world. To get the feel of Cotopaxi you can drive through the wild and beautiful **Cotopaxi National Park,** and up to the parking lot on the mountain itself at 4,600 m (15,332 ft). Serious climbers continue upwards to the *refugio* where they rest before attempting to climb the peak in the early hours of the morning.

Gracious stately homes, such as Hacienda Cusín ABOVE, and numerous waterfalls, as this one in Baños LEFT, stimulate and soothe the senses of visitors to Ecuador.

Another exciting way of coming to grips, so to speak, with Cotopaxi is to take an "up hill by jeep, down hill by bike" tour. **Biking Dutchman Tours** in Quito organizes these hell-for-leather, adventures (see CENTRAL HIGHLANDS, page 113).

Ecuador is a climber's paradise but skill, experience, a guide and the right equipment are all required for the higher mountains. Contact a specialist agency for more information (see HOW TO GET THERE in TRAVELERS' TIPS, page 254).

Soak in a Spring

VOLCANIC ECUADOR OVERFLOWS WITH HOT SPRINGS, NATURAL POOLS AND SPOUTING WATERFALLS. Many are hidden deep in the jungle and are difficult to get to. Near **Miazal** in El Oriente ("The East," referring to the rainforest east of the Andes), there are twin waterfalls, one hot and one cold, like hot and cold showers. Some of the Indian tribes consider waterfalls to be sacred.

The best hot springs within reach of Quito are the **Baños de Papallacta**, two hours by bus or car from the city, just off the road which descends over the rim of the Amazon basin to Baeza. The river here feeds five clean pools ranging from very hot to refreshingly cold. In good weather the view of the snow-capped cone of Volcán Antisana is spectacular.

The small town of **Baños** is another popular hot spring destination a few hour's ride by bus from Quito. Nestled in a valley surrounded by steep, green mountains, this attractive resort has become a favored stopover on the gringo trail in recent years. The main baths are the **Baños de la Virgin** by the waterfall near the Palace Hotel at the southeast end of town. More pleasant are the baths at **El Salado**, about a mile out of town off the Ambato road, which have more pools and are less crowded.

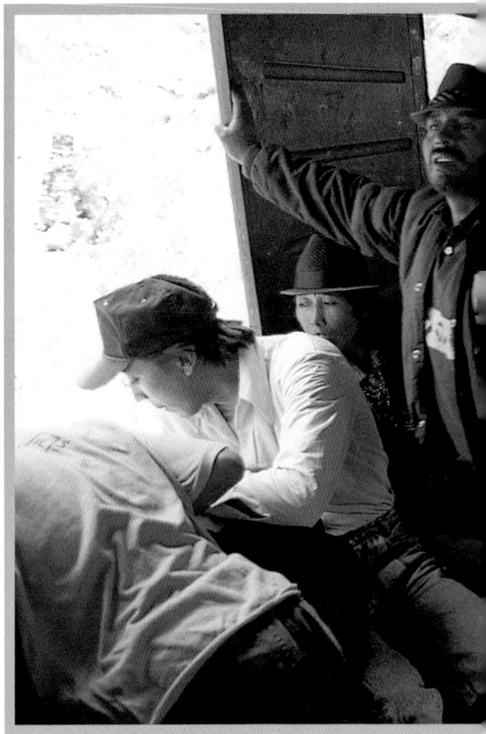

There's nothing like an early morning soak in a hot spring, followed by a shower under a cold waterfall, to set you up for the day.

Mountain Training

ECUADOR BOASTS TWO OF THE MOST THRILLING TRAIN RIDES IN THE WORLD, BOTH OF WHICH WIND UP AND DOWN THE STEEP SLOPES OF THE ANDES. Even more exciting is riding on the roof of the train, ducking your head or lying flat through tunnels and under low branches.

The route from **Ríobamba** to **Guayaquil** takes about twelve hours in

antiquated equipment. The most dramatic section is between Alausí and Bucay, known as the **Devil's Nose**, because of the switchbacks and steepness of the single track.

Under normal conditions, two types of *autoferros* (iron cars) make the vertiginous journey down the mountainside on the **Ibarra–San Lorenzo railway**. However, after damage in the recent El Niño floods there are doubts whether the track will ever be repaired.

The 200-km (124-mile) journey from an altitude of 2,210 m (6,630 ft) to sea level is spectacular and thrilling, though potentially uncomfortable. The toy-like train crosses narrow bridges over deep gorges, clings to the side of precipitous mountains and plunges in and out of some 20 dark tunnels. In a matter of seven to 10 hours (depending on the condition of the mudslide-prone, narrow gauge track) you descend from the thin cold air of the mountains to the heat and humidity of the tropical coast (see THE TRAIN TO SAN LORENZO in NORTHERN HIGHLANDS, page 109).

Buggying on the Beach

WITH SOME 2,000 KM (1,250 MILES) OF PACIFIC OCEAN COASTLINE, ECUADOR IS A PARADISE FOR BEACH LOVERS, and the best way to explore it all is by buggying down the shoreline in a four-wheel-drive vehicle.

If deserted beaches, hidden coves and isolated fishing villages are to your taste, then the coast of Ecuador will suit you well. Most beaches in Ecuador are simply long stretches of empty sand with no signs of tourism or facilities. Ecuador's beach culture has much more to do with fishing communities and shrimp farming than suntans and *discotecas*.

But things are changing. In recent years beach vacations have become increasingly popular with Ecuadorians and foreign visitors and a number of lively beach resorts have sprung up along the coast.

ABOVE: The 12-hour train ride from Ríobamba to Guayaquil is one of the world's most thrilling, particularly the steep switchback section known as Devil's Nose. LEFT: Tourism has not yet reached most of the beaches of Ecuador's Pacific coast.

Atacames in the north has a reputation as a party beach, especially on weekends and at festival times. **Canoa**, further south, is also popular with party-loving beach people, though you can escape to a 20-km (12-mile) stretch of sand if you're looking for peace and solitude.

At the end of the sands is the resort of **San Vicente,** and on the other side of the Chone estuary is the upmarket **Bahía de Caráquez**. Further south is the small community of **Montañita** on Ecuador's most popular surfing beach. **Salinas**, on the tip of the Santa Elena peninsula, is a Miami Beach-style resort popular with rich vacationers from Guayaquil.

Get Hatted

CLIMATIC CONDITIONS IN THE COASTAL AREA AROUND THE TOWN OF JIPIJAPA (pronounced hippy-happa) are conducive to growing a special type of palm plant used for making *toquilla* straw. For centuries the long, uniform and supple fronds of this plant have been used for weaving fine quality white straw hats. But when the hats were exported to Panama in the last century they became known as **panama hats**, though strictly speaking they should be called Ecuador hats.

The very best so-called "panamas," known as *finos* or *ultra-finos*, are woven in or around the town of **Montecristi,** not far from Jipijapa. These are the sort of hats that take one weaver three of four months to weave and which can be rolled up so tightly that they can pass through a wedding ring and spring back into perfect shape.

These days the weaving and finishing of most panamas are done in Cuenca, in the Sierra, though toquilla straw still comes from the coast. Montecristi itself isn't an exciting town but it's a good place to go if you're looking for the finest straw hat money can buy — and at a much better price than in London, Frankfurt or New York.

Cruise the Galápagos Islands

A TYPICAL DAY ON A GALÁPAGOS ISLAND CRUISE STARTS WITH THE SOUND OF MUSIC IN YOUR CABIN AND YOUR EARLY MORNING CALL. After breakfast you board a small dinghy for a short trip to a nearby island.

Immediately you sense that you've arrived in a place like nowhere else on earth.

Prehistoric marine iguanas lounge on black lava rocks while slithery sea lions bask in the sun. Astonishingly, the animals don't run away at the sight of you. Birds peck about at your feet and may even land on your shoulders.

Marine iguanas and the ubiquitous sea lions play starring roles supported by blue-footed and masked boobies. Galápagos doves, mockingbirds, hawks, lava herons, night herons, oystercatchers, swallowtail gulls, various finches, lava lizards and the occasional snake take cameo roles.

After a thrilling encounter with these creatures, you return to the cruise ship for lunch. In the afternoon you put on your snorkel to swim in waters glinting and flickering with millions of tropical fish. You may spot a turtle or two. Or perhaps

ABOVE: Fearless and comical blue-footed boobies are one of the star attractions on the Galápagos Islands. RIGHT: Hats woven by hand in Ecuador from *toquilla* straw, a centuries-old tradition, became known as panamas when they were exported to Panama in the nineteenth century.

a white-tipped shark will cruise silently past you underwater, like a policeman of the deep keeping an eye on things.

From swimming to relaxation: You share the golden beach with sea lions. Family groups of these blubbery torpedoes enjoy long siestas in the sun, their whiskery noses smudged with sand. When they get too hot or hungry, they shuffle down to the water for a swim and a snack. Your own pursuits are even more indulgent.

Back on the cruise ship, you sip delicious fruit cocktails on the deck watching the sun set over the horizon.

Spot a Cock of the Rock

ECUADOR IS CONSIDERED BY ENTHUSIASTS TO BE THE HOTTEST SPOT FOR BIRDING IN SOUTH AMERICA. The country's varying altitudes create a range of microclimates and habitats, from wild *páramo* and mountain forests to coastal plains and dense Amazonian jungles. Some 1,600 bird species have been recorded in Ecuador, about 18% of the world's total and twice the number in Canada and the United States combined. And new bird species are still being discovered.

Birders arriving in Ecuador usually start with some of the lesser-used roads down the slopes of the Andes from Quito. The **old Nono road** towards Mindo becomes the Yes-Yes road when birders encounter a flock of a dozen or more species. The small town of **Mindo** is a mecca for cognoscenti bird-watchers. In the dense surrounding cloud forest some 400 species have been observed, including such trophies as the fabulous scarlet-crested, black-bottomed **Andean Cock of the Rock**, the toucan, golden headed and crested quetzals, the plate-billed mountain toucan, grass-green tanagers and velvet-purple coronet. In the rich subtropical forest there are also howler monkeys, many brilliant butterflies and hundreds of species of orchids.

Multi-chromatic sunrises and sunsets are a feature of the Galápagos Islands. Here dawn breaks over Santa Fé, home to a unique species of land iguana.

Another excellent area to spot the Cock of the Rock is in the vicinity of the **Cascada de San Rafael** — also known as the Coca Falls — on the road from Baeza to Lago Agrio. These are the biggest falls in Ecuador east of the Andes. Reports speak of dozens of the birds coming together and making a raucous racket to attract females. The male with the loudest call and brightest colors generally wins the lady.

A Night in the Jungle

FOR ANYONE VISITING ECUADOR FOR MORE THAN A FEW DAYS, A TRIP TO THE JUNGLE IS A WORTHWHILE AND HUMBLING EXPERIENCE. It is worthwhile because it is an opportunity to glimpse a way of life different in almost every respect to that with which we are familiar, humbling because we are confronted with a totally alien environment which most of us would be unable to cope with alone and unaided.

There are many areas of the Oriente to choose from, with different communities of Indians and a variety of jungle lodges. The prices and level of comfort vary considerably from lodge to lodge though the quality of your stay isn't necessarily proportional to what you pay.

Probably the most comfortable jungle experience is on board the luxurious flat-bottomed riverboat, the **Flotel Orellana**, which cruises the Río Aguarico near the Peruvian border. Run by Ecuador's largest tour company, Metropolitan Touring, the tour includes shore trips, guides, canoe rides, lectures and good food. Metropolitan Touring also runs excellent camps on the shores of **Lakes Iripari** and **Imuya** outside the 606,000-hectare (one-and-a-half-million-acre) **Cuyabeno Wildlife Reserve**.

Several lodges on the Río Napo offer good jungle experiences, including the well-known and upmarket **La Selva Jungle Lodge**, and **Sacha Lodge** and, further downstream, **Yuturi Lodge**. There are also a number of less expensive and more basic facilities along the shores in the tributaries of the R'o Napo offering good jungle experiences.

Upriver, the Napo flows past the jungle town of **Misahuallí**, another good base for rainforest exploration. Jungle tour operators and guides are numerous here, as they are in the nearby town of **Tena**. Facilities range from basic cabaña complexes to upmarket jungle lodges. Aside from exploring the jungle and watching wildlife, popular activities include white-water rafting, panning for gold (but you won't get rich!) and exploring nearby caves.

Budget jungle trips in the upper Napo area can be organized through the Federación de Organizaciones Indígenas (FOIN) who represent many Quichua communities (see under TENA in CENTRAL ORIENTE, page 167). Programs, which range from camping in the jungle to taking part in spiritual ceremonies with a shaman, have been developed in response to the activities of outside tourist operators. Accommodation is usually in traditional Quichua cabañas, and it helps if you speak Spanish.

One of Ecuador's most highly rated jungle lodges is the **Kapawi Ecotourism Lodge** near the Peruvian border in the southeast of the country. This is one of the most remote, unspoiled and pristine parts of the Ecuadorian Amazon basin, so far untouched by logging or oil wells. A visit to Kapawi is highly recommended (see ECOTOURISM in YOUR CHOICE, page 25; KAPAWI ECOLOGICAL RESERVE, page 172).

Scientists believe the rainforest of the Amazon basin could account for between 30 and 80 million species of plants and animals, perhaps as much as half of all the earth's life forms.

The Great Outdoors

Ecuador is a gallery of stunning landscapes. From snow-capped, volcanic mountains and long stretches of unspoiled coastline to Amazon rainforests and the bleak splendor of the Galápagos Islands, the country offers the visitor a breathtaking spectrum of natural wonders.

Some 16% of Ecuador's land area is officially designated as national parkland, nature reserve or special recreation area. The first national park created was the Galápagos Islands in 1959 and the first mainland park was Cotopaxi in 1975. Since then, five more national parks have been created: at Machalilla, Yasuni, Sangay, Podocarpus and El Salado.

In addition there are huge areas of protected nature reserves, the largest being Cotacachi-Cayapas, Cayambe-Coca and Cuyabeno, all in the north of the country, as well as national recreation areas, natural monuments and private reserves.

If you have the time it is well worth visiting four national parks representing the four major ecosystems of the country. The **Galápagos Islands**, with their extraordinary wildlife, are an experience of a lifetime. In the Andes, the most frequently visited national park is **Cotopaxi,** with its magnificent, cone-shaped volcano, the tallest active volcano in the world. The **Machalilla National Park** on the coast is stunningly beautiful, and the **Yasuni National Park** in Amazonia provides a unique insight into rainforest wildlife. Some of the parks and reserves are remote and difficult to reach and facilities aren't well developed. Visitors planning to stay a few days are advised to bring their own camping gear, water and adequate supplies.

The entrance fees for national parks are generally US$10 for a highland park and US$20 for a lowland park. One payment allows multiple entry to the park for a week. Ecuadorian nationals pay considerably less. The entry fee to the Galápagos National Park is US$80, plus an additional tax of US$12.

Even though a portion of the quite high entrance fees goes towards administration and protection, sufficient manpower and equipment aren't available to prevent various kinds of destruction. Areas of some of the parks and reserves have been subject to illegal fishing, oil drilling, mining, ranching and colonization.

For more information on parks and reserves contact INEFAN ☎(02) 548924, the Ecuadorian Institute of Forestry, Natural Areas and Wildlife, which is part of the Ministry of Agriculture. Their main office is on the eighth floor of the MAG building on Amazonas and Eloy Alfaro in Quito.

Tracking through the Andes — what you lose in comfort by riding on top of a train you gain in experience and excitement.

It is worth keeping in mind that even though the national parks and nature reserves embrace most types of Ecuador's varied topography, vast areas of the country outside these demarcations are also extremely beautiful and uncontaminated by the accumulated debris of human occupation and industrialization.

ECOTOURISM

Ecotourism has been defined as tourism that does no damage to the environment and wildlife and benefits the local people. One might add that it should educate and benefit the ecotourist as well. Because of increased concern about environmental issues and evidence of the damaging effects of tourism around the world, the concept is of vital importance and is likely to remain so as long as people travel.

In Ecuador the objectives of ecotourism are relevant throughout the country but nowhere more so than in the Oriente, where cultural differences between tourists and Indian groups are most pronounced, and where corruption can easily occur because of disparities of wealth. It isn't surprising that some Indian groups want little or nothing to do with the "outside world" because they know that any contacts will ultimately be a threat to their way of life.

Visitors interested in the beneficial aspects of tourism and who are sensitive to the effect they have on the environment and people they encounter may wish to consider staying at places that support the principles of ecotourism. The following are examples of places that espouse ecotourist ideas by respecting the environment and working in harmony with local communities.

Kapawi Ecological Reserve, in a remote area of rainforest in Pastaza Province near the border with Peru, was started in 1996 as an association between a major tour operator, CANODROS SA, and an isolated group of Achuar Indians. The goal was to start a trend in ecotourism by pooling resources and sharing benefits while respecting the land

and traditions of the people without damaging the environment.

Under the terms of the agreement CANODROS invested some US$2 million to build a state-of-the-art ecolodge on Kapawi lagoon, which they pledged to hand over to the local Achuar community after 15 years. The company also pays US$2,000 a month as rent to the local people and has promised that the majority of employees on the project will be Achuar. For their part, the Achuar offered wood, palm leaves and materials for the building, to maintain the airstrip and to restrict hunting within the area of the lodge.

The lodge accommodates up to 40 visitors and was built in an Achuar style of architecture without using a single nail. Environmentally friendly technologies, such as solar energy and waste recycling, are also used. In addition a research station has been established in the area with a data center on the Achuar culture, as well as medical, educational and ecological programs.

From the visitor's point of view, Kapawi is a superb introduction to the rainforest and its people. Flexible programs include visits to Achuar communities (see KAPAWI ECOLOGICAL RESERVE, page 172, for more details), hikes

OPPOSITE: High-wire crossing near Baños, a typical Andean footbridge. ABOVE: Rare and unique species of cactus are characteristic of the Galápagos Islands.

in the pristine rainforest, canoeing in the lakes and rivers, where pink dolphins are often seen, and birdwatching in an area where more than 400 species have been recorded.

Alandaluz (winged city of light) **Ecological Resort** is an impressive beachside complex of bamboo and palm-thatch lodges and cabañas on the southern coast of Manabí Province that is on the cutting edge of ecological architecture, self-sufficiency and organic agriculture. The resort's modest brochure printed on recycled paper speaks of dedication to neighboring communities and sustainable strategies.

As well as functioning as a hotel, Alandaluz has training workshops and courses on waste and water recycling, nutrition, compost latrines and ecological architecture. As a measure of its success and influence, some 40 structures in the area have been built in the "Alandaluz style," which is based on the ancestral architecture of the local people. Wood and bamboo is cut during the phase of the waning moon because the materials are thought to contain less liquid during this period and are thus more durable and less attractive to insects.

Alandaluz is situated on a beautiful, empty beach with big, surfable waves and is also convenient for visits to the **Machalilla National Park** and **Isla de la Plata**. When I stopped by the resort, however, it had just been devastated by a storm. Bamboo guest houses had blown away, the palm-thatched main lodge was in tatters and the staff were far too busy clearing up and making repairs to cope with guests, even if they had anywhere to put them. Let's hope this unique resort will be functioning again soon.

Describing itself as an "ecological inn and farm," **Casa Mojanda** is set in 10 hectares (25 acres) of Andean farmland overlooking the mountains of Imbabura and Cotacachi near Otavalo. Visitors are unanimous in their praise of its magical views, friendly welcome, beautiful accommodation and delicious Ecuadorian cuisine made from homegrown produce.

Owners Bettie Sachs and Diego Falconi also run the **Mojanda Foundation**, a not-for-profit organization dedicated to environmental protection in the Mojanda Lakes region and assisting community initiatives in public health, education, organic agriculture and the arts.

There are many other ecotourism establishments, some of which are mentioned in the destination chapters to follow.

Sporting Spree

With extensive areas of wilderness and its varied terrain of mountains, rainforest, coast and islands, Ecuador is one of the great and least expensive destinations for adventure sports. Adrenaline-pumping outdoor activities include mountain climbing, mountain biking, trekking, caving, diving, whitewater rafting, kayaking, paragliding, bungee jumping, surfing, four-wheel-driving, horse riding, and llama trekking.

With 10 peaks over 5,000 m (16,665 ft), Ecuador has a reputation as a country for serious **mountain climbing**. Since the nineteenth century, European and American climbers have come to Ecuador in attempts to conquer both the mountain

LEFT: Courtship ritual of the waved albatross, the largest and one of the rarest birds of the Galápagos Islands. RIGHT: Pacuya camp in the Cuyabeno Wildlife Reserve, northern Oriente.

once thought to be the tallest in the world, **Mt. Chimborazo**, 6,310 m (21,031 ft), and the tallest continuously active volcano in the world, **Mt. Cotopaxi**, 5,897 m (19,655 ft). The German scientist and traveler Wilhelm Reiss conquered Cotopaxi in 1872, while the English climber, Edward Whymper, made the first successful ascent to the peak of Chimborazo in 1880.

Hundreds of people now climb these and other Ecuadorian peaks each year. Conditions vary from mountain to mountain, though climbing is usually best from June to September and in December and January. There are *refugios* on the high slopes of most of the big mountains where climbers rest, preparatory to making their ascents around midnight — in order to reach the peak at dawn when visibility is at its best and before the sun softens the snow. Proper acclimatization and experience is essential before climbing any of the higher peaks. Qualified guides can be contacted and equipment rented in Quito.

For those with little climbing experience there are suitable routes up some of the lesser mountains, such as **Mt. Tungurahua**, 5,016 m (16,703 ft), near Baños. But even this mountain is no easy stroll; several climbers have died on its slopes. A guide is recommended and proper climbing equipment is essential.

If you prefer to admire mountains from a safe distance, the lower mountain slopes and the valleys of the Ecuadorian Andes are excellent **trekking** country. National parks surround most of the mountains, which makes access reasonably convenient. The wild and windswept páramo of Cotopaxi National Park, within easy reach of Quito, is one of the most popular destinations for trekking and camping. If you're lucky you might spot a condor or herds of wild bulls or horses, even a mountain lion. Parts of the park are so remote that you can camp there for a week and not see one other person.

Similar and even better opportunities for wilderness experiences and trekking exist in all Ecuador's national parks, nature reserves and recreation areas. In terms of landscape and wildlife interest these **protected territories** are spectacular. Facilities for lodging and eating, however, tend to be basic if they exist at all, so unless you are going for a one-day trek, bring camping equipment. For information, contact **INEFAN** ☎ (02) 506337, the National Parks administrative authority in Quito.

Outside the national parks more Andes trekking opportunities abound. Go to any hacienda or country inn and there will be plenty of great treks in the surrounding countryside. Aside from good walking shoes, the most vital piece of equipment is a large-scale map of the area where you want to go, which you can buy at the **Instituto Geográfico Militar** in Quito (see QUITO, page 64). The second most important piece of equipment is a strong stick in case you encounter unfriendly dogs. The Indian women who sell goods up and down Avenida Amazonas in Quito sell sticks with brass handles.

Several agencies in Quito arrange treks. Safari Tours, for example, offers a five-day, 60-km (38-mile) Oyacachi hike from the Andes to the Amazon on a 1,000-year-old trail. Another popular trek is the Inca Trail from Achupallus near Cuenca to the ruins Ingapura (see CENTRAL HIGHLANDS, page 112). There are also many good treks around the Lake District near Otavalo, and treks through the jungle are part of most rainforest tours.

As for **mountain biking**, one great ride is the thrilling, mostly downhill run from Baños to Puyo (see CENTRAL HIGHLANDS, page 112). Another is the Biking Dutchman's "up hill by jeep, down hill by bike" Cotopaxi descent (see COTOPAXI NATIONAL PARK, page 118). But there are scores of possibilities for mountain biking in Ecuador. The Dutchman's mountain bikes are excellent machines and well maintained, but those for rent at major tourist towns, such as Otavalo or Baños, should be checked over carefully.

The many rivers gushing down the sides of the Andes offer great scope for exhilarating **whitewater rafting** and **kayaking**. Though relatively new sports in Ecuador, top class water riders come from all over the world to experience Ecuador's wild rivers. Good rivers for rafting and kayaking include the Quijos in Napo province, the Anzu and Bobonaza in Pastaza, the Paute in Azuay, the Toachi and Blanco near Santo Domingo de los Colorados on the west of the Andes, and the Río Puyango near Zaruma in the south.

Ríos Ecuador, based at Tena in the Oriente, has a good reputation for its experienced guides and rafting trips on the Upper Napo and Río Misahuallí for all levels of skill and experience. River Odyssey West (ROW) ✆(02) 458339, in Quito, is also recommended. Details of other rafting and kayaking operators can be obtained from most of the adventure travel companies in Quito.

For another type of spill and thrill, Ecuador claims one of the world's highest **bungee jumps**. Many young Israelis traveling to South America after military service make a point of doing the 87-m (290-ft) "Andes bungee" from a bridge over the Chiche River on the road from Quito to Puembo. The jumps are supervised by trained jumpmasters from Andes Adrenaline Adventures ✆(02) 226071 or 227896 FAX (02) 508369, on Baron Von Humbolt 279, Casilla 17-12-91, Quito. Jumping takes place year round on Saturdays and Sundays between 10 AM and 5 PM. Reservations are required.

You can also contact Andes Adrenaline Adventures for information about paragliding and other adrenaline-boosting activities. For diving information see page 246 in GALÁPAGOS ISLANDS, and for surfing information see page 201 in PACIFIC COAST. For information on other adventure travel opportunities contact the South America Explorers Club (see page 70 for details on membership). Safari Tours ✆(02) 552505 or 223381 FAX (02) 220426 E-MAIL admin@safari.ecx.ec in Quito, is also a good source of knowledge and ideas about adventure travel.

The Open Road

As travel becomes increasingly popular throughout the planet, South America has become recognized a prime destination for those looking for adventurous, exotic and unusual

At 6,310 m (2,1031 ft), Mt. Chimborazo, the tallest in Ecuador, towers over the former capital of Ríobamba. Chimborazo was once thought to be the tallest in the world.

Estelar

experiences at a reasonable cost. The great advantage Ecuador has as a destination is that it offers almost all the attractions of the continent within the confines of a smallish country. In the course of a week or two you can experience the lifestyles, culture and natural beauty of the Andes, the Amazon jungle, the coast and the islands.

Renting a car gives you the most freedom and flexibility to explore the country. But if you decide to take this route, be aware of some hazards and drawbacks. These include confusing road signs or no signs at all, inadequate road maps, dangerous roads and dangerous driving (especially at night). You must always be alert to the possibility of car theft and never leave valuables in an unattended vehicle. Also be aware that if you get in a serious accident in a remote country area you could find yourself on the sharp end of some on-the-spot punishment.

For these reasons self-drive vacations in Ecuador are relatively uncommon. Most people prefer to join a tour group, where transport is provided, or to travel independently by public transport.

Backpacking

The greatest advantage of independent travel is that you meet up with all sorts of people on the road. Even if you start out alone chances are you will spend some time traveling with others. Sometimes you meet, quite unexpectedly, the same people two or three times in different places. Part of the reason for this is that there are a number of regular routes and haunts that have become part of the well-worn "gringo trail."

You encounter fellow travelers on buses, trains, boats and planes, in jungle hostels and city cafés, waiting for a ferry to cross a river, standing in a check-in line at an airport. Inevitably, the same questions are asked: Where are you from? Where are you going? Where's a good place to stay in Baños? Which is the best beach on the coast? Where should I go in the jungle? How do I get the train to go down the Devil's Nose?

Riding on the top of the train down or up the Devil's Nose is one of the great experiences for travelers in Ecuador. So is the train ride between Ibarra and San Lorenzo, when it is running. A few days chilling out in Madre Tierra in Vilcabamba is almost obligatory, as is a stay at the Black Sheep Inn near Latacunga. Jungle trips from Tena or Misahuallí are also on most independent travelers' itineraries.

It is easier than many people think to get around Ecuador using public transport. People of all ages do it and some get by without speaking a word of Spanish, though a smattering of the language does help. During my road journeys in Ecuador I have met travelers ranging from young students to people in their thirties and forties taking time off from their jobs, not to mention gray-haired backpackers, some of whom were women traveling alone.

For independent travelers in Ecuador, a few special considerations are worth bearing in mind. Though Ecuador is considered one of the safest places for traveling in South America, it is always important to exercise caution while on the road, especially in areas that are known to be dangerous (the Old City in Quito, for example). Don't carry valuables (a watch, a camera) that you can do without; avoid traveling with more than the minimum amount of money (see page 255 in TRAVELERS' TIPS).

Living It Up

In Ecuador you can live it up in stylish surroundings and luxury of the highest standard. Some of the historic haciendas in the sierra, for example, are a treat, combining old-style comfort with modern conveniences.

One of the best known is **Hostería La Ciénega**, (also known as Hacienda La Ciénega) 60 km (38 miles) south of Quito. You drive up to this imposing white hacienda along a driveway perfumed by fragrant eucalyptus trees. The dazzling

columns and balustrades, create a solid, yet timeless aura. The private chapel has a massive and ancient carved wooden door. The gardens are filled with bright flowers and a fountain cascades in the inner courtyard. Elegance, charm and good taste characterize the public rooms and bedrooms. Service is good and the food is excellent. What more can you want for a few days of good living?

A similar quality of style and luxury applies to most of the other haciendas. Near Ciénega stands the equally historic **Hacienda San Agustín de Callo**, a former monastery, with breath-taking views of Cotopaxi volcano. Its history began with the Incas who built a temple centuries ago on what became the site of this hacienda. San Agustín is recommended for those who enjoy history, beauty and tranquillity.

An hour's drive north of Quito, near the well-known market town of Otavalo, are the fabulous haciendas of **Guachala**, **Pinsaquí** and **Cusín** (see page 92). For horse-riders, both experienced and novice, treks can be arranged from one to another, giving you the chance to experience a variety of style and comfort.

Though more confined in space, there is plenty of luxury aboard the many **cruise ships** that ply the waters around the Galápagos. Above all a wildlife destination, visitors can enjoy the highest standards of comfort and cuisine as they hop between the islands. The bigger cruise ships tend to be more luxurious but some of the smaller boats have more flexible programs and their more manageable visitor groups lend themselves to better wildlife viewing. Medium-sized boats, such as *Coral I* and *Coral II*, operated by Kleintours, offer a good compromise between comfort and wildlife experiences.

About 100 boats are licensed to operate in the Galápagos Islands. Ones that have been recommended, ranging from luxurious to affordable, include the *Ambassador, Nortada, Encantada, Beluga, Santa Cruz, Isabela II, Reina Sylvia, The Delphin, Letty, Beagle III, Flamingo, Pulsar, Coral I* and *II*, *Angelique, Stella Maris, Gaby* and *Cormorant*. It is important to note that others may be equally good and that standards on each boat can vary from season to season, depending on the crew and guides.

The all-purpose ranchero provides transport between country towns and villages, this one heading for the rough-and-tough mining town of Nambija, near Zamora in the south.

The **jungle lodges** in the Amazon basin offer visitors another style of comfort. Conditions in the jungle are more basic and physically demanding than aboard a cruise ship or in the sybaritic city but it can be equally satisfying and interesting. After a long, sweaty jungle trek, luxury can be as simple as a cold beer and a hot shower.

Jungle lodges known for the high standards of their amenities include the American-owned **La Selva Jungle Lodge**, about three hours by fast private launch from Coca; the luxurious, Swiss-owned **Sacha Lodge**, where many of the amenities of a first-class hotel have been brought into the heart of the jungle on the shores of a lagoon; and the more remote **Yuturi Lodge** , a scenic five-hour journey by motorized canoe down the Río Napo from Coca. Also known for the high standards of its facilities and its commitment to ecotourism is **Kapawi Ecological Reserve** (see ECOTOURISM, page 25, in THE GREAT OUTDOORS).

The ultimate way to explore the jungles without getting your feet wet, as it were, is aboard the enormous, flat-bottomed riverboat, the **Flotel Orellana**, which cruises the Río Aguarico near the Peruvian border. Shore trips, guides, canoe rides, lectures and good food are included.

To really live it up in Ecuador, go to the coast where many Ecuadorians take their vacations. La Costa is the place to party. The beach resorts of **Salinas** (see page 202 for more details) or **Bahía de Caráquez** (page 195) have some of the smartest and most luxurious hotels, but you will probably find the best party atmosphere at the lively but more downmarket resorts of Atacames or Canoa.

Family Fun

Children can enjoy and benefit from a wealth of experiences while traveling in Ecuador. Any adventurous child would jump at the chance of learning to use a blow pipe at a jungle camp, swimming with sea lions on the Galápagos Islands, riding a horse in the Andes, rafting down a jungle river or buggying down the beach in a pickup truck. Many parents do take their children on just these sorts of adventures.

It's possible to take your children along on group tours also, but some tour operators will not take children under the age of 12 on multidestination itineraries and safari-style trips, either for reasons of insurance or because other adults in the group don't want the distraction of having kids about. If you do intend to take children with you on a tour, shop around for a child-friendly operator.

If you are traveling independently there are no legal restrictions on bringing children. But don't forget that independent travel usually involves a lot of waiting around for buses, and then more time squashed in the bus itself. Make sure you bring things to keep children occupied, such as drawing materials or games. Food, too, can be a problem, as children tend not to be as adventurous as adults. Plenty of biscuits, soft drinks, bottled water and bananas, all available locally, are the most practical rations for children on the road.

Health risks are no greater for kids than for adults. A good medical kit is essential with remedies for upset stomachs and a strong antibacterial cream for cuts and scrapes (especially when traveling in the Amazonia), while adults and children alike must be very careful to use mosquito repellent when traveling in the rainforest or in the coastal areas. And don't forget a high factor sunblock and a hat.

If a child is small enough to sit on your lap on a bus trip you won't have to pay a fare, but since some buses are uncomfortable, it might be prudent to pay for a seat. On domestic airlines children under 12 pay half fare, with or without their own seat. Infants under two pay 10% of the fare. Hotels usually give discounts for children and it's always worth bargaining. If two children are sharing a bed it should only be necessary

Elegance and antiques characterize many old haciendas, such as Hacienda Hualiagua de Jijon near Alóag, south of Quito. Some owners have opened their stately homes to tourists.

to pay for one child. You may be able to get a hammock for the kids in smaller places and in lodges. Nights in a hammock are quite an experience. Once along the Pacific Coast or in Amazonia, the better hotels either have pools or access to places where kids can swim. In Quito all the luxury hotels we mention have pools, and while some of them are exclusively for hotel guests, others offer day passes for individuals or families, who may then also use the hotel's other health facilities.

A number of small guesthouses and lodges are run by Europeans who have fallen in love with Ecuador and who have moved home and family to be there. Your kids won't have to look far for playmates. Word of mouth, the Internet and this book will point you in the right direction to find some of them.

Generally speaking, Ecuadoreans are especially friendly to gringos traveling with children. And it's even been reported that travelers with children are less likely to be robbed!

Cultural Kicks

Culture is all around you in Ecuador. In Quito it's in the naïf paintings made by the *indígenas* from Tigua which they sell to tourists — bright and detailed miniature scenes of village festivals, lamas and snow-capped volcanoes. It's in the weavings of the people of **Otavalo**, which they sell on street corners. It's in the baroque churches of the Old Town incorporating Inca motifs, built by artisans under the guidance of Spanish masters. It's in stark, roadside murals warning of the dangers of drug abuse, in modern public sculptures in intersections, in statues of past political and literary figures. Culture is in the cut of a poncho or a strain of Andean pipe music floating on the air.

It is said that the defining aspect of Ecuadorian culture is the fusion of ancient *indígenas* artistic heritage with western thought and sensibilies imported by Spanish colonists in the sixteenth

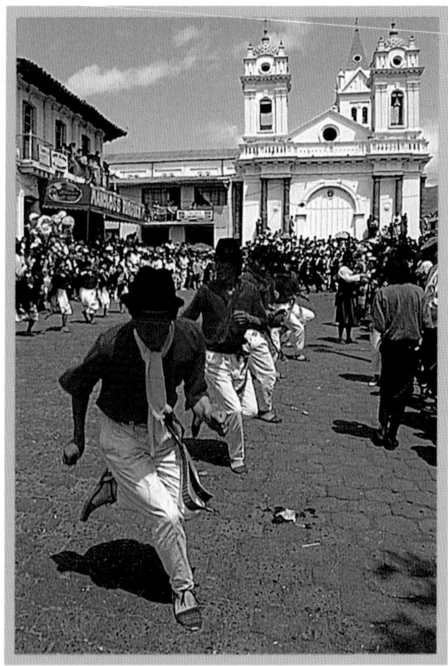

century. Certainly this curious amalgam led to the well-known **Escuela Quiteña**, or Quito School of religious art, which can be seen in churches and museums throughout the country, especially in Quito and Cuenca. Already skilled at carving, painting and working with gold leaf, local artisans executed, and interpreted in their own way, the religious themes of their Spanish masters.

But Ecuadorian culture dates back much earlier than the Spanish invasion of four hundred years ago. To appreciate its depth and history, go see the extraordinary exhibits at the **Casa de la Cultura** museum complex, housed in the strikingly modern, circular glass building in the Parque El Ejido in Quito (see QUITO, page 64). Here you will find a well-displayed collection of artifacts that document Ecuador's ancient coastal cultures dating back nearly 6,000 years. You cannot fail to be impressed by the elegant gold and platinum ornaments, for example, that were made using sophisticated smelting techniques unknown in Europe until hundreds of years later.

Probably the most powerful modern expression of the combination of European and *indígenas* sensibilities are in the paintings of the internationally known Indian artist, **Oswaldo Guayasamín's** harrowing images of suffering Indians some of which are painted in a cubist style. A magnificent display of his paintings can be seen in his private **Museo Guayasamín** ☎(02) 446455 or 452938 in the exclusive Quito inner suburb of Bellavista.

Outside the capital there is plenty more to satisfy the appetites of culture vultures. In **Cuenca**, some of the colonial and religious art and architecture is considered to be the finest in the country. And within a couple of hours' drive the ruins at Ingapirca are the finest example of Inca architecture in the country. Even in Guayaquil, not usually known as a city of culture, there are several excellent museums well worth visiting (see GUAYAQUIL, page 200, in PACIFIC COAST).

You will also find culture in the Amazon rainforest and its indigenous people, its architecture, in the techniques of making blowpipes and dugout canoes, the ritual brewing of manioc beer and the mystic use of the hallucinogenic plant, *ayuaska*. On the coast there are many sites where archaeologists are researching long-forgotten civilizations. A world away on the northern coastline, in Esmeraldas province, black culture with its marimba music and voodoo, brought by castaway slaves from Africa, is still thriving.

Festive Flings

Music, parades, dressing up, beauty contests, dancing in the streets, drinking, feasting, bull fighting, cock fighting, firecrackers — the Ecuadorians love a good party and there's nothing like a fiesta to generate the right mood. For gringos, fiestas are a great opportunities to join in and have fun. Villages and towns all have their own festivals days, usually a local saint's day, while there are certain times of the year, notably Carnival in the days before Lent, when the whole country celebrates.

Street parades OPPOSITE and equestrian events BELOW are highlights of Ecuadorian fiestas.

The following are some of the main annual festivals, though don't be surprised if you happen upon a festival in the country about which nobody seems to know the significance. It could be some ancient ritual dating from pre-Hispanic times. In the list below, an asterisk (*) signifies a public holiday. But if the holiday falls in the middle of the week it is usually moved to a Friday or a Monday to make a long weekend. And if it falls on a Saturday or Sunday it also moves to a Friday or Monday. Though it's fun to visit a town at festival time accommodation fills quickly so it's advisable to make reservations.

January 1 *New Year's Day**. Most of the excitement will have taken place on New Year's Eve so this tends to be a quiet day.

January 6 *Epiphany**, also known as The Festival of the Three Kings.

February 27 *National Unity Day* commemorates the Battle of Tarqui.

February or **March** *Carnival* takes place in the week before Lent. This is the biggest festival in Ecuador. Frenzied water fights in which nobody is spared are an Ecuadorian specialty. The people of Cuenca seem particularly fond of soaking each other. The only way to save yourself a drenching is to stay indoors or go to Ambato, where water throwing was banned because it became too rough. Instead, a festival of fruit and flowers takes place in Ambato in the last two weeks of February.

March or **April** On *Palm Sunday*, a week before Easter Sunday, people throughout Ecuador buy palm fronds in the market and weave them into ornaments. During *Semana Santa* (Holy Week) religious processions are held. The colorful *Good Friday* procession in Quito is spectacular with penitents and flagellants dragging crosses through the streets. Holy Thursday, Good Friday and Easter Saturday are public holidays.

March 4 Annual *Peach Festival* in Gualaceo.

April 21 Ríobamba celebrates the *Battle of Tapi* with an agricultural fair at around the same time.

May 1 *Labor Day**.

May 24 *Independence Day** marks the anniversary of the Battle of Pichincha in 1822 when Ecuador won independence from Spain.

June *Corpus Christi* is celebrated in many central highland towns usually on the ninth Thursday after Easter. Combining pre-Christian harvest celebrations, it's a major festival in the Cotopaxi and Tungurahua provinces and elsewhere. Ornate masks and headdresses are sometimes worn and a dance procession takes place from Salasaca to Pelileo near Baños.

June 24 The *Festival of Saint John the Baptist* is celebrated most actively in Otavalo and its surroundings. There's dancing in the streets during the nights leading up to festival day, and on its eve people dress in the strangest of costumes, from blond gringos to cartoon characters. Ritual battles and stone throwing take place outside the town in which people have been known to get injured or even killed. The festival may have originated as a pre-Inca solstice celebration.

June 29 The *Festival of Saint Peter and Saint Paul* tends to merge with the Saint John the Baptist Festival in parts of Imbabura Province. Bonfires are lit in the streets on the festival eve. Some areas associate themselves with Saint John, some with Saint Peter and others with Saint Paul. Saint Peter is the patron saint of Cayambe, where there are big parades and a ceremony for the "delivery of roosters," a throwback to feudal times. Similar fiestas, which probably originated as harvest celebrations, take place in other parts of the highlands such as southern Chimborazo Province.

July 24 *Birthday of the Great Liberator, Simón Bolívar**.

July 25 *Foundation of Guayaquil Day* is a wild celebration in the city with beauty pageants, fireworks and parades that combines with the previous day's national holiday.

Poncho Plaza at Otavalo market, the biggest and best for hand-woven textiles, clothing and indigenous crafts. The busiest market day is Saturday, though Friday is also active.

de LOS CHASKIS
VIVERES CENTENARIO
POR MAYOR Y MENOR

August 10 *Quito Independence Day**.
September The *Fiesta del Yamor* takes place in the Otavalo area, in the early part of the month with plenty of razzle and dazzle and the election of a Fiesta Queen.
September 23–24 *Fiesta de la Mamá Negra*, Latacunga's major festival, also known as the fiesta of La Virgen de las Mercedes. Men dress up as women and blacken their faces in one of Ecuador's most colorful festivals. Two weeks later there's another big parade in honor of Mamá Negra.
October 9 *Guayaquil Independence Day**.
October 12 *Anniversary of Columbus' Discovery of the Americas**.
November 1 *All Saints' Day**.
November 2 *All Souls' Day** is marked by the laying of flowers and gifts in cemeteries and lighting candles in honor of ancestors.
November 3 *Cuenca Independence Day**. Combining with the preceding national holiday this is Cuenca's biggest celebration.
November 11 *Latacunga Independence Day* includes parades and a bullfight.
November 18 *Loja Independence Day* includes week-long festivities and cultural events.
December 6 *Quito Foundation Day** is celebrated in the first week of the month. Bullfights take place at the Plaza de Toros. (Local *indígenas* aren't much interested in the historical implications of this festival.)
December 16 The lively annual *Baños Festival* takes place around this date. It is also a festive time when townspeople pay homage to their local saint.
December 25 *Christmas Day*. Celebrations lead up to New Year's Eve when effigies are burned in the streets.

Shop till You Drop

After a day or two in Ecuador your impression might be that the country is one big bustling bazaar selling handicrafts, bags, leather goods, ponchos, sweaters, wall hangings and woven waistcoats to tourists. But as you travel further and see more of the country, away from the main tourist areas, you will see that most markets are geared towards local people, and that the merchandise on offer is of greatest interest to those who want to buy, say, plastic buckets or aluminum saucepans.

Every town or village in Ecuador, it seems, has a weekly market day. As much as places where people come to buy and sell goods, they are meeting places and the main social event of the week. People living miles away, up in the mountains or down in some hidden valley, will make a point of going to market once a week where they will shop, meet their friends and drink. Mostly it's the women who do the shopping, while the men do the drinking. Towards the end of the day you are bound to see more than one drunken *vaquero* (cowboy) swaying in his saddle as his faithful horse plods along the familiar road back home, with the dog trotting along behind.

For overseas visitors, markets are great places to experience Ecuador's incredible diversity. Costumes of the various *indígena* groups alone, seen on figures moving gracefully through the crowds, passing by baskets of fruit and squeaking guinea pigs, are as confusing as they are fascinating. Does the black poncho on that man mean he's from Salasaca? Does the wide white felt hat on that woman come from Saquisilí or Saraguro? The Indian names of these places are as elegant as the costumes of those that live there. Markets are great places for people watching and getting a feel for the country, never mind the shopping.

Ecuador's best-known market at **Otavalo**, and the one most popular with tourists is, in fact, very good for shopping. Saturday is the day to visit. One of the plazas in central Otavalo becomes the Plaza de Ponchos where, amid the maze of brilliant textiles, you're bound to find a few items will that take your fancy. Myriad small shops and stands invite you to look at their handmade goods — ponchos, woolen blankets, woven wall hangings, handknitted sweaters, scarves, gloves, hats, shirts, shawls, embroidered blouses,

table cloths, string bags, baskets, ceramics, sandals, leather goods, carvings, beads, buttons, bric-a-brac, and more.

The bad news is that tourists arrive here by the busload from Quito, which means you'll have to bargain hard. And get there early if you want the pick of the best.

As well as a great place for shopping, Otavalo is a photographer's dream. The bold colors and striking designs of the Andean textiles and wall hangings, combined with the elegant costumes and strong faces of the Otavaleños make for powerful graphic images. But it's important to be sensitive to your subjects. If possible, ask permission before you photograph somebody.

The Thursday market at **Saquisilí**, north of Latacunga, is considered to be one of the biggest and best in Ecuador. Though there are a few tourist items for sale, the main interest is the animal market, the atmosphere and the people who come from way out in the hills. West of Latacunga, the Saturday market at **Zumbahua** is also very colorful and not often visited by tourists. The local Indians wear felt porkpie hats and red or striped ponchos and shawls.

Other markets worth visiting include the Monday market at **Ambato**; the Saturday market at **Ríobamba** (note the tagua nut carvings and the shigra bags); the Thursday market in **Cuenca** at Plaza Rotary; the **Gualaceo** Sunday market; the Calle Cuenca market on Wednesdays and Saturdays in **Quito**; and the daily Bahía black market in **Guayaquil**. Be aware that markets are stalking grounds for pickpockets and sneak thieves, so hold tight to your bags and cameras at all times.

Short Breaks

If you're flying into Quito or Guayaquil for a few days on business it is worthwhile, if you have time, to spend an extra day or two outside the city. From Quito a good choice would be to visit a **hacienda** (see TOP SPOTS, page 11), most of which are around an hour's drive from the city. Any reputable travel agent in Quito will be able to make the arrangements. **Angermeyer's Enchanted Expeditions** ☎(02) 569960 FAX (02) 569956 is one such agency.

If you also want to buy presents to take home then head north to one of the haciendas near **Otavalo** (Cusín, Guachala or Pinsaqui) so that you can visit the famous handicraft market on Friday or Saturday. For a close encounter with the world's tallest active volcano head south to one of the haciendas near Cotopaxi (La Ciénega or San Agustín de Callo). To cycle down the volcano the Biking Dutchman's "uphill by jeep, downhill by bike" one-day tour is highly recommended.

If you are interested in birdlife, then head for the small town of Mindo on the western slopes of the Andes, just 40 km (25 miles) northwest of Quito as the condor flies. In the cloud forest around the town some 450 species have been observed. Nearby is the Bellavista Cloud Forest Reserve, a dome-shaped ecolodge on stilts with lots of windows and big

Religious icons and souvenirs on sale at Plaza San Francisco in Quito's Old Town.

balconies (see MINDO AND MAQUIPUCUNA RESERVES, page 89, and SPOT A COCK OF THE ROCK, page 18, in TOP SPOTS)

Baños is another popular place for a few days' break from Quito. This small town surrounded by green hills on the flanks of the Andes has long been famous for its hot springs. There are also several good restaurants, hotels and a reasonably happening nightlife. There are plenty of good walks and bike rides outside the town. Frequent buses from Quito take about four hours, though you might have to change in Ambato.

For a short trip from Guayaquil your best bet is to head for the beach. The rather tacky resort of Playas is about two hours away by bus, while the upmarket resort of Salinas, 150 km (95 miles) west of Guayaquil, is popular with the rich and glitzy. This is the place for salsatecas, ceviche and a bit of deep-sea fishing. If you're into the surfing scene, continue up the coast to catch the waves at Montañita, Ecuador's leading surfing beach, which attracts a young crowd from far and wide.

Galloping Gourmets

Because of its physical and cultural diversity, Ecuador is blessed with a wide range of fruits, vegetables and edible creatures. The Andes are the birthplace of the potato, for example, and several hundred species are grown here. The Incas knew ways of treating potatoes so that they could be stored for many years. They valued the potato not only as nurishment, but as a unit of time measure, the unit being the length of time it took to cook one.

As for tropical fruits, you will see and taste delicious varieties you never knew existed. The various forms of passion fruits, melons, mangoes, papayas, pomegranates, kiwis, kumquats, custard apples, bananas, guavas, and tamarinds number in the thousands. My favorite is a berry-sized tomato known as *tomate del árbol* (tree tomato) which makes a delicious fresh fruit drink. Another unusual fruit is a *vavaco*, which looks something like a papaya but tastes more like a pineapple. *Naranjilla*, a greenish orange type fruit, also makes wonderful juice (*jugo*), as do *maracuyá, taxo*, white *guanabana* and *mora* (blueberries).

Before the Spanish introduced cattle, the favored meat in Ecuador was guinea pig, or *cuy*. It's still an Ecuadorian delicacy. Whole grilled guinea pigs (teeth bared, eyes closed and paws intact) are said to be tasty and sweet — something like a cross between a chicken and a rabbit. Ecuadorians enjoy discussing the best places to eat *cuy*. Some say Latacunga while others favor the *cuy* from Ambato or Baños.

More acceptable to European and American palates are some of the great soups of the highlands. *Locro de papas*, usually known simply as *locro*, a thick potato and cheese soup, is delicious and requires no culinary courage to consume. *Yaguar locro*, a potato soup made with blood sausage, avocados and onions, is equally tasty. *Fanesca*, rich soup made with fish, eggs, beans and grains, is traditionally eaten during Holy Week.

Another sierra favorite among Ecuadorians and foreigners is *llapingachos*, potato pancakes or patties made with cheese and onions. And for a quick snack, *empanadas*, wheat flour pasties stuffed with cheese or meat, are filling and appetizing and can be bought inexpensively at a *panadería* (bakery). *Empanadas de morocho* are corn meal empanadas, usually filled with meat. The most typical mountain cooking is fried pork and roast pork — *fritada* and *hornado*. If you are really hungry order a *chugchucaras*, a specialty of Latacunga, which is a big plate of fried pork with *mote* (corn), bananas, fried potato pancakes, popcorn and porkskin with a couple of eggs on top.

With its abundance of seafood, fresh fruits and vegetables, the best cuisine in Ecuador is found on the coast. The greatest glory of the coastal cuisine is *ceviche*, which is fresh fish or shellfish marinated using various recipes combining lime or lemon, chili, onions,

coriander (*cilantro*) and perhaps other spices. Though the best ceviche comes from the coast, from Manabí Province in particular, it is popular throughout the country and indeed along the length of the Pacific coastline of South America.

Ceviche can be made from fish, shrimp, lobster, clams, mussels, oysters or mixtures of all of these. If you like Japanese sushi and prawn cocktails you are sure to enjoy ceviche. But it should be said that some people avoid ceviche because it is believed that it sometimes carries cholera bacteria. If you are concerned, avoid *ceviche de pescado* (fish) and *ceviche de concha* (clam) which are not even lightly cooked before marinating. Stick with *ceviche de camarón* (prawn) and clean-looking establishments.

Even if you avoid ceviche altogether there are still plenty of great seafood dishes to enjoy on the coast. Try *viche*, for examples (not to be confused with ceviche), a soup of fish, crab, crawfish, conch and calamares with peanut and banana. Similarly, *cazuela* is a mixed seafood stew made with peanut sauce and green cooking bananas (*verdes*) served in clay pot. A very thick cazuela can also be made into a flan-type pie, a real delicacy.

Esmeraldas Province is known for its *encocado* (made with coconut) dishes. You can have *encocado de pescado* (fish), *encocado de camarón* (prawn), *encocado de jaiba* (blue crab) and the supreme *encocado de cangrejo* (blue mangrove crab, found only in Esmeraldas). Another coastal specialty is *encebollado*, a hearty tuna soup eaten for breakfast; it's said to alleviate hangovers.

All Ecuadorian meals are served with a small side dish of hot sauce (*salsa picant*) made in various ways with chili peppers (*ají*). The spiciness of the sauce varies from place to place, so proceed with caution.

Typical alcoholic Ecuadorian drinks include various fruit concoctions made with a powerful sugar cane spirit (*trago*) as a base. A popular one is *canelazos*, which is a hot cocktail of trago, mixed with cinnamon, sugar and lime. Pilsener and Club (both good) are the national beers, while the most popular bottled

A multiplicity of fresh fruits LEFT and plenty of pork RIGHT are important ingredients of the varied Ecuadorian cuisine.

mineral water is Güitig. Unfortunately for a country which produces it, coffee is not well prepared in Ecuador, the most popular form being a concentrated liquid called *escencia,* to which hot water or milk is added. You can get proper coffee in some of the better hotels and a few coffeeshops in the cities.

Special Interests

For **naturalists**, Ecuador offers almost every conceivable vacation option. And there are many special interest trips such as ornithology, wildlife, scuba diving or rainforest tours organized on a regular basis from Great Britain or the United States. A look at the small advertisements in the back pages of your favorite special interests magazine will reveal a number of options.

English companies that specialize in such tours include **Cox & Kings** ☎ 0171 873 5000 FAX 0171 630 6038, Gordon House 10 Greencoat Place, London SW1P 1PH; **Birdquest** ☎ 01254 826317 FAX 01254 826780, Two Jays, Kemple End, Birdybrow, Stonyhurst, Lanc. BB7 9QY; **Penelope Kellie** ☎ 01962 779317 FAX 01962 779458, who represents a number of Ecuadorian tour operators in Great Britain; and **Galápagos Adventure Tours** ☎ FAX 0171 261 9890, 37–39 Great Guildford Street, London SE1 OES.

There are also possibilities to pursue language courses. Spanish courses are offered at a large number of language schools in the capital and also (at a slightly less expensive rate) in Otavalo and Baños.

Taking a Tour

Dozens of overseas travel companies offer packages to Ecuador while as many operators within the country offer a wide variety of tours. Very often the two categories are connected, with an overseas operator working with a tour company in Ecuador. Generally, it is more cost-effective to arrange a tour when you get to the country, but this might pose problems for those with limited time or those who don't speak Spanish. If this is the case, it will probably be better to shop around for a tour operator at home.

Most tours sold by overseas operators are of excellent value and include the best that Ecuador has to offer. They range from upmarket tours of the Galápagos Islands and hacienda riding tours to bird-watching expeditions and jungle adventures. Many operators also arrange customized itineraries.

If you have **three weeks** available and want an overall experience of the country, I recommend that you start with a week on the Galápagos Islands. Follow this with a week in Quito and the Sierra, visiting Otavalo or Cuenca, including a couple of nights at a hacienda. Then spend three or four nights at a jungle lodge in the Oriente, and end your vacation relaxing on the coast, perhaps at Bahía de Caráquez. Although Ecuador is topographically extremely varied it is also compact, so it is easy to get around, either by plane or by road.

A good starting point for planning a trip to Ecuador is to check out your local newspapers and travel magazines for tour companies specializing in Latin America. Your local Ecuadorian embassy should also be able to supply you with some general information. (For a partial listing of tour operators putting together vacations from Great Britain, the United States and Germany see HOW TO GET THERE, page 254, in TRAVELERS' TIPS.)

Some 95% of the 8,000 sq km (3,088 square miles) of the Galápagos Islands are national parklands. Visitors are restricted to designated sites.

Welcome to Ecuador

WHATEVER YOU WANT IN A VACATION, Ecuador has it: wild nature, mystical mountains, magical rainforest, volcanic islands, extraordinary wildlife, adventure travel, fascinating history, luxurious haciendas, great hotels, exotic cuisine, long empty beaches, colorful nightlife, wonderful people… Shall I go on? About the only thing that Ecuador hasn't got is good golf courses.

Ecuador has been aptly described as a big country in a small space. Certainly, it looks small on a map of South America — it's the second smallest state on the continent after Paraguay — but if you put a tracing of it over a map of Europe you'll find it's bigger than about 20 countries, including the United Kingdom.

Ecuador's greatest attraction is its diversity. You don't have to be a birdwatcher or orchidologist to appreciate the place, but if you are, you'll be in heaven. In terms of numbers of avian (1,600) or orchid (3,500) species alone, Ecuador is a world leader.

Ecuador is also a world-class destination for mountain climbing. Ten of the country's mountains are over 5,000 m (16,665 ft), and half that number are active or potentially active volcanoes. Twenty-five summits are over 4,000 m (13,332 ft). There are plenty of challenges out there.

There are many excellent rivers for rafting and kayaking enthusiasts. Whether it's the thrill of white water or the magic of drifting quietly through a rainforest, Ecuador has plenty of both on its many rivers that gush down the slopes of the Andes.

Beaches, it has too, aplenty. Most of them are long, wide and empty, without a tourist or traveler, or even a local to be seen. But dotted up and down the coast are a number of resorts, some luxurious, but many of them not much more than a handful of bamboo bars and straw *cabañas*. During festivals and holidays, La Costa is the place to party.

You should visit the Galápagos Islands at least once in a lifetime. The magic of the archipelago has often been described, but seldom captured in words. Charles Darwin, whose theory of evolution was inspired by these islands, described them as "infinitely strange, unlike any other islands in the world." And he wrote that the natural history of the archipelago was "very remarkable: it seems to be a little world within itself; the greater number of its inhabitants both vegetable and animal being found nowhere else."

Darwin was also a fan of rainforests. "In tropical forests, when quietly walking along the shady pathways, and admiring each successive view, I wished to find a language to express my ideas," he wrote. "Epithet after epithet was found too weak to convey to those who have not visited the inter-tropical regions the sensation of delight which the mind experiences." In Ecuador there are many ways of exploring the rainforest and experiencing this "sensation of delight," from the luxury of jungle lodges or a floating hotel to staying with a family of local *indígenas*.

A land of contrasts may be a cliché but it's true in the case of Ecuador. From the Amazon to the Andes is not only a huge change in altitude, which leaves you breathless when carrying your bags, but it's also a cultural jump from a culture of animist hunter gatherers, in some parts of the rainforest, to baroque churches and slick city skyscrapers.

Set in a high plateau surrounded by mountains, Ecuador's capital, Quito, is the loveliest city in the Andes where it's always spring. With an abundance of colonial-era buildings, The Old City of Quito is a designated World Heritage Site, while the new town has all the facilities of any modern city, including fine hotels, great shopping, good restaurants and a vibrant nightlife.

Finally, don't forget that Ecuador is the home of the misnamed panama hat. Let it not be forgotten that panamas are made in Ecuador. (They were named after the country of Panama because that's where they were sold in the middle of the nineteenth century when the world started to appreciate them.) Buy yourself a panama when you're in Ecuador, or a poncho or a hammock or any of the fabulous handwoven products produced in the country.

PREVIOUS PAGES: Known to local people as Taita (father), Mount Chimborazo LEFT is the tallest peak in Ecuador's Avenue of Volcanoes. An *indígena* from Salasaca RIGHT, possibly of Bolivian descent. OPPOSITE: Flamingo on Floreana Island in the Galápagos.

The Country and Its People

ECUADOR IS AN ABUNDANTLY DIVERSE COUNTRY on the northwest of the South American continent which is bisected horizontally by the equator — from which its name derives — and vertically by the volcanic Andes mountains. The country is relatively small in terms of the land area delineated by its borders: at 270,670 sq km (104,208 square miles), it is only a bit larger than Great Britain and no bigger than the state of Nevada in the United States. But if you imagine it's mountainous topography as a hugely magnified, crumpled handkerchief, and if that handkerchief were to be smoothed onto a flat surface, you would see that the surface area of the country is considerably greater than it appears on a map.

Ecuador's size is illusory in more ways than this. The density of its mountainous areas, its equatorial location and its position at the meeting point of two major Pacific currents are factors that help create a diverse pattern of microclimates and a rich repository of plant and animal life. If countries were ranked according to the size of their bird population rather than their human population, for example, Ecuador — with some 16,000 recorded avian species — would be bigger than the United Sates and Canada combined. If countries were measured by the number of orchid species, Ecuador — with some 3,500 orchids — would rank second in the world after Colombia.

Taken to extreme, of course, the above line of thought becomes absurd. Measured in terms of the populations of some unique species of large turtles, pink dolphins, marine iguanas and other endemic creatures, Ecuador becomes the biggest country in the world — or even the only country in the world. What this concept does indicate, however, is that Ecuador is enormously wealthy in terms of biodiversity. Indeed, some areas of the country, particularly where the slopes of the Andes meet the rim of the Amazon basin, are considered to be the most biodiverse areas on earth.

LAND BEFORE MAN

In geological time, Ecuador is a relatively young country formed by the collision of tectonic plates just a few million years ago. The clash of these subterranean titans threw up the great mountain system, the Andean *cordillera*, that forms the 6,500-km (4,000-mile) western fringe of South America. Like the Himalayas, these young, rugged and sharp-ridged mountains aren't yet time-hardened nor ground smooth and smaller by the relentless impact of wind and water. Meanwhile, underground, the titanic plates continue to shift around making Ecuador constantly vulnerable to sudden earthquakes and volcanic eruptions.

Lying 1,000 km (625 miles) off the Pacific coast, the Galápagos Islands were created of the solidified lava from erupting undersea volcanoes. It is thought that they are attached to a slowly moving tectonic plate, named Nazca after a pre-Incan coastal state. Below Nazca lies the stationary Hot Spot in the earth's magma. As Nazca inches its way to the southeast, nudged by other titans to the north and west, Hot Spot shoots torpedoes up from its hull, so to speak, creating new volcanoes and, possibly, new islands. This theory fits with the fact that the younger, more volcanically active islands such as Fernandina and Isabela, are on the northwest side of the archipelago, while the older ones, such as Española, are to the southeast. It also supports the now current belief that Galápagos Islands have never been physically attached to the mainland.

Including the Galápagos Islands, Ecuador consists of four contrasting regions, each one distinctly different from the others. The **Galápagos** are arid, volcanic outcrops patterned with moon-like lava flows and twisted rock formations. No soft Pacific palms fringe their rocky shores. Plants and creatures here that have adapted to these harsh conditions are tough and hardy — thick-skinned iguanas, giant armor-plated tortoises, blubber-bound sea lions, spiny acacia, spiky cactuses, saltbush and scalesia.

The coastline and the coastal plain, simply called **La Costa**, present a less fierce face — marshland, mangrove swamps (or what is left of them after the invasion of shrimp

PREVIOUS PAGES: Beaming seller of colored yarn LEFT at Latacunga market. Panama hat supremo, Homero Ortega RIGHT, from Cuenca. OPPOSITE: Ancient volcanic crater in the highlands of Santa Cruz Island, Galápagos.

farms), creeks, estuaries and long stretches of empty beaches swathed with palm trees. The hot and humid coastal plains were thickly forested before man arrived with his machete to create banana, cacao, coffee, sugar cane and rice plantations. As these plantations encroached further upon the forest, Ecuador became a full-fledged banana republic and is now reputed to be the world's leading exporter.

Upwards and eastwards, the flanks of the Andes are clothed in mists and residual areas of thick cloud forests threaded with

silvery waterfalls. In the highland valleys, the **Sierra**, the face of the landscape takes a more worn and hewn look. Tilled and retilled for centuries before the Incas and the Spanish came along, the ancient, geometric fields, which are terraced on the steeper slopes, transform the valleys into tapestries woven in pastel shades of brown and green. Splashes of deep red on the ponchos of Indian women herding sheep provide a vivid color contrast, while llamas grazing by high mountain lakes embellish the pastoral scenes. Above the valleys tower snow-white peaks, stern and dangerous, the world's tallest active volcanoes.

Over the other side of the mountains, the eastern slopes of the Andes stretch towards the great Amazon basin, the world's largest rainforest. The word itself, Amazonia, resonates with deep mysteries and hidden dangers. The Ecuadorians call this vast area of their country El Oriente, The East. The discovery of oil in the Oriente in the 1970s has led to the building of new roads, destruction and contamination of huge tracts of virgin forest and increasing numbers of "colonists," as well as new diseases, cultural decimation and anger within the local indigenous populations. Rivers flowing down the Andes and through their tribal lands eventually link up with the mighty Amazon River on its 3,200-km (2,000-mile) journey across Brazil and into the Atlantic Ocean.

HISTORICAL BACKGROUND

Who were the first South Americans, and when did they arrive on the continent? It is thought that the first humans to set foot here were descendants of Asian nomads who crossed from Siberia to Alaska over the Bering Strait. Over many generations these travelers moved down the American continent, through the Isthmus of Panama and into South America.

Some historians say the first evidence of man in South America comes from eastern Brazil and dates back 30,000 years, while others believe that man has inhabited the continent for as long as 50,000 or even 80,000 years. It is further suggested that some of the first settlers may have been Polynesians who sailed across the Pacific many thousands of years ago and landed on the western coast.

The earliest firm evidence of human presence in Ecuador is thought to be Stone Age tools found in the Quito area dating from around 9000 BC. But the first signs of settled, pottery-making communities date from about 3000 BC, when the Valdivian tribes inhabited central areas of the coast. Artifacts and figurines made by the Valdivians can be seen in museums in Quito and Guayaquil.

Curiously, Valdivian pots are similar to Jomon pots made during a similar period on the Japanese island of Kyushu. Later coastal cultures made figurines that strongly resemble Asian Buddhas, and clay model houses that look like pagodas. But theories that there were long-distance travel connections between the respective cultures require further investigation.

What is certain is that many cultures, each with their own language, customs and style of artifacts, developed in coastal areas, sometimes trading with each other, sometimes fighting. The Machalilla Culture, for example, extended along the coasts of southern Manabí and the Santa Elena peninsula, lasting from about 1500 to 800 BC. An idiosyncrasy that the Machalilla people shared with some other coastal cultures was their practice of deforming their skulls as a beauty technique in order to increase the slope of the forehead and make the nose protrude.

In the same area, but at a later period, people of the Manta culture made balsa wood boats and sailed as far as Chile and Mexico, trading pink spondylous shells from which they made jewelry. It is possible, even probable, that Manteños also sailed to the Galápagos Islands. The people of the La Tolita Culture (600 BC to 400 AD), from northern Esmeraldas, created beautiful gold and platinum jewelry using techniques that Europeans didn't develop until thousands of years later. Studies of these Ecuadorian coastal cultures indicate that they were the first of their kind to develop in South America and helped shape the civilization of the continent.

In the Sierra, a similar mixture of tribal groupings developed, each with their own language, traditions, craft techniques and style of dress. In the south of the highlands, around present-day Cuenca, the Canari Indians produced sophisticated textiles, such as *ikat* weaving, which is found nowhere else in the world except in Guatemala and Indonesia. The Canari also trained powerful military forces, which they deployed against the rising power of the Inca state towards the south in the 14th and 15th centuries. In time, however, the powerful, disciplined and highly organized Incan forces defeated the Canaris and achieved their ambition of dominating the fertile valleys of the northern Andes.

The Spanish Conquest

In what was for them a lucky coincidence, the first Spanish explorers landed on the Pacific

OPPOSITE: Pottery at a craft market in Cuenca. ABOVE: The Inca ruins at Ingapirca are the most important of their type in Ecuador. The original structure functioned as a fort, a temple or an observatory, or perhaps all three.

Coast of South America in 1526, the year of the death of the great Inca chief, Huayna Capac, who left his empire divided between two sons, Atahualpa in Quito and Huáscar in Cuzco in the south. While two halves of the Incan empire were fighting each other the Spanish stepped into a vacuum of power. Although Spanich forces were small, their superior weapons, armor and fearsome horses never before seen on the South American continent, gave the them a powerful advantage.

Many local tribes joined the Spanish in their fight against their Incan masters. For their part, the Spanish used every means at their disposal to assert their power. Though accounts of it differ in detail, one story is worth repeating because of its great historical importance. When the conquistador, Francisco Pizarro invited the leader of the northern part of the Inca empire, Atahualpa, for negotiations in Cajamarca in Peru, the Spanish promptly arrested him. Atahualpa arranged a huge ransom, enough gold to fill his prison cell and twice that amount in silver. Taking the treasure, the Spanish summarily put the Inca on trial charged with incest, polygamy, worshipping false gods and other counts that were crimes to the Spanish, but not to the Incas.

Atahualpa was found guilty and executed on August 29, 1533. In the last moments of his life the Inca chief converted to Christianity in order to qualify for the lesser sentence of execution by garroting instead of the more painful and prolonged death by burning. This duplicitous and tragic event was the blow that felled the once-mighty Inca Empire.

The Incas continued fighting the Spanish for two years after the death of their leader, but with ruthless efficiency the Spanish soon defeated the Inca forces and destroyed their buildings, replacing them quite rapidly with Spanish-style houses and Christian churches. When the Spanish leader, Sebastián de Belalcázar, marched on the kingdom of Quito, he found the city in ruins. The Inca leader, Rumiñahui, had ordered the destruction of the city rather than leave to the Spanish the sacred Inca temples dedicated to the worship of the sun and the moon. Quito was refounded by the Spanish as Villa de San Francisco de Quito in 1534, and the following year Rumiñahui was captured, tortured and executed.

In the early days, the province that is now the country of Ecuador was ruled by Spanish authorities in Lima, Peru, who themselves answered to the King of Spain. But in 1563 the colony was granted the status of Audencia de Quito, a judicial and political body with considerably more autonomy, and more powers to deal directly with Madrid.

As the city grew in stature it developed its own school of art, the Quito School, which combined Spanish religious traditions with local Indian inspiration. Paintings and sculptures produced at that time are still among Quito's greatest treasures. At the same time, the colonial masters expropriated large areas of land to form estates and used the Indians as a source of forced labor, while at the same time trying to convert them to Christianity. Observing the skill of the Indian weavers, the colonists established weaving workshops and imported new machinery and sheep to make wool.

Without much change, the colonial feudal system continued to operate for some three hundred years. In the eighteenth century there were several uprising by oppressed Indians, but it was external changes that eventually disturbed the equilibrium. The French Revolution, Napoleon's conquest of Spain, and the United States War of Independence fueled a nascent nationalism among liberal thinkers in South America, including Ecuador. People of Spanish origin who were born in Ecuador also resented the privileges of the Spanish-born elite who held the top positions of power in the country. With a growing demand for independence, the days of all-powerful, expatriate Spanish rulers were numbered.

INDEPENDENCE

Rumbling discontent turned to open violence. Supported by the "Great Liberator," Simón Bolívar, who had already fought for and won the liberation of his birthplace, Venezuela, Ecuador achieved freedom from colonial rule in 1822. In the final, decisive battle, the Ecuadorian leader, Antonio José de Sucre (after whom Ecuadorian currency is named), defeated Spanish colonial forces in the Battle of Pichincha and took Quito. Guayaquil, incidentally, had achieved independence two years earlier. Initially Ecuador became part of the Bolívar's Federation of Gran Colombia, which included Colombia and Venezuela, but the federation broke up in 1830 and Ecuador at last became a completely independent nation.

As in most post-colonial periods, things did not run smoothly in the early days of the Ecuadorian republic. Constitutions were written and rewritten, presidents came and went and power struggles that have characterized the country ever since soon emerged. Liberal-conservative polarization largely reflected traditional conflicts between the progressive and commercial values of the Guayaquileños and the rest of the coast and more established, conformist beliefs of the Quiteños and the highlanders.

Two politicians who served as president at the end of the nineteenth and the beginning of the twentieth centuries exemplified

these divisions. Gabriel García Moreno, known as the father of Ecuadorian conservatism, was from Guayaquil, but his early liberal ideas shifted to the right when he married into an aristocratic Quito family. Elected president for the first time in 1860, he sought to unify the nation through the Roman Catholic Church. Education and welfare were placed in the hands of the church, ties to the Vatican were strengthened and in 1861 Catholicism was declared the state religion. At the same time Moreno embarked on some progressive projects, includ-

In Ecuador, you can usually tell where someone is from by their hat. OPPOSITE: A Cañari woman with child. ABOVE: At the animal market at Otavalo.

ing the building of schools and hospitals and the construction of the Guayaquil to Quito railway. Moreno's political career and second presidential term came to an abrupt end in 1875 on the steps of the presidential palace where a crazed farmer hacked him to death.

Personifying the liberal side of Ecuadorian politics, the career of Eloy Alfaro Delgado, who was born in Montecristi on the coast, was similarly fated. Elected president in 1897, Alfaro's first move was to create a secular constitution and to eliminate the Church's power of censorship. He exiled clergy, seized church lands for the state, instituted civil marriages and divorce and broke the special links with the Vatican. He built ports and roads and oversaw the completion of Moreno's railway project, which provided an important link between the coast and the highlands.

Alfaro's first presidential term was followed by more than a decade of political instability during which power was tossed back and forth between Alfaro and several opponents. In 1911 Alfaro returned from exile in Panama, attempted another coup d'état, and was lynched on the streets by a pro-clerical mob.

MODERN TIMES

Since independence, mostly civilian governments have run Ecuador. But there have been a number of military coups and for some periods, notably from 1926 to 1931, 1963 to 1966 and 1972 to 1979, military regimes were in overt control.

The military also played behind-the-scenes roles in the extraordinary political situation in early 1997 when the then president, Abdala Bucarám, former mayor of Guayaquil who called himself "El Loco" (the Madman), was forced out of office. An unprecedented popular uprising took place in which hundreds of thousands of people took to the streets in protest against the president's outrageous conduct and massive and blatant corruption. Congress, supported by the military, relieved the Madman of his post for reasons of "mental incapacity."

For one day during this chaotic transition period, when Bucarám refused to leave the presidential palace, three people claimed the presidency: the recalcitrant Bucarám, the vice-president, Dr. Rosalía Ortega, who had automatically succeeded to the post, and a new president, Fabian Alarcon, who had been appointed by the Senate. In spite of the political chaos, the crisis was solved in an intelligent Ecuadorian way, without a shot fired on the streets and with just one casualty. Fabian Alarcon was later confirmed as interim president until new elections.

Modern Ecuador has been fortunate not to have suffered any major civil or international wars. The one exception was a border conflict with Peru. This is a result of what Ecuador claims to have been an unfair treaty in 1942 in which Peru was granted Amazonian territory claimed by Ecuador. There are good reasons to believe that Ecuador is right in its claim, but there are equally good reasons to think that Ecuador will never get the territory back in contravention of an acknowledged international treaty. Every year or so, it seems, there are vicious border clashes over the issue, the most recent occurring in 1995.

Internally, one of the major issues concerns oil exploration in the Oriente and rights of the local Indian populations. These are tough political issues that aren't likely to go away for some time.

THE RIVER OF LIFE

The extraordinary ethnic diversity of Ecuadorians is nowhere more apparent than on the streets of Quito. Sitting outside a café on the busy, exhaust-filled main street of Avenida Amazonas on a weekday lunchtime, the river of Ecuadorian life flows past. The first people to catch your eye as a visitor will be the indigenous peoples in traditional costumes and pork-pie hats selling trinkets and paintings on the sidewalks. Probably they are *indígenas* from Chimborazu Province in the highlands, where they make colorful Tigua paintings on leather — brilliant miniatures of fiestas under snow-capped volcanoes; tourist art, to be sure, but charming in its way, a glimpse into the surreal and dreamtime mind of the Quichua Indian.

There are estimated to be about two million highland Quichua-speaking Indians in

Ecuador, mostly descended from the various tribes who lived in these parts of the Andes before the Inca invasion. Some are descendants of the Incas themselves, such as the black poncho-wearing, white-hatted folk from Saraguro, and others will have ancestors who were *mitmakuna*, peoples who were transferred by the Incas from other areas as educators, military personnel or administrators, or simply because they were considered to be troublemakers.

Quechua, spelled with an "e," is the language of the Quechua peoples, the language imposed by the Incas. Part of the Andean-Equatorial family of languages, it is *lingua franca* among *indígenas* in Ecuador, Bolivia, Columbia, Argentina, and Chile. There are several dialects, one of which is Quichua, with an "i," which is commonly spoken in Ecuador. Quechua and Quichua are different transcriptions and are often used interchangeably. If this sounds complicated, it is.

ABOVE: Time out for a shoe shine in the backstreets of Quito's Old City.

During the colonial days the Quichuas (or Quechuas) worked in feudal conditions on the estates of the big haciendas, and some still do. But with the land reforms of 1964, most of the estates were broken up and local Indians lost their jobs and security. Now they farm their small holdings in the mountains or come to Quito to sell trinkets on the streets.

Many of Quito's fast-growing population of about three million have come from the countryside in the last 30 years and few of them have regular work. The 1970s and 1980s saw a huge increase in the urban unemployed. Though as a visitor you may not see slums, there are many deprived areas in the city without running water, sewage systems or electricity.

Trinket-selling Quichuas are only a small minority of the crowds on Avenida Amazonas. Most are office workers and business people, smartly dressed in western clothes, busy, walking fast to get things done on their lunch breaks or to grab a hamburger at a fast food joint. These are olive-skinned *mestizos,* mixed race peoples who make up the majority of Quito's growing middle class.

Although they might have some Spanish blood, young mestizos are generally not much interested in the colonial past or the festivals that celebrate the founding of their city by the Spanish. They identify themselves as Ecuadorians and are less an ethnic category than a segment of the social spectrum. Making up about half of the population, it is mostly mestizos that you will meet in Ecuador.

Down the street from where we sit, ladies from Otavalo, in their crisp, clean embroidered blouses, bright glass necklaces and long dark skirts, set up stands selling sweaters, shawls and ponchos. They feel themselves more Otavaleño than Ecuadorian and are proud to wear their traditional costume. Otovaleños are the success story of the Quechua Indians. Otavalo textiles are almost an international brand name and are

ABOVE: The river of Ecuadorian life flows along Quito's Avenida Amazonas. RIGHT: Plaza de la Independencia in the Old City.

sold all over the world. Otovaleños run their own businesses and gain professional qualifications as doctors, accountants and archaeologists. Some of them drive around in new BMWs.

A tall black woman in a very short skirt strides past. Perhaps she's a model or a visiting pop star from the United States, or maybe she works here in Quito in the nighttime entertainment business. Blacks are a very small minority in Quito. They come from the coast in Esmeraldas province, where for centuries they existed more or less as an independent state cut off from the rest of the country. Descended from slaves who escaped from a shipwreck off the coast in the sixteenth century, they have retained many aspects of their African culture, in particular the intricate rhythms of marimba music. Another community of blacks, heirs of local plantation workers, lives in the Chota Valley in the northwest of the country.

You won't see many people from the Oriente in central Quito. The *indígenas* from the rainforest only come here when they have to, which could be for a protest meeting about the damage being done by oil companies to their traditional homelands. The Huaorani from the Napo area have been particularly active in this respect. Organized by CONAIE (Confederation of Indian Nations of Ecuador), protests were also held in 1992 against the 500th anniversary of Columbus' discovery of the Americas that the *indígenas* consider to have led to a brutal conquest.

There are several tribal groupings living in the Ecuadorian Amazon, ranging from the Cofáns, the Siona and the Sequoia in the north to the Huaorani in the central areas south of the Napo River, and the Shuar (also known as Jivaro) and Achuar in the Pastaza river area in the south. Each have their own customs and language, but many people speak Quichua and some Spanish. Other Quichua-speaking tribes, the Awa, the Cayapas, the Colorados, live in the coastal lowlands but their numbers are dwindling.

Roughly speaking, whites, or *blancos*, make up 15% of Ecuador's racially mixed population of some 11 million, with the *indígenas* accounting for 40%, mestizos 40% and blacks, five percent. A few pureblood whites are descended from the Spanish rulers, but in most of the old families there are some traces of Indian blood. Many whites have arrived in Ecuador in the recent past to work as English teachers, perhaps, or in the oil industry.

Other immigrants to Ecuador include the Chinese, some of whose families arrived at the beginning of the century to help build railways. Lebanese are also an important group of new Ecuadorians, most of whom live in Guayaquil. The former president, Abdala Bucarám is from a Lebanese family. The Ecuadorian river of life that flows down Avenida Amazonas includes all shades, from black to white.

ARTISTS AND ARTISANS

The Spanish conquistadors were no doubt pleasantly surprised when they arrived four and a half centuries ago to find a land of weavers and craftsmen. Certainly today visitors become very excited about hand-

woven Ecuadorian clothes and handicrafts. Everywhere you go, it seems, there's something to buy. You might be driving up through mountains on some remote dusty track and suddenly, spread out on the grass beside the road, will be a checkered carpet of handwoven items of woolen clothing minded by a handful of mountain *indígenas* in colorful, bulbous ponchos.

The first market most serious shoppers head for is Otavalo, about two hours by bus or car north of Quito. This is one of the world's great markets where you can buy

many Ecuadorian products — not only the well-known Otavalo-made items, but textiles and handicrafts from all over the country. What you might not find, however, are everyday items that local people wouldn't think about selling at big markets or to foreigners. The avid craft connoisseur has to look beyond Otavalo to the specialist craft villages and the smaller country markets.

Northern Ecuador is known for exquisitely embroidered skirts, blouses, tablecloths and napkins. Many of them are made in the west of Imbabura Province and can be bought in the markets of Otavalo and Ibarra. Excellent leather goods of all sorts, such as bags, purses, jackets, belts, trousers, even saddles, are made in Cotacachi, north of Otavalo, and can be bought from the shops and workshops in the village. For woodcarvings, go to San Antonio de Ibarra where the locals make everything from sculpture to furniture.

Ikat textiles, made with a sophisticated weaving technique in which the thread is tied and dyed in sections, are one of Ecuador's specialties. The process is used to make shawls, *macanas* (carrying cloths), ponchos and blankets. Good *ikats* are made in the Cuenca region, though the best *paños* (shawls with macramé figures) and scarves come from Gualaceo, and fine macanas are made in the Salcedo region.

Wool or cotton tapestries (*tapices*), often depicting images of *indígenas* and mountain scenes, are made around the village of Salasaca, near Baños and in the Otavalo area. Salasaca and Cañar are known for their double-sided belts (*chumbis*), while knitted sweaters, gloves, socks and hats as well as woven ponchos, blankets and other woolen items are made throughout the sierra. *Shigra* straw bags are made in the central sierra.

Panama hats are woven in villages around Cuenca although they come from the Montecristi area on the coast, and some of the best ones are still made there. Cuenca is also known for its large, lidded reed baskets. Near Montecristi, the village of Pujili produces honest reproduction pre-Columbian figurines as well as (so it is said) fake antiques. Ceramics for everyday use are made in many places throughout the country, but some high-end work is produced in Cuenca. Quichua *indígenas* in central Oriente make coiled bowls and pots with hand-painted designs of Quichua life and mythology. Chordeleg near Cuenca specializes in filigree jewelry, while Saraguro is known for its decorative shawl pins (*tupus*).

CONTEMPORARY ART

After the Spanish conquest, Ecuadorian craftsmen adapted their skills to decorate the great new churches and monasteries of Quito. Adding their own taste and imagination to European techniques of carving and painting, they helped create the School of Quito, which became influential throughout the New World and is characterized by realistic and gruesome scenes of martyrdom.

The techniques Quito craftsmen learned from the Spanish are the historical foundation of contemporary Ecuadorian painting and sculpture. There is also an interesting parallel in terms of the subject matter. While the theme of most early Quito art was Christian suffering, many twentieth century Ecuadorian artists have also portrayed suffering, but they have replaced the suffering of Christian martyrs with the distress and exploitation of the indigenous peoples.

The internationally famous artist Oswaldo Guayasamín, the son of an *indígena* himself, is the leading exponent of the indigenist school, an artistic movement that was prominent from the 1940s to the 1960s. Many of his powerful, cubist-influenced paintings depict pain and poverty and some have strong political messages. One of a series of panels he made for the Congress building in Quito shows a skull under a Nazi helmet inscribed with the letters "CIA." In spite of official protests and threats from the United States his work remains intact and *in situ*. Guayasamín's work can be seen at his museum in Quito (see WHAT TO SEE, page 73, under QUITO).

Other leading artists who were part of the indigenist movement include Eduardo Kingman whose tactile, colorful paintings explore the essence of *indígena* sorrow and exclusion. Camilo Egas, a versatile painter expressed the dignity rather than the sorrow of his indigenist subjects. Some of Manuel Rendón's fine and wide-ranging body of work was also indigenist in content.

Of the above artists, Oswaldo Guayasamín, now in his eighties, has returned to the roots of Ecuadorian painting with a massive mural project for the interior of a chapel near his museum in Quito, while the others have moved on to paint in that big studio in the sky. Prominent among a new generation of painters are the abstract expressionists Marcelo Aguirre, Ramiro Jácome and Carlos Rosero and the surreal landscape artist Charles Egas.

Places to see modern art in Quito include the Casa de la Cultura Museo Guayasamín and the Museo Camilo Egas (see under QUITO, page 66, in ANDEAN HIGHLANDS), La Galería on Juan Rodriguez No. 168 and Diego de Almargo, Art Forum on Juan León Mera No. 870 and Wilson, CDX on Juan León Mera and Baquedano Esquina, and at the weekend open-air art displays in Parque El Ejido on Avenida Patria, a few blocks west of the Casa de la Cultura. The city of Cuenca holds a biannual arts festival in November on years ending with even numbers.

OPPOSITE: Craft items made by the Cofán Indians. ABOVE: Paintings by internationally-known artist Oswaldo Guayasamín in his museum in Quito.

Andean Highlands

A TWIN CHAIN OF ANDEAN PEAKS, THE AVENUE of Volcanoes, cuts through the center of Ecuador, from north to south, like the dislocated spine of some fossilized creature, each vertebra a volcanic peak. A series of wide, intensely cultivated, densely pop-ulated valleys lie between the parallel rows of mountains. These are the food baskets of Ecuador that for thousands of years have produced grain, fruit, vegetables and dairy products for the high sierra. As you pass through the fertile highland basins you'll see a panoramic patchwork of fields planted with all manner of crops. Stretching across some of these fields are huge plastic greenhouses used for one of the country's fastest-growing export businesses, the cultivation of flowers.

The Avenue of Volcanoes also cradles the main thoroughfare that runs up and down the spine of the country. For centuries local Quichua Indians and other *indígenas* have trudged this route, or ridden it on mules and donkeys, carrying crops from the fields, and produce to market. So they do today, many still wearing traditional costumes of handwoven shawls and wide-brimmed hats, and carrying huge loads on their backs. But more often these days they travel in cars, trucks or flashy, honking, dangerously speeding buses. Today this dusty, often pot-holed, sometimes smooth road that follows the ancient route is part of the rather grandly named Pan-American Highway (theoretically it's possible to journey through North and Central America and down the South American continent without leaving the highway).

Traveling up and down the Pan-American Highway (known as "the Pana") through the Avenue of Volcanoes is a pleasure for any visitor who spends some time in Ecuador. To visit the famous tourist market at Otavalo, you pass north from Quito along the Pana by car or bus. To get to the popular spa resort of Baños you must go south through Ambato. If you want to stay at one of the fine *haciendas* of the Sierra you must take the road south or north. To go in another direction would mean hurtling down the steep slopes of the Andes, either towards the upper reaches of the Amazon basin to the east, or to the coastal plain in the west. The Pana is indeed Ecuador's main transport artery.

For many foreign travelers the most dramatic and fascinating features of Ecuador are its mystical, majestic mountains. Some 30 peaks in the vicinity of the Avenue of Volcanoes, some still smoldering, give the area one of the highest concentrations of volcanoes in the world. Much of the time these peaks are draped in swirling clouds and mists because, it is said, the mountains are shy and modest. But on a clear day the views over green fields to the snow-crowned peaks are spectacular.

At 6,310m (21,031 ft), Chimborazo, Ecuador's tallest mountain, presides over the western chain of mountains, Cordillera Occidental. It was believed to be the tallest mountain in the world until Mt. Everest was surveyed in the mid-nineteenth century. Indeed, every Ecuadorian schoolchild knows that Chimborazo, which means "mountain of snow," is the world's tallest mountain if measured from the center of the earth — remember the earth bulges around the equator! The English climber, Edward Whymper first climbed Chimborazo, in 1880.

The tallest peak of the eastern, and geologically older chain, Cordillera Central, is the stunning and almost perfectly symmetrical cone of Cotopaxi, which means "shining peak." At 5,897m (19,654 ft), it is the world's tallest continuously active volcano. It has erupted some 50 times since 1738, and scars

PREVIOUS PAGES: Fertile valley in the Andean Highlands near San Pablo Lake LEFT and local highland style RIGHT. OPPOSITE: Broad valley in the Avenue of Volcanoes. ABOVE: The snow-capped peak of Mt. Chimborazo.

and lava flows from past volcanic activities can be seen in its vicinity. The 1877 eruption produced mudflows which traveled 100 km (62 miles). In 1997 people living near Cotopaxi reported that the snowcap was melting, fearing that the mountain would erupt again and destroy their homes and farms.

The upper part of Cotopaxi is permanently covered in snow and often hidden by clouds that at night are sometimes lit up by fires in the 360-m (1,200-ft) crater. The base of the volcano stands in open mountain grassland, the páramo, which is part of the bleak, yet beautiful 34,000-hectare (84,150-acre) Cotopaxi National Park. Only 50 km (31 miles) from Quito, this is Ecuador's most frequently visited national park. The German scientist and traveler Wilhelm Reiss first climbed Cotopaxi in 1872.

QUITO

Ecuador's capital, Quito — the name itself resonates with wonder and romance — is regarded as the most beautiful and stylish city in the Andes. Your first glance from the air, as you descend towards Aeropuerto Mariscal Sucre, reveals an urbanized, South American Shangri-La stretching along a high valley beneath a string of white-topped mountains. Taking a bus or taxi into town from the airport, you pass steel-and-glass office blocks, luxury hotels and shopping malls with supermarkets, fast food franchises and multiplex cinemas. At the same time you may experience the sickness of almost all major cities: traffic jams and pollution.

Further south, in the old part of the city, you come upon a world of cobbled streets, ornate baroque churches and colonial-style mansions with tiled roofs and quiet courtyards with tinkling fountains. You have now passed from the New City to the old. Together the old and new form a fast-growing, modern metropolis woven into the fabric of an old Spanish colonial town. On the sidewalks office workers in smart suits talk on mobile phones, while local *indígenas* in colorful traditional costumes sell blankets, ponchos, chewing gum and lottery tickets. Million-dollar apartments owned by oil company executives and drug money launderers coexist with slums in impoverished barrios, where the poor and unemployed from the countryside live.

Aside from its high altitude, the most striking geographical feature of Quito is the length of the city and its bottleneck narrowness. From north to south it stretches some 30 km (19 miles), yet it is only three to five kilometers (two to three miles) wide. To the north is the residential and business district of the new town, to the south is an area of industry and low-cost housing, while at its heart is the historic center of the Old City. This narrow strip of urbanized land is wedged between the steep slopes of Mt. Pichincha to the west, and a deep canyon formed by the river Machángara to the east. In recent years the urban carpet has spread up the slopes of the mountain to the west and into the Los Chillos valley on the eastern side of the city.

Despite pollution in parts of the city at certain times of the day, Quito has an almost perfect climate best described as perpetual springtime. By midday the temperature usually reaches a pleasant high of about 22°C (72°F) while average nighttime temperatures are 11°C (52°F). Since the city is only a few miles south of the equator, there is little climatic variation throughout the year, though in the so-called winter months (October to May) it often rains in the afternoon. In spite of the agreeable climate, clouds often veil the surrounding mountain peaks. Quiteños say that they have two types of weather: either sunny with clouds, or cloudy with sunshine.

In general, Quito's fine climate makes for good health and a feeling of well-being, but it takes most visitors a day or two to adjust to the altitude. At nearly 3,000 m (10,000 ft) above sea level, this is the third highest capital in the world after La Paz in Bolivia and Lhasa in Tibet. You might find yourself out of breath carrying your luggage at the airport or walking up your first steep slope. Other symptoms of altitude sicknesses are headaches, nausea and lassitude. To deal with the problem, avoid alcohol and cigarettes, drink plenty of water, and lie down a lot. Almost everyone recovers quickly but if you're not better within a day or two you're obviously not cut out for high altitudes, so cut your losses and head downhill!

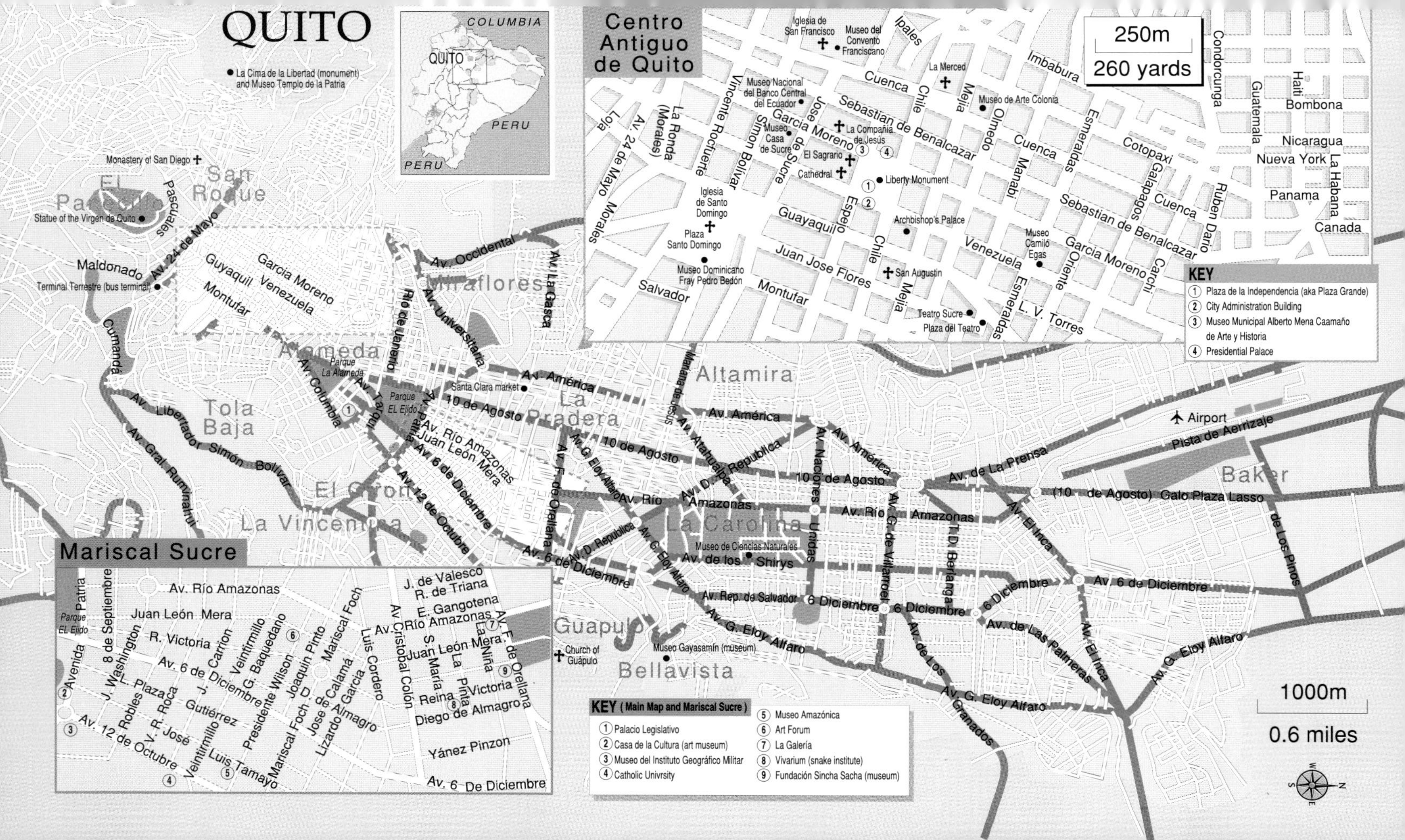
QUITO
La Cima de la Libertad (monument) and Museo Templo de la Patria
COLUMBIA
QUITO
PERU
PERU
Monastery of San Diego
San Roque
El Panecillo
Statue of the Virgen de Quito
Pascuales
Av. 24 de Mayo
Maldonado
Terminal Terrestre (bus terminal)
Garcia Moreno
Guyaquil
Venezuela
Montufar
Cumandá
Alameda
Parque La Alameda
Av. Columbia
Av. Tarqui
Parque EL Ejido
Av. Patria
Tola Baja
Av. Libertador Simón Bolívar
Av. Gral. Rumiñahui
El Girón
La Vicentina
Av. Occidental
Av. La Gasca
Miraflores
Río de Janerio
Av. Universitaria
Santa Clara market
Av. América
La Pradera
10 de Agosto
Av. Río Amazonas
Juan León Mera
Av. 6 de Diciembre
Av. 12 de Octubre
Av. F. de Orellana
Av. G. Eloy Alfaro
Av. Río Amazonas
Av. D. Republica
Av. Atahualpa
Mañana de Jesús
Altamira
Av. Naciones Unidas
La Carolina
Museo de Ciencias Naturales
Av. de los Shirys
Av. Rep. de Salvador
6 Diciembre
Av. G. de Villarroel
T.D. Berlanga
Av. de La Prensa
(10 de Agosto) Galo Plaza Lasso
Av. El Inca
de Los Pinos
Airport
Pista de Aerrizaje
Baker
Av. de Las Palmeras
Av. de Los Granados
Guapulo
Church of Guápulo
Museo Gayasamín (museum)
Bellavista
1000m
0.6 miles
Centro Antiguo de Quito
250m
260 yards
Iglesia de San Francisco
Museo del Convento Franciscano
Ipales
La Merced
Imbabura
Condorcunga
Guatemala
Haiti
Bombona
Nicaragua
Nueva York
La Habana
Panama
Canada
Cuenca
Chile
Mejia
Museo de Arte Colonia
Olmedo
Esmeraldas
Cotopaxi
Galapagos
Ruben Dario
Museo Nacional del Banco Central del Ecuador
Jose de Sucre
Garcia Moreno
La Compañia de Jesús
Sebastian de Benalcazar
Manabi
Museo Casa de Sucre
El Sagrario
Cathedral
Liberty Monument
Loja
Av. 24 de Mayo
Morales
La Ronda (Morales)
Vicente Rocfuerte
Simon Bolívar
Iglesia de Santo Domingo
Plaza Santo Domingo
Espejo
Guayaquil
Archbishop's Palace
Museo Camilo Egas
Oriente
Carchi
Venezuela
Juan Jose Flores
San Augustin
Museo Dominicano Fray Pedro Bedón
Salvador
Montufar
Teatro Sucre
Plaza del Teatro
L. V. Torres
KEY
1 Plaza de la Independencia (aka Plaza Grande)
2 City Administration Building
3 Museo Municipal Alberto Mena Caamaño de Arte y Historia
4 Presidential Palace
Mariscal Sucre
Parque EL Ejido
Avenida Patria
8 de Septiembre
Av. Río Amazonas
Juan León Mera
J. Washington
R. Victoria
L. Plaza
Robles
R. Roca
V. E. José
Av. 12 de Octubre
Av. 6 de Diciembre
J. Carrion
Veintimillo
Gutiérrez
Luis Tamayo
G. Baquedano
Presidente Wilson
Joaquin Pinto
Mariscal Foch
Jose Calamá
D. de Almagro
Lizardo Garcia
Luis Cordero
Av. Cristobal Colón
J. de Valesco
R. de Triana
E. Gangotena
Av. Río Amazonas
Juan León Mera
S. María
La Niña
La Pinta
Reina Victoria
Diego de Almagro
Av. F. de Orellana
Yánez Pinzon
Av. 6 De Diciembre
KEY (Main Map and Mariscal Sucre)
1 Palacio Legislativo
2 Casa de la Cultura (art museum)
3 Museo del Instituto Geográfico Militar
4 Catholic Univrsity
5 Museo Amazónica
6 Art Forum
7 La Galería
8 Vivarium (snake institute)
9 Fundación Sincha Sacha (museum)

Quito has all the attractions and amenities of most major cities. For tourists, the best-known and most useful area is Mariscal in the New City, a series of streets running off and parallel to Avenida Río Amazonas, between the major cross streets of Avenida Patria and Avenida Franciso de Orellana. Here you will travel agencies, airlines, funky bars and restaurants, nightclubs, inexpensive hostels, the best and most expensive hotels, trendy galleries and exciting crafts and clothing shopping. Indeed, there is very little that Quito lacks. It even has its fair share of that common city blight, pickpockets, which means that visitors must take special care of themselves and their possessions at all times. In particular, it's advisable to avoid walking alone through the streets at night.

BACKGROUND

The takeover of the northern highlands around present-day Quito by the conquistadors was for the Spanish partly a matter of lucky timing. Only a few decades before the first Spaniards landed on the coast in 1526 many of the tribes of the area had been forced into the Inca Empire. At that time the far-flung empire itself was engaged in civil war as a result of rivalry between the two half-brothers, Atahualpa and Huascar, respective leaders of the northern and southern territories. The Spanish exploited divisions among the Incas, murdered Atahualpa and won the support of the newly conquered tribes, who had no loyalty to their recently acquired Inca masters. In addition, Spanish firearms and cannons gave the "bearded white strangers" huge superiority in battle.

In 1534, Sebastián de Belalcázar, a lieutenant of the conquistador Francisco Pizarro, marched from the south up the spine of the Andes towards Quito. Near Ríobamba, he and his cohorts met a huge Incan army, the largest Inca force ever gathered against the Spanish, which they managed to evade under the cover of night.

OPPOSITE: The Church and Monastery of San Francisco, dedicated to Quito's patron saint, is the city's largest colonial building and the oldest Christian structure in South America.

Continuing north, the Spaniards gathered local tribespeople into their ranks and entered Quito in early December. They skirmished with the Inca general, Rumiñahui (Face of Stone) who, realizing he was going to be defeated, burned down the Inca palace rather than leave it intact for the Spanish. On December 6, the Villa de San Francisco de Quito was officially founded on the ashes of the Inca town. Rumiñahui was captured, tortured and executed.

Though they retained the name Quito, which is derived from the Quitus, one of the tribes in the area, the Spanish lost no time in creating a new city in their own image. On the foundations of Inca houses they built their own churches and convents, monasteries and mansions, using Inca stones from the rubble for the floors and façades. Construction of the magnificent Church of San Francisco began within weeks of the Spanish takeover, making it the oldest church in South America. In the traditional Spanish way, they built streets radiating from a main square in the center of the city, and they divided the city into 200 lots, one for each conquistador.

In order to embellish their grandiose buildings the Franciscans soon established the Quito School of Art, the first of its kind in South America. Local artists and craftsmen learned to make exquisite wooden polychrome sculptures and paintings, many of them characterized by savage Christian themes of martyrdom and mutilation. Quito's churches and museums contain a wealth of beautiful but gruesome renditions of Christ on the cross, and scenes of diabolical tortures that are part of a religious art movement that flourished throughout the Spanish colonial period. At the end of the sixteenth century Quito became the seat of the royal *Audencia*, a governmental court, and was known as the "Cloister of America" because of the collection of religious edifices that occupied a quarter of the Old City. In one square kilometer in the center of Old Quito there are 17 major Christian places of worship, while there are an estimated 86 churches in the whole city.

In 1978 UNESCO designated Old Quito as a World Heritage Site in recognition of the importance of its old colonial center. De-

velopment in the historic area became more strictly controlled, and a number of conservation projects were undertaken. There is still much to be done. A recent report by the Getty Conservation Institute, which is also involved in projects in the Old City, tells of deterioration, pollution, overcrowding, overuse and lack of sanitation and maintenance. From dawn to dusk, the city center is an overcrowded corridor for transporting people and products between south and north. Leaded fuel turns the place into a veritable gas chamber, the report said, affecting everyone and everything. "Some buildings are used as warehouses, others are treated like dumpsites. A chaotic mass of cables, billboards, posters, and other miscellanies dangle from walls and balconies, concealing the beautiful, orderly seventeenth to nineteenth century façades."

Don't let such strong words put you off. As the Getty report says, prostitutes and petty criminals are beginning to give way to street performers and spectators. Tourism is on the rise, and pickpockets seem to be on the decline. Although the Old City has problems, its colonial architecture matches its splendid Andean setting like a jeweled pendant hanging from a magnificent mountain chain. The jewel might need some polishing, but tourists would do well to see the Old City of Quito as more than a mere staging-post on the way to the Galápagos Islands.

GENERAL INFORMATION

Independent travelers who want to get off the beaten track will find the non-profit **South America Explorers Club** (SAEC) to be an excellent source of advice, information and up-to-date travel news, as well as a place to meet fellow travelers. Annual membership is US$40 for a single person and US$60 for a couple. For this outlay, members get a comfortable place to relax in a restored colonial building in central Quito, tea and coffee making facilities, a good lending library and bookshop for maps and books about Ecuador, access to members' trip reports, knowledgeable and friendly staff, a mailing address and use of computers for e-mail, occasional talks and lectures, copies of the club's journal, use of members' notice board, advice on where to stay, facilities for storing equipment, etc. As a working and social base in Quito, I found the SAEC clubhouse to be invaluable. The club's headquarters are at 126 Indian Creek Road, Ithaca, NY 14850 USA. (There is another clubhouse in Lima, Peru.) The SAEC in Quito new town is at Jorge Washington 311 and Leonidas Plaza, Mariscal Sucre (postal address: Apartado 17-21-431, Eloy Alfaro, Quito, Ecuador) ☎/FAX (02) 225228 E-MAIL explorer@SAEC.org.ec (members use member@SAEC.org.ec). The office is open from 9:30 AM to 5 PM, weekdays only. Non-members are allowed a tour but only members are allowed to use the facilities. No references are required and you can join on the spot. A taxi from the airport to the SAEC costs about US$4.

Less useful, but free, are the three CETUR (Corporación Ecuatoriana de Turismo) offices in Quito. The main office ☎ (02) 224972 or 507559, Avenida Eloy Alfaro 1214 and Carlos Tovar, is open between 8:30 AM and 5 PM, Monday to Friday. Similar hours apply for the CETUR office ☎ (02) 514044 in the old town, on Venezuela and Chile, but CETUR's airport office ☎ (02) 246232, is open from 7 AM to 7 PM. Hotel reservations can be made from the offices in the old town and at the airport.

The **British Council** ☎ (02) 508282 or 508284 or 540225 at Amazonas 1646 and Orellana in the new town, is another well-known Quito institution. It has book and video lending libraries, English language newspapers, e-mail and Internet services, and a useful notice board (where I found an excellent Spanish teacher). It also stages art events and has a good vegetarian café, *La Galeria*. Non-members can use most of the facilities and the café, but there is an annual membership charge of about $16 for each of the two libraries. The libraries and information services are open from 7 AM to noon and 3 PM to 8 PM, Monday to Friday.

Most travelers in Ecuador rely heavily on the extensive, inexpensive network of **buses** for trips throughout the country. With Quito as the main transport hub, the starting point for most long-distance journeys is the bus terminal, **Terminal Terrestre**, at Maldonado and Cumandá, a few hundred meters south of Plaza Santo Domingo in the old town. Finding the terminal might be the most difficult part of your journey since it isn't clearly marked on some maps. When using the terminal for the first time it's probably best to take a taxi, which from most parts of Quito won't cost more than three or four dollars. Once you're familiar with the terminal, you can take the new trolley bus along 10 de Agosto to the Cumandá stop and walk down the steps. The most reliable information about buses can be obtained at the terminal, where each bus company has an office. There are frequent buses to all the main towns and cities making it unnecessary to buy tickets in advance except on major holidays and festivals. Just show up with a destination in mind (or not, if you want to be truly adventurous) and you'll find a bus going there shortly. Because there are usually thick crowds at the bus terminal keep an especially sharp eye on your belongings.

Trains are not as fast or practical as buses for getting around the country, the rail network is limited and trains don't run often. However, there are some spectacular train journeys, and passengers can have the unusual and exciting experience of riding on the roof of an ancient coach. One of the better rides is from Quito to Cotopaxi National Park, and onwards down to Ambato and Ríobamba. At present this is only a weekly service which leaves at 8 AM on Saturdays, but there is also a service to Cotopaxi which returns on Sundays. The old, decrepit, but charming **Quito Railway Station** is on Maldonado south of the old town. Take a taxi or buses No. 1 or 2 heading south. For more information on train rides, see MOUNTAIN TRAINING, page 14, in TOP SPOTS.

Within Quito **bus** and **trolley** transport is simple and inexpensive but, as always, you must be careful with your bags and wallet. The new trolley system, with its arched, glass-walled stops, runs along 10 de Agosto in the new town and along Guayaquil and Montufar in the old town. After running through the central corridor of the city, the trolleys branch off onto different routes to the suburbs. For the airport, take the trolley to Estación Norte and change to the Rumiñuahi route heading north. At about US$0.20 per ride, the trolleys are inexpensive, but still about twice the price of standard **city buses**. *Ejecutivo* and *Selectivo* bus services are a bit more expensive. Most buses run along the north-south city axis and have the name of their destination on a placard in the window: The No. 1 Aeropuerto bus goes to… well, where you would expect.

Taxis are inexpensive compared to most other places in the world, but make sure that the driver uses his meter. If he claims it's broken, negotiate the fare beforehand or find another taxi. Don't be put off by horror stories of passengers being mugged by taxi drivers. Such rare incidents occur when the

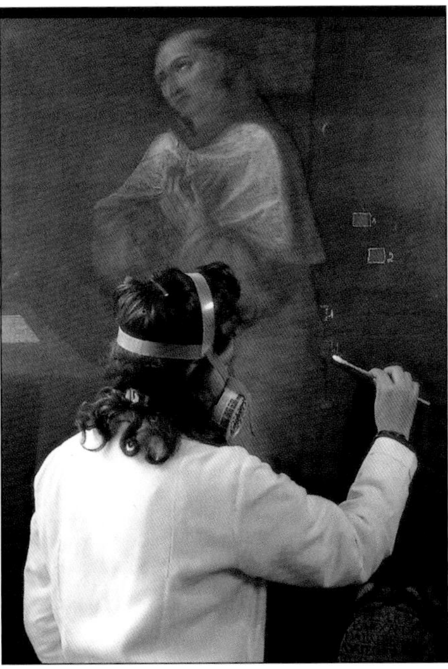

passenger is very drunk and/or it's an illegal cab. Only take the yellow cabs with a red taxi sign on top. Most taxi drivers are friendly but if you don't like the look of one, don't get in the cab. If you want to be extra safe, only use cabs from lines outside major hotels. At night, taxi fares are up to 50% more than during the day.

As in other countries, **car rentals** are easily available in Ecuador, though I'm surprised that anyone bothers. The idea of driving on unfamiliar, badly signed Ecuadorian roads, where the Highway Code is unconventional isn't my idea of fun. But I've

Restoration works in Quito. UNESCO has designated the city's Old Town as a World Heritage Site.

met people who enjoyed the adventure, while others thought it was a nightmare. Most of the major car rental companies (including Hertz ✆ (02) 560628, Budget ✆ (02) 584237 and Avis ✆ (02) 550238) have offices at the airport and downtown. A small car costs about US$35 per day including mileage or US$10 per day plus US$0.10 per kilometer. Four-wheel-drive vehicles are also available. Check carefully on insurance, tax, drop-off and other charges. The cost of gasoline in oil-producing Ecuador is low, about US$0.34 per liter (US$1.50 per gallon).

Heaven forbid that you will need these numbers, but **in an emergency** dial ✆ 01 for the police ✆ 11 for general and ✆ 31 for a Red Cross ambulance. Recommended hospitals are Hospital Voz Andes ✆ (02) 241540 or 241540 and Hospital Metropolitano ✆ (02) 431520 or 431521 or 431457. Both are English speaking, as are these recommended doctors: Wallace Swanson ✆ (02) 449374 or 470830, John Rosenberg ✆ (02) 521104 and Renato Leon ✆ (02) 238342 or 552080.

If your hotel doesn't have facilities for international and long distance domestic telephone calls, you will have to go to the telecommunications company, EMETEL (see page 257 in TRAVELERS' TIPS). Its Quito offices are at Avenida 10 de Agosto and Colón in the new town, Benalcazár and Meija in the old town, at Terminal Terrestre and at the airport.

Because Ecuador is such a great place for shopping, many travelers find themselves sending home their new purchases. If you're in this situation and are staying in the Mariscal area, go to the post office on the ground floor of the big, modern building at Reina Victoria and Colón. Don't seal your packages, and bring packing tape with you in case of inspection. The maximum weight is 20 kg (44 lb) and 70 x 30 x 30 cm (20 x 12 x 12 inches) is the maximum size. Another recommended Correo (post office) is Marítimo Aduana, on Ulloa 273 and Ramírez Dávalos, next to the Santa Clara market. Quito's two main post offices are on Espejo, between Guayaquil and Venezuela in the old town, and at Eloy Alfaro 354 and 9 de Octubre in the new town. All *poste restante* mail for Quito goes to the Espejo branch unless marked "Correo Central, Eloy Alfaro." But it's better to have mail sent to you care of SAEC (see above) or care of American Express, Apartado 2605, Quito. A curious quirk of the Ecuadorian postal service, or an indictment of it, is that many Quiteños use a private arrangement with Lufthansa whereby mail with Ecuadorian postage can be dropped off at the airline office on 6 de Diciembre 955 and 18 de Setiembre to be sent on the next flight. Mail and packages can also be sent by FedEx (Federal Express) ☎ (02) 251356 or 253552, OEMs ☎ (02) 543468 or 569741 or DHL ☎ (02) 565059 or 565060.

Several international airlines fly in and out of Quito. Check your travel information pack for your local contact. Since many flights tend to be overbooked it's a good idea to re-confirm at least 72 hours before your flight, and to get to the airport two hours before departure. Don't forget there is a US$25 departure tax for international flights, payable in dollars or sucres.

The main local carrier is TAME (Transportes Aeros Militares Equatorianos) ☎ (02) 509382 or 509384 or 509386 to 8, which flies to all major cities and the Galápagos Islands. The main office is at Amazonas 13-54 and Rábida, Sixth Floor. SAN-SAETA ☎ (02) 564969 or 550291 or 565005 or 565008, at República de El Salvador 880, Edificio Almirante Colón, also has flights to the Galápagos, Guayaquil and Cuenca. Domestic flights are relatively inexpensive.

Quito is relatively well served by international airlines, all having main offices in Quito, and some with subsidiary offices in Guayaquil:

Aerolineas Argentinas ☎ (02) 543257 or 543269
Air France ☎ (02) 524201
American Airlines ☎ 0561144
British Airways ☎ (02) 540000 or 540902 or 550739
Iberia ☎ (02) 560456 or 560546 to 8
KLM ☎ (02) 455233 or 455560 or 455550 or 455551
Lufthansa ☎ (02) 508682
Varig ☎ (02) 250126 or 240384

You can cash **travelers' checks** and **change money** at most banks and *casas de cambio* (money changers), and the rates aren't significantly different. Most banks are open between 9 AM and 1:30 PM on week-days. Moneychangers are usually open until about 6 PM. Some major hotels will cash travelers' checks for non-residents, which can be very helpful if you are strapped for cash on a weekend. The Hilton Colón International at Amazonas and Patria has a good service but it's a good idea to dress neatly if you want to use their facilities. **Automated Teller Machines** (ATMs) are becoming more common in the big cities. If you need to get sucres with your Visa card, for example, go to the cash machines behind the Banco Guayaquil on Colón and Reina Victoria.

Finally, if you really get into trouble, you might need help from your embassy. Indeed, if you are going to be in the country for some time, it is a good idea to register with your embassy, and leave a photocopy of your passport so it can be replaced quickly in case of loss. Some embassies also have current advice on places to avoid and tips for safe traveling. See page 254 in TRAVELERS' TIPS for further information, embassy addresses and phone numbers.

WHAT TO SEE AND DO

As the oldest and arguably the most beautiful city in the Andes, Quito has a wealth of attractions. The **art** and **architecture** of the Old City is world renowned, the **museums** are a source of endless fascination, the **shops** and **markets** are a bargain hunter's paradise, and Quito's **nightlife** is one of the world's best-kept secrets. A few days in Quito are enough to get a good taste of the city, but a lifetime isn't enough to decipher all its mysteries.

The first thing any visitor should do in Quito is to make a determined effort to take it easy. The excitement of a new place, limited time, high altitude dizzyness and a desire to do everything at once may conspire to make you immediately want to rush out and explore the city. But altitude affects young and old, fit and unfit equally, so first let your body adjust to the thin air and subtle vibrations of this ancient mountain realm.

Museums

If there is any meaning to the concept of the one-unmissable-city-sight, I would say that in Quito it's the **Casa de la Cultura** museum complex, housed in its striking circular building, largely made of glass, in the Parque El Ejido on the corner of Avenida Patria

Religious souvenirs are popular with Catholic visitors who come from all over the country to see Quito's magnificent churches.

and 12 de Octubre. As part of the complex, the **Museo Nacional del Banco Central del Ecuador** is a great place to start any exploration of Ecuador. It offers a wide cultural and artistic perspective on Ecuador's proud history — and some exhibits, such as an extraordinary ceremonial gold mask, will make your chin drop. Most impressive of the bank's museums is the **Sala de Arqueología**, with its dioramas and well-displayed artifacts from the pre-ceramic era (4000 BC) through the end of the Inca era (AD 1533). Techniques for working gold and platinum were astoundingly advanced for their times. Also fascinating is the uncanny similarity of some of the museum's objects to those found in Asia, and in Japan in particular, which leads to speculation that in ancient times there were links between the cultures across the Pacific Ocean. As for Incan gold itself, nobody can fail to be impressed by the beauty and sheer weight of the body adornments. Though not to be condoned, it's not surprising that the Spanish became carried away in their cruel quest for El Dorado. Further sections on colonial, Republican and modern art give a quite different perspective on Ecuadorian culture, as do the separate Casa de la Cultura museums of musical instruments, modern art and traditional dress from the indigenous cultures. Hours at the **Banco Central Museums** ☎ (02) 223259 are Tuesday to Friday, 9 AM to 5 PM; Saturday to Sunday: 10 AM to 3 PM, and admission is 10,000 sucres. Hours at the **Casa de la Cultura** museums ☎ (02) 565808 are: Tuesday to Friday, 10 AM to 6 PM; Saturday and Sunday, 10 AM to 3 PM, and admission is 3,500 sucres, free on weekends. The cultural complex also has a movie theater and a concert hall.

Perhaps on another day, to avoid instructional overdose, visit another outstanding Quito museum, **Museo Guayasamín** ☎ (02) 446455 or 452938, José Bosmediano 543, Bellavista, a cultural multiplex covering pre-Columbian, colonial and contemporary art but on a smaller, more personal scale than the Banco Central or Casa de la Cultura, above. The best of the museum is the powerful, harrowing paintings of the internationally-known Indian artist, Oswaldo Guayasamín, while the pre-Columbian and colonial sections are his private collection. The museum is housed in a private compound in the exclusive Bellavista area of the city, and the pretty garden is embellished with Guayasamín's bronze sculptures. High-quality prints, posters and jewelry are for sale. It is open 9:30 AM to 1 PM and 3 PM to 6:30 PM, Monday to Friday, and 9:30 AM to 1 PM on Saturdays, and admission is 3,000 sucres. Another museum devoted to the work of a fine Ecuadorian artist is **Museo Camilo Egas** (1889–1962) ☎ (02) 514511, on Venezuela 1302 and Esmeraldas in the old town. The museum, owned by the Banco Central, has been undergoing renovations so it's best to check to see if and when it's open.

Because the city is so rich in art, particularly religious works from the colonial era, there is a plenitude of museums devoted to the subject. One of the finest is **Museo de Arte Colonial** ☎ (02) 212297, also known as the Casa de la Cultura Ecuatoriana, on Cuenca 915 and Mejia in the old town. This stylish seventeenth-century colonial mansion contains a delightful collection of fine work by some of the best artists of the School of Quito. It is closed on Mondays and Saturday and Sunday afternoons, and admission is 2,000 sucres. Just a few blocks south, the **Museo Municipal Alberto Mena Caamaño de Arte y Historia** ☎ (02) 214018, housed in a Jesuit mansion that later became the barracks of the Spanish garrison, also has many fine paintings of the Quito School. In what used to be prison cells in the basement, a gory waxworks made in France depicts the execution of nationalist martyrs who were imprisoned here for nine months. Located near Espejo 1147 and García Moreno, the museum is a little hard to find. It is open Tuesday to Saturday, 9 AM to 5 PM and admission is free. More masters of the Quito School are exhibited at an excellent little museum attached to the Catholic University on 12 de Octubre, opposite Calle J. Carrión, though the main focus of **Museo de Jacinto Jijón y Caamaño** ☎ (02) 529240 or 529250, extension 128 or 242, is the archaeological collection bequeathed by the estate of the renowned Ecuadorian archaeologist of the same name. It is open Monday to Friday, 9 AM to 4 PM and admission is 1,000 sucres.

Just two blocks south and east of the old Spanish garrison in the old town is the former home of the greatest hero of Ecuador's battle for independence, Mariscal (Marshal) Sucre, after whom Ecuadorian currency is named. The house is now a museum, **Museo Casa de Sucre** ☎ (02) 512860, full of weapons, uniforms and other military paraphernalia, as well as colonial, republican and contemporary art. Located at Venezuela 573 and Sucre, the museum is open Tuesday to Friday from 8 AM to 4 PM, with an hour and a half lunch break from noon. On Saturday it's open from 8 AM to 1 PM and admission is 3,000 sucres. Mariscal Sucre won the decisive battle for independence on the slopes of Volcán Pichincha on May 24, 1822, where the **Museo Templo de la Patria** now marks the victory spot. Along with military and historical artifacts, there is an impressive mural by Eduardo Kingman and an eternal flame in honor of those killed in the battle. From the adjoining monument, **La Cima de la Libertad** (Summit of Victory) there is a splendid view over Quito. The museum was built and is managed by the Ministry of National Defense. Check with CETUR or a travel agent for hours as there appear to have been some changes recently.

Also with a military flavor is the **Museo del Instituto Geográfico Militar**, which has a geographical museum and a planetarium with shows several times a day. The Ecuadorian military make excellent and detailed country maps that are on sale at the institute which is open Monday to Friday, 8 AM to 3 PM. The institute is on top of a hill at the end of Paz and Miño southeast of Parque El Ejido. Take a taxi or hike up the hill and don't forget to bring your passport, which you have to leave at the gate. Entrance to the museum is free, but there is a small charge for the planetarium.

Another unusual institute in the new town, which appeals to those who love retiles, is the **Vivarium** ☎ (02) 452280 or 210863 or 230988, in the heart of the Mariscal tourist area on Reina Victoria 1576 and Santa María, a living showcase of many of the species found in Ecuador. These include deadly fer-de-lances and anacondas, as well as iguanas, turtles and tortoises (a vivarium is an artificial enclosure for keeping or raising living animals). The slinky beauties welcome visitors every day except Mondays but take a rest at lunch time. The cost of an encounter is 4,000 sucres but they prefer that you call ahead. The

The colonial art section of the Guayasamín Museum in Quito, run by Oswaldo Guayasamín, Ecuador's best-known painter.

best natural history museum in Ecuador, but sadly not equal to the splendor of the country's wildlife, is the **Museo de Ciencias Naturales**, which has recently moved to the east side of Parque La Carolina on Rumipamba 341 and Los Shyris. It is open Monday to Friday with a short lunch break and on Saturday mornings, and admission is 5,000 sucres, free on Saturdays.

Unfortunately Indian tribes from the Amazon aren't well-represented in Quito's museums. The **Museo Amazónica** ☎ (02) 562633, 12 de Octubre 1430 and Wilson, formerly known as the Museo Shuar, has a small but interesting collection of artifacts, weapons, costumes, photographs, videos and books on Indian cultures. It is open mornings and afternoons from Monday to Friday, but closed at lunch time. The museum of the **Fundación Sincha Sacha** ☎ (02) 230609, a non-profit organization supporting Amazonian cultures on Reina Victoria 1780 and La Niña, has ethnographic artifacts, information on the peoples of the rainforest and a gift shop. It is open all day from Monday to Saturday.

Churches

Most of Quito's greatest treasures are housed in resplendent churches, some of which have museums attached. Named after Quito's patron saint, the huge **Iglesia de San Francisco**, on Plaza de San Francisco in the old town, is Quito's oldest church, though not much of it is that old as it has been extensively rebuilt after earthquake damage. The church has more than one hundred Doric columns and fine cloisters. Much great and valuable art of the Quito School are contained in the church and the separate museum, **Museo del Convento Franciscano** ☎ (02) 211124. The museum is open mornings and afternoons from Monday to Friday with a long break for lunch.

Similarly, the beautiful seventeenth century church and convent of **San Agustín** on Chile and Guayaquil has a museum in the convent next to the church that contains important paintings of the Quito School. In 1809, the first treaty of independence from Spain was signed in the church's beautiful cloister. Also highly recommended is the recently restored **Monastery of San Diego** on Calicuchima 117 and Farfán, to the east of the giant virgin on the hill. Visitors, who have to ring the doorbell to get attention, are given a guided tour of the monastery complex and the monks' quarters. Christ eating *cuy* for his Last Supper is depicted in one of the paintings. It is open Tuesday to Sunday mornings and afternoons, with a two-hour lunch break, and admission is 5,000 sucres. There are also some fine art objects at **Museo Dominicano Fray Pedro Bedón** on the Plaza de Santa Domingo in the old town. **Iglesia de Santo Domingo** is

noted for a handsome façade and domes that are particularly impressive when floodlit at night.

Quito has many noteworthy churches, particularly in the old town. On García Moreno, just a block from the Plaza de la Independencia, is the magnificent **La Compañía de Jesús**, richly carved and sculpted, and considered to be the loveliest church in Ecuador. Its massive altars, baroque columns and ceilings are laden with gold leaf, but some of its most precious treasures are kept in the vault of Banco Central and are only displayed on festival days. Nearby is **La Merced**, built to commemorate the eruptions of Volcán Pichincha that threatened to destroy the city. Paintings in the church show scenes of erupting volcanoes. The cloisters are especially beautiful. The **Municipal Cathedral** itself is not as ornate as many of the older baroque churches, though it contains several interesting historical points of

OPPOSITE: Quito's cathedral towers above the streets of the Old Town. ABOVE: Old Town architecture.

interest, such as the tomb of Mariscal Sucre. The main chapel of the cathedral, the beautiful **El Sagrario**, which has recently been restored, is now an independent church.

One of my favorite Quito churches isn't in the old town, but in the old village of Guápulo right on the edge of the city looking down over Los Chillos valley. There is a peaceful atmosphere in the seventeenth century **Church of Guápulo**, beautiful paintings and sculpture and a superb carved pulpit. From this church Francisco de Orellana set off on a expedition which eventually took him down the Amazon river and across the South American continent to the Atlantic, making him the first to complete such a journey. A statue of Orellana stands in the square in front of the church, having been moved recently from higher up the valley. From this point you get a sense of the scale of the "earthly paradise" of South America, as Christopher Columbus put it, "which no one can enter except by God's leave."

Walking the Old Town

Walking the streets, stopping where you fancy, and perhaps getting lost a few times is the best way to get the feel of a city. If you do this in Quito, however, don't bring anything of value with you, keep your camera hidden, and only bring a few dollars and sucres. Pickpocketing and bag slashing are special skills of the city. Generally speaking though, Quito isn't dangerous for tourists as long as they don't carry tempting targets for petty thieves. The less you have to lose the safer and freer you will be. Don't walk about the old town alone at night, and take special care wherever you are.

A good place to start any walking tour is in the steep, narrow cobbled streets of the old town where whitewashed, blue-trimmed houses with red-tiled roofs rub shoulders with churches, convents and museums. The heart of *Casco colonial*, as it's called, is the tree-lined **Plaza de la Independencia**, or **Plaza Grande**, which is overlooked by a number of distinguished civic buildings and is the setting for the Victorian-style **Liberty Monument** in the middle of the square. The **Presidential Palace**, the **Archbishop's Palace**, the modern **City Administration Building** and the **Cathedral** command the locus of the old town, yet much of the real power of the city has long since moved northwards to the new town where most banks, big business and embassies are now located. Many of the big old mansions in the old town, once home to the rich and famous, are now tatty, rundown, divided up and rented to tenants.

You can poke your head inside the Presidential Palace, also known as the **Government Palace**, and glimpse a huge mural of Francisco de Orellana cruising down the Amazon. Echoing Quito's pride in this event is a sign on the cathedral's wall saying, "Quito's Glory is the discovery of the Amazon River." Not surprisingly, the Ecuadorians resent the fact that a large chunk of the territory through which the great river flows, which once belonged to Ecuador, is now part of Peru.

Most of the great churches and convents are within a few minutes' walk of the Plaza Grande. **La Compañía** is just a block away and **Iglesia de San Francisco** is not much further. Walking south from the square along Venezuela or Garcia Moreno you will come to the historic **La Ronda** on Juan de Dios Morales, so named because it was once famous for its serenading musicians. Though rather rundown and unsafe these days, there are some charming Spanish-style houses with balconies, reminiscent of Barrio Santa Cruz in Seville, and on some of the walls there are tile portraits of famous musicians and composers.

Crossing Avenida 24 de Mayo, you come to the foot of a hill known as **El Panecillo** (little loaf of bread), formerly a sacred Inca site for sun worship. Today the hill is dominated by the huge, winged statue, of the **Virgen de Quito** trampling on a dragon, the city's most prominent landmark. It's a stiff, half-hour walk up to the statue but it's advisable to take a taxi up from the old town, not just to save your breath but because there have been a number of robberies on the path. Ask the driver to wait while you survey the city below.

Walking north from Plaza Grande, passing **Teatro Sucre** in **Plaza del Teatro**, you come to **Parque la Alameda**, which marks the beginning of the new town. In the middle of the park is the **Quito Observatory**, the oldest on the continent and still in use, which can be visited on Saturday mornings. There are several interesting statues in the park, including one of the Great Liberator, Simón Bolívar. Next to the park is the new **Palacio Legislativo**, where elected representatives debate national issues and in which outgoing president, Abdala Bucarám, barricaded himself in an unsuccessful bid to hold on to power in 1997.

Just beyond the government building, **Parque El Ejido**, Quito's biggest downtown park, is a good spot to take a break, maybe have an ice-cream or a hot sweet potato and watch a game of football or volleyball. This is a popular spot for Quiteños, especially on weekends when there's an open-air art market at the north end of the park. It's also a transition point from the old to the new town. From here traffic and pedestrians flow down the wide Avenida Amazonas, lined with sidewalk cafés, modern shopping malls, luxury hotels, tourist shops, travel agents, restaurants, trendy bars... As you continue north all the way out to the airport, you're into twentieth century Quito.

People from Tigua, near Latacunga, sell their paintings on the streets of Quito.

WHERE TO STAY

Where to stay in Quito will be one of your most important decisions on a trip to Ecuador. The capital is the tourist and transport hub of the country, and the base from which to make various excursions: to the highlands, the rainforest, the pacific coast or the Galápagos Islands. Visitors often find themselves coming in and out of Quito several times, so their hotel becomes a home base. Obviously it's important that it's a comfortable establishment where you receive a friendly welcome, where messages are kept for you and where you can leave excess luggage you don't want to take on the road.

It's also important that your hotel is in a relatively safe area, which is why most of those recommended here are in the new town. The majority are in the Mariscal quarter because this is the most popular place for tourists, where the best shops, restaurants and hotels are located. There aren't many places to go in the old town after 9 PM and walking back at night, alone, is not my idea of fun.

There are many hotels that offer excellent value for money. However prices tend to vary from published rates according to season, exchange rates and your personal negotiation skills. Most of the more expensive hotels quote prices in United States dollars while less expensive places tend to charge in sucres. Whether or not the 10% tax and 10% service charge are included in the price of the room should be established before making reservations. It's also important to note that whether you like it or not, Ecuadorian nationals are often charged less than foreigners. Prices given here are for foreigners.

As for star ratings for hotels, this is a complex and sometimes arbitrary affair, and doesn't always indicate quality, service or value for money. Because of this I have divided Quito hotels into simple categories of Expensive, Moderate and Inexpensive. The fact that a hotel isn't included in this listing is no indication that it is below standard. Since things move fast in the hotel business we cannot take responsibility for changes in prices, phone numbers or even quality of service. To the best of my knowledge all the hotels listed, except some of the less expensive hostels, have English speaking staff, STD phones and facilities for storing luggage.

Expensive

By far the most expensive hotel in Quito is the Swiss-run **Oro Verde** ☎ (02) 566497 FAX (02) 569189, 12 de Octubre 1820 and Cordero, where a room (for one or two people) costs around US$250. Casino, a swimming pool and excellent restaurants are part of the deal. Favored by those who choose

the most expensive on principle, the hotel was hosting a well-known pop group last time I was in its glitzy lobby. Non-residents can while away an evening at the plush casino, enjoying drinks on the house, for minimum bets of a few thousand sucres.

Also in the top range is the **Colón International (Hilton)** ☎ (02) 560666 FAX (02) 563903, on Avenida Amazonas and Patria, where rooms are around US$150 and facilities include pool, fitness center, business center and everything else you expect from a modern first-class hotel. For about US$50 less per night you can stay at the brand-new **Alameda Real** ☎ (02) 562345 FAX (02) 565759, Roca 653 and Amazonas, where most of the rooms are suite-sized with bar or kitchenettes and some have computer terminals. It is popular with business people and upmarket tour groups.

Hotel Quito ☎ (02) 544600 FAX (02) 567284, Avenida Gonzalez Suarez 2500, isn't as centrally located as the above hotels but, it has good views, gardens and a nice pool. Though the hotel has a loyal clientele it also has its detractors who say the service isn't as good as it should be. Rooms start from about US$100. Also in the high end is the modern and luxurious **Tambo Real** ☎ (02) 563820 FAX (02) 554964, Avenida 12 de Octubre and Patria, just opposite the United States Embassy, where rooms are around the US$100 mark and there is a casino and good restaurants.

My own favorite luxury hotel is at the bottom of the expensive range. With wooden balconies looking like apartments in an alpine resort, is the small, European-style **Hotel Sebastian** ☎ (02) 2232400 FAX (02) 222500, nicely located on Almagro 822 and Cordero. Double rooms start from US$83 and a suite for three is US$108. The atmosphere is warm and the staff is friendly.

Moderate

I have to admit I'm prejudiced in favor of **Café Cultura** ☎ (02) 504078 FAX (02) 224271 E-MAIL sstevens@pi.pro.ec, Robles 513 and Reina Victoria, where I often stay in Quito. Owned and run by an couple who forsook the London media scene to restore a beautiful colonial mansion in the heart of Mariscal, this 16-room hotel, formerly the French Cultural Center, is seeped in atmosphere, comfort and style. They even serve an authentic English cream tea, complete with fresh cream, jam and scones, for the equivalent of about $1.60 — surely the world's best cream tea deal. Room rates, including taxes and service: single, US$38; double, US$50; triple, US$62; suite, US$65; family suite (four to five persons), US$68.

If you prefer airy colonial mansions to air-conditioned concrete boxes where you can't open the windows, you should try **Santa Barbara** ☎ (02) 564382 FAX (02) 275121 E-MAIL hplaza@uio.satnet.net, 12 de Octubre 2263, whose rates are similar to those of Café Cultura, or **Hostel Plaza Internacional** ☎ (02) 524530 FAX (02) 505075, on Leonidas

Plaza 150 and 18 de Septiembre E-MAIL hplaza @uio.satnet.sat, also similarly priced, both of which are multi-lingual and recommended by SAEC. Another recommended converted mansion is **Palm Garden** ✆ (02) 523960 FAX (02) 568944, on 9 de Octubre 923 and Cordero, whose rates are higher but has beautiful restaurant, bar and gardens.

The **Alston Inn Hotel** ✆ (02) 229955, Juan León Mera 741 and Baquedano E-MAIL alston @uio.satnet.net, in a prime position for shopping, bars and restaurants, is another favorite of mine in the Mariscal. It has good service, clean, comfortable rooms and is reasonably priced. Single, US$19; double, US$24; triple, US$28; taxes included. Nearby is **Hotel Casino Chalet Suisse** ✆ (02) 562700 FAX (02) 563966 on Reina Victoria and Calama Esquina, whose rates are a little higher, but boasts a sauna, Swiss-style restaurant and a small casino.

Rates are truly reasonable at the **Hotel Ambassador** ✆ (02) 561777 FAX 503712, Avenida 9 de Octubre 1052 and Colón, where singles start from about US$20. **Hostal Charles Darwin** ✆ (02) 592384, in a quiet location on Colina 304 and Orellana, is in a similar range as is **Hostal Camila's** ✆ (02) 225412 FAX (02) 225412, on 6 de Diciembre 1329, between Roca and Carrión, which is newly-renovated and well recommended. **Hostal Los Andes** ✆ (02) 550839, Muros 146 and Gonzales Suarez, is in a quiet, upmarket residential area and is a little less expensive than the above.

Other recommended and reasonably priced hotels, hostels, hostals, inns, pensións, posadas and casas (the words are almost interchangeable and don't necessarily indicate the nature of the establishment) include: **Rincón** (corner) **Escandinavo** ✆ (02) 222168 or 540794 or 225965, on Leonidas Plaza 1110 and Baquerizo Moreno, where Scandinavian languages are spoken; **Casa Helbling** ✆ (02) 226013, Veintimilla 531 and 6 de Diciembre, which is popular with Swiss and Germans; the oddly named **Gd'Oro** ✆ (02) 543033 FAX (02) 565725, on Santa Rosa and Armero, which is next to the Universidad Central; and the Italian-owned **Hostal del la Rábida** ✆ (02) 222169 FAX (02) 220426, La Rábida 227 and Santa Maria, near the British Council.

In the old town, the best hotel is **Hotel Real Audiencia** ✆ (02) 512711 FAX (02) 580213, on the corner of Plaza Santo Domingo on Bolívar 220. Recently refurbished, this clean, excellent value establishment has a bar, restaurant, fine views and rooms from US$20.

Inexpensive

The good news is that there are a large number of inexpensive and excellent-value hostels in Quito. The bad news is that some of them are grubby, small-roomed, thin-walled and unsanitary. Those mentioned all have some positive attributes but aren't necessarily perfect in every way. Most of them have luggage storage and kitchen facilities and are good places to meet and exchange information with other travelers.

The **Magic Bean** ✆ (02) 566181, Foch 681 and León Mera, is a well-known Quito hangout for the well-scrubbed backpacker who is prepared to pay a little extra for comfort and cleanliness. But the accommodation is limited and whenever I've tried to stay it's been full. Dormitory rooms are about US$7 per person, while a double costs US$20, including breakfast for two. The coffee is excellent (hence the name) at the pleasant outside restaurant, which is right in the center of the Quito bar and travel agent circuit.

A Canadian woman introduced me to **Posada del Maple** ✆ (02) 544507 or 237375, Juan Rodriguez 148 and Almagro, where I stayed happily for a couple of weeks. This is a well-located hostel in a quiet street at the center of Mariscal. There are good facilities, friendly atmosphere and a pleasant courtyard, but the rooms are nothing special and English is *not* spoken. US$6.50 for dormitory accommodation, US$18 for a double, including breakfast. It is popular with American Peace Corps volunteers.

Just down the road is **Loro Verde** ✆ (02) 226173, Juan Rodriguez 241 and Almagro. Though the name is remarkably similar to that of the most expensive hotel in town, the two are at opposite ends of the spectrum. Loro Verde describes itself as "Bohemian

Hotel Oro Verde, Quito's most luxurious and expensive hotel.

with a great family atmosphere." Prices are similar to Posada del Maple.

For the real thing in backpackers' hostels, **El Centro del Mundo** (The Center of the World) ℂ/FAX (02) 229050, Lizardo García 569 and Reina Victoria, has it all: good music, party room, futons, sun deck and rock-bottom prices. Rates are US$4 per night for dormitory beds, US$12 for doubles and US$15 for triples. Also popular with young backpackers is **El Cafecito** ℂ (02) 234862, centrally located on Luis Cordero 1124 and Reina Victoria, with a vegetarian café downstairs. In a similar range, **El Taxo** ℂ (02) 225593 on Foch 909 and Cordero, is run by artists and good for long-term stays.

The women-only hostel, **Hostal Eva Luna** ℂ (02) 234799 E-MAIL admin@safari.ecx.ec, at Pasaje Roca 630 between Amazonas and Juan León Mera, is clean, comfortable and secure at US$5.50 in a shared room. Just into the old town, the best known hostel is **Hotel Belmonte** ℂ (02) 516235, Antepara 413 and V. León, a legendary backpackers' meeting place which some rave about.

Apartment Hotels

For long stays, fully furnished service apartments with TV, laundry, etc. are very convenient. Check out Apart-Hotel Amaranta ℂ (02) 560585 FAX (02) 560586; Apartamentos modernos ℂ (02) 553136; Apartotel Mariscal ℂ (02) 528833; Residencial Casa Oriente ℂ (02) 546157; Apart Hotel Panorámico ℂ (02) 542425; Apartamentos Calima ℂ (02) 524036. Many of them are booked well in advance.

WHERE TO EAT

The are plenty of good restaurants in Quito and listed below are some recommendations. Note that it is rarely necessary to make reservations, except in the most expensive of places, and many smaller restaurants do not have phones so we don't give many phone numbers.

Ecuadorian

If you want Ecuadorian food in style and comfort try **La Choza** ℂ (02) 230839, Avenida 12 de Octubre 1821 and Cordero, opposite the Hotel Oro Verde, whose name, which means "hut," belies its quality. Main dishes here are between US$5 and US$10. It is open Monday to Friday for lunch and dinner (until 9:30 PM) and Saturday to Sunday between 2 PM and 4 PM. The equally fancy **Mare Nostrum** ℂ (02) 37236, Foch 172 and Tamayó, located in a beautifully restored mansion fitted out with coats of armor and a big log fire, serves excellent seafood. Try *mariscos* (seafood) in coconut.

In Quito, everyone has their favorite restaurant for *ceviche* (marinated seafood), an Ecuadorian specialty. Some people swear by **El Viejo José** (Old Joe), Reina Victoria and La Pinta, while others prefer **El Viejo Jorje** (Old George), which was opened in the same area by a disgruntled employee of Old Joe. Still others say you should go to **Su Ceviche**, Juan León Mera and Calama, where you can sit at an outside table and eat the best ceviche in town. Somebody else insists that **El Cebiche** surpasses them all.

Other recommended restaurants serving Ecuadorian cuisine are **Las Redes**, on Amazonas and Veintimilla, which is down to earth and of good value; **Rincón La Ronda**, at Belo Horizonte and Almagro; and **Taberna Quiteña**, on Amazonas 1259 and Cordero, the last two having live traditional Andean music.

European and American

Most of the luxury hotels have fine but expensive European-style restaurants. Best value are brunches at **Café Quito** in **Hotel Quito** and at **Hotel Oro Verde**, and the Sunday buffet is excellent at **Hotel Colón**. Top choice, however, for all around presentation, atmosphere and superb Mediterranean food is **La Viña**, behind the Oro Verde Hotel on Isabela La Católica. Lunch for two, almost as good as you would get anywhere in London, is about $48 including wine. Also in the expensive category, look out for **Rincón de Francia**, **Le Bistro**, **Rincón de Borgoña** and **Amadeus**.

The best straight grills are at **Texas Ranch** on Juan León Mera and Calama, which has really good steaks; **Columbia** on Colón and Amazonas; **Shorton Grill** on Almagro and Calama; and **El Toro Partido** on Veintimilla and 9 de Octubre. **La Terraza de Tártaro** ℂ (02) 527987, on the top floor of the Edificio Amazonas on Veintimilla 1106 and Amazonas, also has good steaks and splendid views of Quito through wide picture windows.

For Italian, try **Il Grillo**, Cordero and Reina Victoria, which has good atmosphere and tasty pastas. **Il Risotto**, on Almagro and Pinto, has an excellent reputation as do **Portofino**, on Calama between Juan León Mera and Reina Victoria, and **Pavarottis**, on 12 de Octubre and Salazar. I don't recommend pizzas in Ecuador because (in my experience) they can cause stomach problems. But if you must, try **Ch' Farina** on Amazonas and Naciones Unidas, which is very popular with local Quiteños.

For Spanish food, **La Paella Valencia**, on República and Almagro, is superb though expensive, and **El Mesón de la Pradera**, in a restored hacienda on Orellana and 6 de Diciembre, is well worthwhile. For New York deli food, go to **The American Deli** near Portugal and Naciones Unidas. For its breakfasts, baked potatoes, home-made pasta and vegetarian food, **Super Papa**, attached to the Alston Inn Hotel, Juan León Mera 741 and Baquedano, is rightly well-known. **Fast food** outlets serving burgers, hot dogs and fried chicken are all over town.

As a final tip for the real gourmet, ask at your hotel about **Mucki's** ☎ (02) 320789 at El Tingo, about 20 minutes drive outside of Quito. This German-run restaurant is said to be simply The Best.

Latin American

For Cuban food **Bodeguita de Cuba**, Reina Victoria and La Pinta, is fun and feisty while **Havana**, on Portugal and El Salvador, is well recommended. Mexican food, though much hotter than Ecuadorian, is very popular. Among the best restaurants are the **Taco Factory**, on Whymper and Orellana, and **Chili Taqueria**, on Juan León Mera and Jorge Washington.

Asian

As in almost every city in the world, there's a host of Chinese restaurants (*chifas*) in Quito. Some of the best are **Casa China** on Cordero and Tamayo, **The Asia** on Amazonas near Plaza de Toros, **Hong Kong** on Lizardo Garcia and Eduardo Xaura, and **Chifa Mayflower** on Carrión and 6 de Diciembre. Also highly recommended is **Mágico Oriental**, 9 Octubre and Jorge Washington. For the best sushi in town, which of course isn't cheap, **Tanoshi** in Hotel Oro Verde is an excellent choice. The **Fuji**, on Robles and Juan León Mera, isn't too bad and has a takeout service. Also recommended, though not strictly Asian, is **Al Arabe**, on Reina Victoria and Carrion, for Middle Eastern food. Although it has delicious Indonesian and Indian items on the menu, the Dutch-run vegetarian restaurant **El Holandés**, on Reina Victoria and Carrión, isn't exclusively Asian either since it also does Greek and Italian dishes. But is the sort of restaurant that a weary budgeted traveler would pray for — inexpensive, tasty and safe.

Quito's nightlife is one of the city's best-kept secrets.

Cafés

Most of the big luxury hotels have good coffeeshops, some of them open all day and night, which are good places for cooling off and meeting people. At the small café/hotel **Café Cultura** you can indulge yourself with homemade breads and scones, and read or chat in an interesting atmosphere. **Magic Bean**, Foch and Juan León Mera, has the same combination and is also a pleasant place to meet other travelers and pick up information. More downmarket but with a similar formula is **El Cafecito**, on Luis Cordero 1124, which serves snacks, light meals and drinks.

Art Forum, on Juan León Mera and Wilson, combines a pleasant café with a gallery, and **Grain de Café**, General Baquedano and Reina Victoria, has homemade pies and the best cheesecake in town. **Death Before Decaf**, a chic little place on Lizardo Garcia and Juan León Mera, does great coffee and exotic teas, but at the time of writing was reinventing itself into another sort of outlet. The quiet and airy **Gallery Café** at the British Council, Amazonas and Pinta, serves vegetarian snacks. **Chantilly**, Roca and Amazonas, is a good upstairs café with light snacks and pastries while **Lennon**, on Calama and Juan León Mera, is well recommended.

For good cappuccino and a huge selection of delicious ice cream, as well as homemade chocolate truffles, go the **Corfú** on Portugal, probably the best place for ice cream in Quito. Treat yourself to bagels at **Mister Bagel**, Portugal and Shyris, or get some of the best *empanadas* in town at **Tianguez**, a new, first-rate café on Plaza San Francisco in the old town, where you can relax and buy souvenirs after a neck-bending church tour. For good views and a Bohemian atmosphere go to **Café Guápulo**, in the village of that name on the edge of the city. For people watching, take a table on one of the four or five outside cafés between Nos. 400 and 500 on Amazonas.

NIGHTLIFE

Quito's nightlife is one of its best-kept secrets. Some Ecuadorians are surprised to learn how much goes on after hours in their own capital. My own guide to dark-time entertainment was an Anglo-Ecuadorian American citizen, Francisco Mallinson, a man-about-Quito who is no slouch in researching the city's clubs and bars. The following classifications are based on what Frank calls his "rowdiness rating."

In the two-star category for **cafés**, **pubs**, **bars** and **clubs** (the cafés listed above being in the one-star range), the upmarket and arty **Café Libro**, Almagro and La Pradera, has literary posters, cool music with live jazz on Thursdays and folkloric events on Fridays. **El Pobre Diablo**, Santa María and Juan León Mera, also with a somewhat arty atmosphere, is as friendly as a Dublin pub. Try the top-class Irish coffees. The young crowd at **Aladdin**, Almagro and Cordero, enjoys smoking hookahs outside on the terrace. The **Rock Café**, Juan León Mera and Lizardo Garcia, where travelers can often get jobs working at the bar, also caters mostly to a young crowd. **Kizomba**, Almagro and Lizardo Garcia, has good atmosphere and Brazilian music. **La Reina Victoria**, Reina Victoria and Roca, is an English-style, English-owned pub with darts, draught beer and sandwiches.

Turning up the volume into the three-star rowdiness category, the **Saravá**, behind Hotel Quito, has good atmosphere, good service, good music and caters to over 25-year-olds. **Varadero** bar and restaurant, next to the La Bodeguita de Cuba on Reina Victoria and Pinta, appeals to a similar crowd

and has plenty of exotic South American cocktails from Cuba Libres (rum and Coke) to Canelazos (cane alcohol flavored with lime and cinnamon). **Arribar**, Juan León Mera and Lizardo Garcia, is a fairly rough joint with very loud music and a pool table. **Ghoz**, La Niña and Reina Victoria, has several pool tables, table football, dart boards, video games and good Swiss snacks. Other bars worth checking out in reasonable proximity to the above in the new town are **Shock**, Juan León Mera and Niña; **Booms**, Juan León Mera and Foch; and **Zima**, Santa Maria and Juan León Mera. A little further afield are **Tropicana**, Whymper and Orellana; **The Cave**, La Granja and Amazonas; **Ramon Antigua**, Veintimilla and Isabela La Católica; and **Alcatraz**, Santa Maria and Reina Victoria.

In the four-star "really kickin'" action and rowdiness range, where you have shout in people's ears to make yourself understood, there are many lively clubs in the Mariscal area. On Friday and Saturday nights **Tequila Rock** and **Tequila Rock Underground**, Reina Victoria and Santa Maria, are bursting, as is the nearby **Papillon**, Santa Maria and Almagro. **Zoo**, Niña and Reina Victoria, is a popular spot, and so is **Limon & Menta**, Santa Maria and Juan Leon Mera. Other currently "in" spots among the clubbing crowd

Lively bars, clubs and *salsatecas* abound in the Mariscal section of the New Town.

are: **Gasoline**, Salazar and Tamayo; **Final**, Gonzalez Suarez and Camino Guápulo; **No Bar**, Calama and Amazonas; **Ku**, Orellana and Yanez Pinion; and **Joy**, República and America.

On the salsa scene, the best beats and the prettiest girls break out at **Seseribó**, Veintimilla and 12 de Octubre, considered to be the hottest salsateca in town. Screaming on its heals is **Cali Salsateca**, Almagro and Orellana, where those Latin rhythms pulse through the night into the early hours. For a genuine *peña* show with folkloric music and dancing, the reasonably priced **Nuncanchi Peña**, opposite the Universidad Central, Avenida Universitaria and Armero, is a popular choice. There are performances most days except Sunday and Monday.

Entry to many clubs requires an ID or credit card and there is often a cover charge of up to 30,000 sucres. In most clubs entry is entirely at the discretion of the doorman. Popularity ebbs and flows in the club and pub world so many of those that are hot today may be gone tomorrow.

HOW TO GET THERE

Most intercontinental visitors to Ecuador arrive at Quito's Aeropuerto Mariscal Sucre. International carriers who fly into the city regularly include American Airlines, Continental, Iberia, KLM, Lufthansa, Air France, AOM (French Airlines) and the South American airlines Copa (Panama), Avensa (Venezuela), Avianca (Columbia) Lacsa (Costa Rica), Viasa (Venezuela), LAB (Bolivia), AeroPerú and Cubana. Ecuadorian airlines flying internationally in and out of Quito are TAME, Ecuatoriana and SAETA.

Facilities in the airport terminal include a cafeteria, gift shops, an EMETEL telephone office and a CETUR tourist information office where reservations for hotels can, theoretically, be made. If it's your first visit to Ecuador and you're not on an organized tour you might feel more secure making reservations before you arrive, although even in peak season there are always rooms available in Quito. Some travelers just hop in a cab and ask the driver to take them to a suitable hotel or hostel.

A taxi from the airport to the center of town, a distance of about 10 km (six miles), should be about 16,000 sucres (US$4–5). Some drivers try to charge more for journeys from the international terminal so bargain hard, or just walk down to the domestic terminal where fares tend to be less expensive. Alternatively, you can stroll over to Avenida 10 de Agosto in front of the terminal where you can flag down a metered taxi or take a southbound bus.

If you're leaving Quito by air on an international flight, don't forget there is a departure tax of US$25, payable in cash in either dollars or sucres. There is no departure tax on domestic flights, nor if you are leaving the country over land.

EXCURSIONS FROM QUITO

From Quito there are many fascinating places you can visit on a day trip, or if you prefer, you might stay a night or two.

LA MITAD DEL MUNDO

In 1736 a team of scientists sponsored by the French Academy of Sciences arrived in Ecuador with the most up-to-date astrolabes, compasses, telescopes and other scientific instruments. Part of their mission was to calculate the precise position of the notional equatorial line as it passed through the country. They also wanted to take readings to resolve contemporary disputes about the shape of the earth. The work of the eight-year Geodetic Mission in Ecuador showed that the earth did indeed bulge in the middle, as English scientist Isaac Newton had predicted. At the same time the scientists helped lay the foundations for the metric "system" that eventually became the global standard.

Busts of these twelve learned scientists (nine members of the Academy of Science in Paris, two Spanish mathematicians and one Ecuadorian scientist) can be seen be seen at **La Mitad del Mundo** (The Center of the Earth), some 15 km (nine miles) north of Quito. More prominent than the busts, though, is the massive 30-m (100-ft) high obelisk of volcanic rock capped with a brass globe four meters (13 ft) in diameter. This ta-

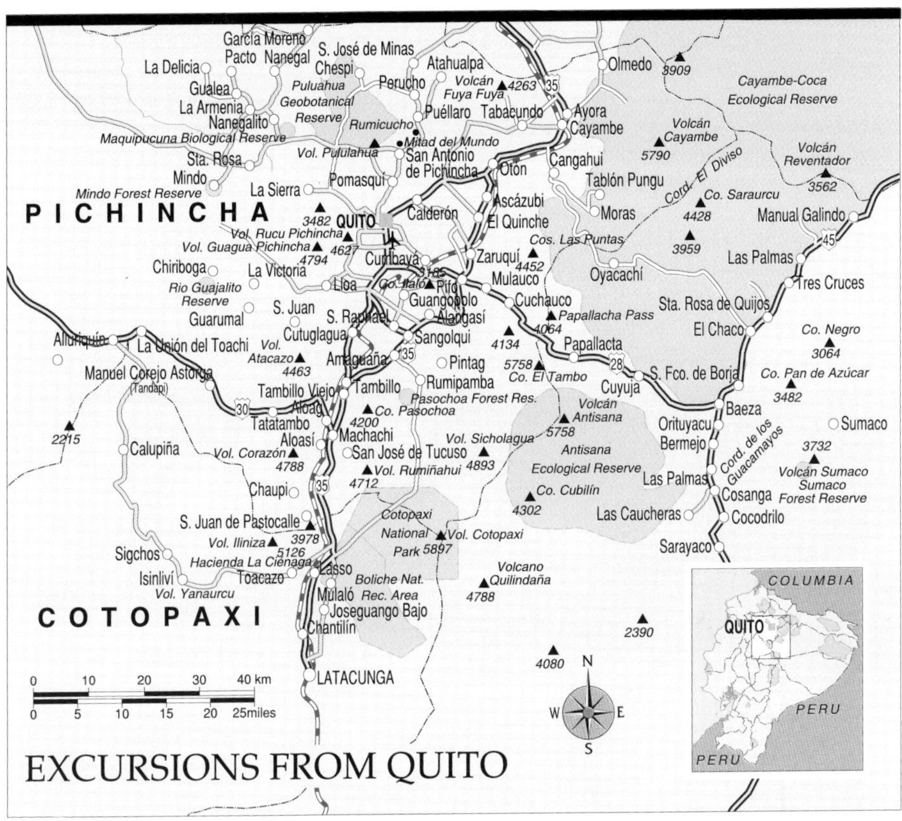

EXCURSIONS FROM QUITO

pered tower was built in 1986 to replace a smaller one erected in 1936 to mark the 200th anniversary of the Geodetic Mission. The massive monument straddles the equatorial line as delineated by the scientists.

The most popular activities for visitors to La Mitad del Mundo are walking the equatorial line, being photographed on both sides of the world at the same time, or just jumping from one side of the earth to the other. There is also a deep fascination among visitors about whether water turns in opposite directions in the southern and northern hemispheres as it drains from a basin or flushes from a toilet. Efforts to resolve this riddle — and to achieve a straight flush exactly on the equatorial line — keep children occupied for hours.

The complex of facilities surrounding the monument at La Mitad del Mundo has developed a theme park atmosphere. Partially built as a typical **colonial town**, there are gift shops, restaurants, a tourist office, a **planetarium**, a very good **model of Old Quito** and even a **bullring**, which is used occasionally. But the main attraction is the monument itself that houses an excellent **ethnographic museum**. After buying a ticket (1,000 sucres), visitors take the elevator to the ninth floor to an observation deck for a panoramic view of the surrounding hills. Walking down the stairs, you pass through the museum with dioramas and displays of ethnic costumes and artifacts that give a vivid and informative picture of Ecuador's great diversity of peoples and cultures.

The best restaurant in the complex is **Equinoccio**, which is near the entrance. Here you can get typical, well-prepared Ecuadorian food, accompanied by live Andean music. This is a good place to sink your teeth into the national delicacy, *cuy* (roasted guinea pig, a favorite of the Incas), as you will not find it on the menu at many Quito restaurants. Equinoccio isn't cheap: a typical meal with beer costs about US$10. If you want to pay less there are snacks available in the complex and some inexpensive *comedores* (eating rooms) in the nearby village of San Antonio.

On the other side of the village is a small **solar museum**, open only by appointment, containing an intriguing solar chronometer and other astronomical gadgets. Those interested in seeing the museum should contact its curator, Oswaldo Muñoz of Nuevo Mundo Expeditions ☎ (02) 552839 in Quito. Incan and pre-Incan artifacts indicate that the early inhabitants studied the path of the sun and were aware of the significance of the equator, as well as the special magic of this location. They were also able to predict eclipses as far ahead as this present century.

Interestingly, it has been suggested that the equator has shifted in the last two thousand years due to a wobble of the earth on its axis. According to this theory, a pair of peaks known as **La Marca**, just five kilometers (three miles) north of La Mitad, were on the previous line, as was the nearby pre-Columbian solar observatory of **Rumicucho**, the ruins of which are currently being excavated by the Banco Central. Possibly connected to this cosmic pattern is another site further to the east, **Cochasquí**, where there are tombs that look like truncated pyramids and where, even these days, there are dance festivals on solstices and equinoxes.

Further east on the same path is the 5,790 m (19,300 ft) peak of **Volcán Cayambe**, the third-tallest mountain in Ecuador and the highest point in the world on the equator. There is an enormous cylinder on the flanks of the mountain, where at noon on solar equinox the sun makes no shadow in the circle. Whatever the significance of these ancient sites, the ghosts of inhabitants past still cast their magic. As you look up to the sky, you can imagine the heavens stretching equally and infinitely from pole to pole while the earth spins beneath your feet.

Buses from Quito to La Mitad del Mundo leave from the El Tejar bus stop in the old town. You can also get on them as they pass along Avenida América in the new town. But they tend to be very crowded, especially on weekends, so you are better off sharing a taxi or contacting a travel agency in Quito to join a guided tour. Some tours include some of the sites mentioned above, as well as the nearby crater of the extinct **Volcán Pululahua**, an impressive spectacle, some 300 m (1,000 ft) deep and four kilometers (just over two miles) in diameter, at the bottom of which is a village and a beautiful old hacienda.

Hiking Around Quito

For the fit and energetic there is no shortage of good hiking and climbing trails near the capital. The closest crater is **Rucu Pichincha** (4,627 m or 15,422 ft), which is a hard day's hike if you want to return to Quito by nightfall. To climb the crater summit of the active volcano **Guagua Pichincha** (4,794 m or 15,980 ft) takes longer and requires an overnight stay in the hut below the summit. It is important to be aware that there have been a number of robberies, muggings and rapes on the roads leading out of the city suburbs, as well as attacks by dogs, so it is advisable to go with a large group and to take a taxi or a jeep for the first stretch up into the hills. If you are thinking of taking either of these hikes, check first for the latest information on the best routes and current conditions at one of the agencies specializing in climbing or with the South America Explorers Club.

For easier hiking in nearby countryside, **Pasochoa Forest Reserve** is a subtropical forest area less than an hour's drive southeast from Quito. Popular for school outings, the reserve attracts some 20,000 visitors per year. Several mapped trails criss cross an extinct volcanic crater rich with plants and wildlife. There are camping and hostel facilities in the park, but no shops or restaurants. For maps and more information contact **Fundación Natura** ((02) 447341, an associate organization of the WWF-World Wide Fund for Nature, in Quito, Avenida América 5653 and Voz Andes, which runs the reserve.

Mindo and Maquipucuna Reserve

The small town of **Mindo** on the western slopes of the Andes, just 40 km (25 miles) northwest of Quito as the condor flies, is a mecca for cognoscenti bird-watchers. In the dense surrounding cloud forest some 450 species have been observed, including such trophies as the fabulous scarlet-crested Andean cock of the rock, the toucan barbet, the plate-billed mountain toucan and the velvet-purple coronet.

But you don't have to be a dedicated "twitcher" to appreciate Mindo's charm. If you prefer, you can simply enjoy the novelty and privacy of staying in a luxury treehouse *cabaña* 10 m (33 ft) above the ground high, in the cloud forest canopy. Here in your bamboo aerie you can lie under your mosquito net while listening to a chorus of toucans sounding like the screeching of rusty nails being clawed from old lumber. Or you can just wander forest paths observing the unique ecosystem of the western slopes of the Andes, enjoying nature at its most abundant. **Río Mindo** gushes down the steep mountainside, blazing a foaming path for hair-raising white water rafting.

But if it's birds you're after, your man is Vinicio Pérez, birdman extraordinare, who usually can be found by asking around at the few bars in town, or you can leave a message with Vinicio's sister in Quito ((02) 612955, who should know the top twitcher's whereabouts. If he takes you birding, be prepared to get up at 5 AM and walk for two hours up steep slopes and through thick undergrowth. Your reward should be a magnificent arboreal show staring the incredible crimson-coated Andean cock-of-the-rock chorus line.

If you want to stay in a tree house in Mindo, contact **Hostería El Carmelo de Mindo** ((02) 538756 FAX (02) 408355 in Quito. Their best cabañas are around US$50 per night but they also have less expensive ones and camping facilities and dormitories for US$5 to US$8. Horse riding is available. More upmarket and expensive is **Mindo Gardens Lodge** ((02) 230463 FAX (02) 564235, though it has been closed for a while and may not have reopened yet. There are also several less expensive, more basic places where you have to bring your own sleeping gear. Mindo shows all the signs of becoming increasingly popular with travelers and nature lovers in the years to come.

About 32 km (20 miles) north of Mindo, on the same western slopes of the Andes, is the **Maquipucuna Biological Reserve**, most of which is primary cloud forest. In this wildlife-rich area, species of close to 2,000 plants, of some 322 birds, more than 200 butterflies and 45 mammals have been recorded. It's no wonder that Maquipucuna

Within a couple of hours' drive south of Quito, La Cienega is one of Ecuador's oldest and finest haciendas.

attracts naturalists like moths to a flame. For information about lodgings, prices and transport to the area contact **Fundación Maquipucuna** ☎ (02) 507200 or 507202 FAX (02) 507201 E-MAIL abi@maqui.ecx.ec. in Quito at Baquerizo 238 and Tamayo, PO Box 17-12-167.

Some gringos fall in love with the wild jungle landscapes and decide to make the places their home. In 1991, British backpacker, Richard Parsons, bought a 300-acre (120-hectare) abandoned farm in the Maquipucuna area for a song. Using eucalyptus logs

and bamboo, and with the help of local labor and his wife Gloria, Parsons constructed an ecolodge shaped like geodesic dome on stilts, with lots of windows and big balconies. Built on three levels and roofed with thatch, there are five triple rooms on the first floor and dormitory rooms above. Perched on the edge of a steep hill, the futuristic cupola looks out over the thick jungle carpet of the **Bellavista Cloud Forest Reserve** where tanagers, toucans and other birds of this paradise flash brightly among deep shades of green. Prices range from US$29 per person with three meals. For more information and reservations ☎/FAX (02) 509255 in Quito or ☎ (09) 490891 at Bellavista (which can be difficult) E-MAIL aecie3@ecnet.ec.

Although little known and difficult to get to get to, the Antisana Ecological Reserve, 57 km (36 miles) southeast of Quito, offers breathtaking scenery of the páramo and views of the eponymous, snow-capped mountain where wild horses roam and condors cross the sky. This dramatic wilderness is a great place for riding, hiking, camping and living in the wild. Visitors must bring their own supplies, though there's a lodge owned by a water company where it's possible to stay. Access is by car only (4-wheel drive recommended) and a permit is required. For more information contact **Fundación Antisana** ☎ (02) 433851 in Quito, Mariana de Jesús and Carvajal. You can also get special permission to enter the territory of Hacienda Pinatura, owned by Carlos Delgado who can be contacted at Avenida de Diciembre 1024 in Quito. Or make inquiries on the way to the reserve at Píntag, where you can find a guide.

Hot Springs

Volcanic Ecuador overflows with hot springs, natural pools and spouting waterfalls. Some of the best are hidden deep in the jungle and aren't easy to get to. Near Miazal in Morona Santiago Province, there are twin waterfalls, one hot and one cold, like hot and cold showers. Indian tribes consider waterfalls to be sacred. Waterfall aficionados should contact Jean Brown of **Safari Tours** ☎ (02) 552505, Calama 380 and Jean León Mera, who is currently writing a book about waterfalls.

The best hot springs within reach of Quito are the **Baños de Papallacta**, two hours by bus or car from the city, just off the road that descends over the rim of the Amazon basin to Baeza. The river here feeds five pools ranging from very hot to refreshingly cold. In good weather the view of the snow-capped cone of Antisana is spectacular. The entrance fee of US$2.50 includes use of changing rooms and showers. There's also a restaurant specializing in fresh trout and cabañas with private thermal baths and kitchen facilities. Call ☎ (02) 438033 for reservations. Adequate places to stay are also available at Papallacta village, a couple of kilometers (about a mile) from the baths. Buses from Quito's Terminal Terrestre to Lago Agrio or Tena will drop you off at Papallacta, but you might have to pay the fare for the whole journey. If you're coming the other way, from a jungle expedition perhaps, the baths provide fine therapy before returning to the capital.

About an hour by road from Quito are the thermal pools of La Merced and El Tingo, but they tend to be overcrowded on weekends. Far better are some private pools at Ilaló, just a few kilometers from La Merced, where US$2 gives access to cleaner and less-crowded facilities. Buses run from Quito to the above places. If possible, avoid weekends.

THE HACIENDA LIFESTYLE

The word *hacienda* conjures up images of grand country estates, huge houses, cobbled courtyards, horsemen with wide-brimmed sombreros, masses of servants and old-fashioned luxury. And that's exactly what haciendas are all about, except that today many of the grand Ecuadorian haciendas have become hotels.

There are several splendid haciendas within easy reach of Quito that you can either visit for a meal or stay at for a night or more. My first Ecuadorian hacienda was **Hostería La Ciénega** ((02) 541337 or 549126, 74 km (46 miles) south of the Quito, a huge and splendid Spanish-style stately home that is approached down a long avenue of towering eucalyptus trees, said to be the oldest eucalypti in the country. Soft music accompanies your entrance to this whitewashed palace with its two-meter (seven-foot) thick volcanic stone walls. A beautifully-kept inner garden with central fountain and bright, exotic plants and flowers lifts your spirits. You feel a sense of tranquillity and grace, as if you have been transported back in time to an age of courtesy and gentle hospitality. The private chapel with its massive carved wooden door has heard the prayers of countless generations over four centuries. La Ciénega has provided food and lodging to some of the most powerful and influential men in Ecuador's history, including the country's first president, Juan José Flores. Charles-Marie de la Condamine, leader of the French geodetic mission, was here in the mid-eighteenth century, while the great German naturalist and explorer, Alexander Von Humbolt, made it his home at the beginning of the nineteenth century. You can add your name to this illustrious guest list by paying US$50 for a double room at this luxurious country chateau.

OPPOSITE: Bathing in hot sulfur springs at Baños. ABOVE: Hacienda Hualiagua de Jijon, an oasis of graceful living.

Lunch and dinner are about US$11 each, and horse riding is US$1.50 per hour. For further information contact Assistant Manager Miguel Ponce ✆ (02) 541337 or 549126 FAX (02) 228820 E-MAIL hcienega@uio.satnet.net.

If you want to throw a house party for a small group of friends and money is no object, the former monastery of **Hacienda San Agustín de Callo** ✆/FAX (02) 503656 or (03) 719160 should be on your list of possible locations. This extraordinary old colonial building's walls were made by Incas for a temple that originally at this magical site in the shadow of the world's tallest active volcano, Volcán Cotopaxi. Guests here live like the owners, and with the owners, sharing the big, comfortable living room with views of the great mountains. One wall of this room is made of dark, volcanic stones that the Incas cut so precisely that you cannot squeeze a needle between them. Photographs of the owner, Señor Plaza, in action in the bullring are displayed, as well as a lovely portrait of his daughter, Mignon Plaza, who now runs the hacienda, painted by Ecuador's most famous artist, Oswaldo Guayasamín. The room I slept in had classic Inca stone work, fine murals (even in the bathroom), an open fireplace and antique furniture, which made for an atmosphere and a depth of relaxation that couldn't be matched in a modern concrete hotel. Meals are served in an elegant dining room, all four walls of which are made of the Inca blocks — you feel as if you're eating inside a pyramid. The Ecuadorian food at San Agustín is renowned, particularly memorable being the simple but delicious *locro de papa*, potato soup. San Agustín is also famous for its parties and festivals. Traditional dancing, music and bullfighting are part of the summer solstice celebration in June. The day-visit to San Agustín, "the house party hacienda," is US$6 and includes drinks and snacks. About US$80 per person per night includes all meals. Phone for more information and reservations, or make reservations through most travel agents in Quito.

The above haciendas, Ciénega and San Agustín, are quite close to each other, near the village of Lasso, just over an hour's drive south of Quito. Other recommended haciendas south of Quito include **Hualilahua**, **San José de Cobo**, **Puchalitola**, **Santa Ana del Pedregal** and **La Fontana**. For more information about these, contact a local travel agent.

There are also several fine haciendas north of Quito. One of the best known is **Hacienda Cusín** ✆ (06) 918013 or 918316, founded in 1602 and beautifully restored by its present English owner, Nicholas Millhouse, who bought the estate in 1990. All rooms are fitted out with locally-made furniture and tapestries, the garden is particularly ravishing and the food is excellent. All 40 guestrooms, suites and cottages (including those in the adjoining **Monasterio de Cusín**) have private bathrooms and garden views and most have fireplaces and beamed ceilings. Dinner is served in a baronial-style hall under chandeliers and candlelight. French windows in the library and reading room look out onto a garden where jasmine, agapanthus, bougainvillea, hollyhocks and phlox bloom among the native orchids and lounging llamas. Services include horses (which are well looked after), mountain bikes, squash, Spanish lessons and nannies. Aside from wallowing in residential luxury, there are plenty of interesting walks and trips to make in the surrounding area, and the famous Otavalo market is nearby. About US$100 per person per night includes meals and some horse riding. For more information and reservations call ✆ (06) 918013 or 918316 FAX (06) 918003 E-MAIL hacienda@cusin.com.ec.

Horse riding, an essential part of the old hacienda way of life, is becoming an increasingly popular pastime with guests of the new hacienda hotels. And since many guests are interested in visiting more than one hacienda, the owners and managers are developing a system whereby you can ride from one to another, while arrangements are made to tranport your luggage. "Every day another horse, every day another hacienda" is the motto of this system. For more information about traveling between the haciendas on horseback, contact Hacienda Cusín (see above). Also participating in the scheme, **Hacienda Pinsaquí**, just a few hours from Cusín by horse, is proud of its equestrian facilities. Its enthusiastic owner, Señor Pedro Freile, was known to ride his white stallion into the lounge to greet guests or to the cellar bar for a drink. Unfortunately the convivial stallion died recently and Sr. Freile has now acquired a splendid chestnut Arab that no doubt will be trained to perform similarly.

Pinsaquí is a 200-year-old mansion that reminds me of an Indian maharajah's palace with 16 enormous guestrooms, old-fashioned baths, beautiful furniture, fine gardens and excellent food. It also has plenty of history: an important treaty between Colombia and Ecuador was signed in the house and "The Liberator," General Simón Bolívar, was a frequent guest. Double rooms are around US$100 per night. For more information and reservations ☏ (06) 920387 or 921797 FAX (06) 920387, or contact one of the Quito travel agents.

Eccentricity seems to be a characteristic of many aristocratic hacienda owners, and I hope Diego Bonifaz, a former government minister and *patrón* of **Hostería Guachala**, won't be offended if I include him on the fringes of this group. A fine mind accompanies his nonconformity, and Señor Bonifaz is a notable historian and expert in rural affairs. He is also the imaginative manager of the oldest hacienda in Ecuador, which looks like a movie set for a costume drama set in the time of the conquistadors. A wide, cobbled courtyard sprouting a few weeds and wild flowers is overlooked on one side by a covered arcade that is used as a dining area. The white walls of the long corridors in the low-lying, rustic mansion are decorated with stag heads, riding tackle, native weavings and old photographs. There's even a fascinating archive of 400 black-and-white photographs taken by Diego's grandfather at the beginning of the twentieth century. There are two medieval chapels. The first one had been eternally desecrated when used for a profane party, so a second had to be built. The ancient messuage also boasts a large indoor swimming pool heated by solar power. Llamas patrol the outside walls of Guachala, of which there are several different types, as Bonanza explained to me. The llama, the alpaca and the guanaco are of the genus lama, while the vicuna has its own genus, vigunae. In some Indian communities a child would have a llama to carry it to school, Diego said, but once the child became too heavy for the llama, he or she would have to kill and eat the llama. To learn more about llamas and other subjects from Diego Bonanza, go stay at Hostería Guachala. Double rooms start at US$40, breakfast is US$3 and lunch and dinner are US$10. For more information and reservations contact ☏/FAX (02) 563748 or toll free in the USA and Canada ☏ (800) 451-6034.

Space doesn't allow me to list all the Ecuadorian haciendas, but a mention should be made of some of the other, better-known, northern ones. These include the recently-opened **Zuleta**, which is a working,

high-altitude farm and has a textile workshop, **La Vega**, **La Mirage**, **Ingenio San José** and **San Vicente**, all of which have their own unique charm and special attractions. Further details of these can be obtained from travel agents in Quito.

ABOVE: Hacienda Cusín, north of Quito, has been tastefully restored by its English owner.

Northern Highlands

THE TWO NORTHERN PROVINCES OF THE SIERRA, Imbabura and Carchi contain some of the most stunning scenery in Ecuador. Majestic volcanoes, wild páramo, deep green valleys and mystical lakes form a panoramic background to diverse Andean cultures. Colorful markets, traditional costumes, haunting music and ancient handicrafts are surviving facets of a lifestyle that predates the Spanish conquistadors and even the Incas.

OTAVALO

This small town, about two hours north of Quito on the Pan-American Highway, is one of the most popular destinations for visitors to Ecuador because of its world-famous market for indigenous crafts, textiles and clothing. The population of the town is around 50,000 people, most of whom are *mestizos*, but about twice as many Quichua-speaking Otavaleños live in the surrounding areas and flood into town on market days.

BACKGROUND

Indígenas in the Otavalo area have been spinning and weaving for longer than anyone knows. After the Inca conquest 500 years ago, after a long and fierce resistance by the Otavalans, the Incas extracted a textile tribute. Though the Incas were only in control for about 40 years, this was long enough for them to leave their mark. The Quichua language spoken by the Otavalan Indians comes from the Incas and the elegant women's costume, which is still universally worn, is said to be closer to Inca dress than any in the Andes today. After the Spanish defeated the Incas in the middle of the sixteenth century, they set about exploiting the weaving skills of the Otavalans by setting up textile workshops (*obrajes*) where hundreds of *indígenas* were forced to work unbearably long hours. Some of the workers were less than 10 years old and committed suicide to avoid the intolerable conditions.

The Spanish introduced modern machinery, including treadle looms, as well as sheep, wool and techniques of production weaving. From the early eighteenth century many haciendas operated weaving workshops, and at the beginning of the twentieth century Otavalan weavers began making imitation British tweeds. Land reforms in 1964 gave weavers more independence, tourism began to develop in the area and the weaving industry started to take off. Today the Otavalo *indígenas* are considered to be the most prosperous indigenous group in Latin America. They own many businesses in Otavalo, including crafts shops, restaurants, bars and travel agencies, and they have developed an international network to sell their products to neighboring countries as well as North America, Europe and Japan.

More than 80% of Otavalan *indígenas* are thought to be involved in the textile industry in some way, whether weaving and spinning at home or working with one of the larger production houses or retail outlets. Others have become lawyers, doctors and engineers. The head of the prestigious Archaeology Department of the Banco Central is an Otavalan *indígena*. The Otavalan weaving phenomenon is a fascinating story of how a small indigenous community has pulled itself out of the trap of poverty and developed its own successful, world-wide business operation.

PREVIOUS PAGES: Countryside LEFT near Otavalo. Weaver RIGHT from Agato near Otavalo. OPPOSITE: Tahuantinsuyo workshop in Agato. ABOVE: Poncho Plaza in Otavalo.

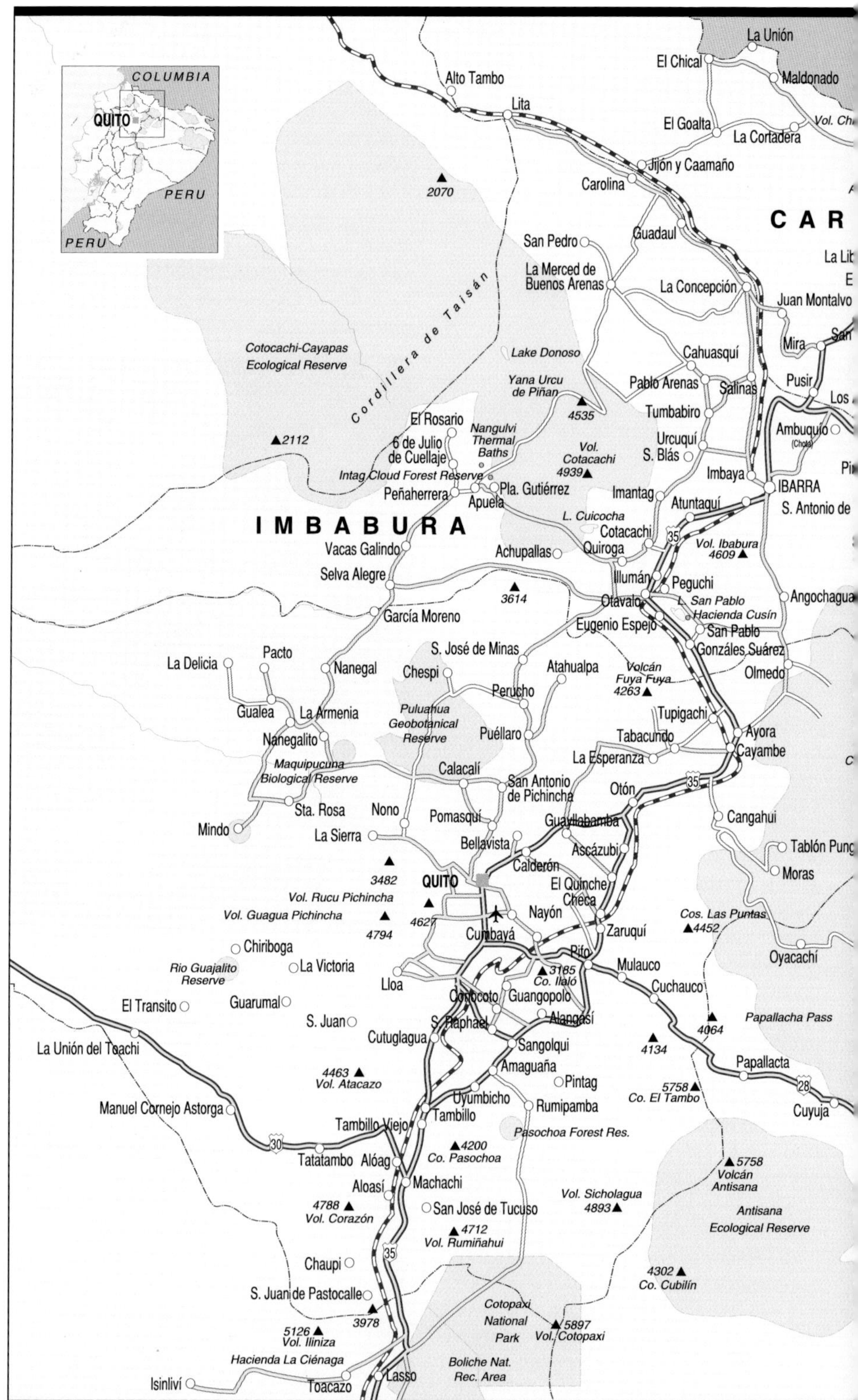
COLUMBIA
QUITO
PERU
PERU
IMBABURA
CAR
Cordillera de Taisán
Cotocachi-Cayapas Ecological Reserve
La Unión
El Chical
Maldonado
Alto Tambo
Lita
El Goalta
La Cortadera
Jijón y Caamaño
Carolina
2070
Guadaul
San Pedro
La Merced de Buenos Arenas
La Concepción
Juan Montalvo
Mira
Lake Donoso
Cahuasquí
Yana Urcu de Piñan
Pablo Arenas
Salinas
Pusir
Tumbabiro
4535
El Rosario
Nangulvi Thermal Baths
Ambuquío
Urcuquí
S. Blás
2112
6 de Julio de Cuellaje
Vol. Cotacachi 4939
Imbaya
Intag Cloud Forest Reserve
Pla. Gutiérrez
IBARRA
Peñaherrera
Apuela
Imantag
Atuntaquí
S. Antonio de
L. Cuicocha
Cotacachi
Vacas Galindo
Achupallas
Quiroga
Vol. Ibabura 4609
Selva Alegre
Illumán
Peguchi
3614
Otavalo
L. San Pablo
Angochagua
Hacienda Cusín
García Moreno
Eugenio Espejo
San Pablo
S. José de Minas
Gonzáles Suárez
Pacto
La Delicia
Nanegal
Chespi
Atahualpa
Volcán Fuya Fuya 4263
Olmedo
Perucho
Gualea
La Armenia
Pululahua Geobotanical Reserve
Tupigachi
Ayora
Nanegalito
Puéllaro
Tabacundo
Cayambe
Maquipucuna Biological Reserve
La Esperanza
Calacalí
San Antonio de Pichincha
Otón
Sta. Rosa
Nono
35
Mindo
Pomasquí
Guayllabamba
Cangahui
La Sierra
Bellavista
Ascázubi
Tablón Pung
3482
Calderón
QUITO
El Quinche
Moras
Vol. Rucu Pichincha
Checa
4627
Vol. Guagua Pichincha
Nayón
Cos. Las Puntas 4452
4794
Cumbayá
Zaruquí
Chiriboga
Oyacachí
Rio Guajalito Reserve
La Victoria
Pifo
3185 Co. Ilaló
Mulauco
Lloa
Cuchauco
El Transito
Guarumal
Conocoto
Guangopolo
Alangasí
4064
Papallacha Pass
S. Juan
S. Raphael
La Unión del Toachi
Cutuglagua
Sangolqui
4134
Amaguaña
Papallacta
4463 Vol. Atacazo
Pintag
5758 Co. El Tambo
28
Uyumbicho
Cuyuja
Manuel Cornejo Astorga
Tambillo
Rumipamba
Tambillo Viejo
Pasochoa Forest Res.
30
4200 Co. Pasochoa
Tatatambo
Alóag
5758 Volcán Antisana
Machachi
Aloasí
Vol. Sicholagua 4893
Antisana Ecological Reserve
4788 Vol. Corazón
San José de Tucuso
4712 Vol. Rumiñahui
35
Chaupi
4302 Co. Cubilín
S. Juan de Pastocalle
Cotopaxi National Park
3978
5897 Vol. Cotopaxi
5126 Vol. Iliniza
Hacienda La Ciénaga
Boliche Nat. Rec. Area
Isinliví
Toacazo
Lasso

While achievin…
Otavalan *indígenas*…
maintain their cultu…
tions. Most visibly, …
unique traditional costu…
favor calf-length white…
blue ponchos, rope sand… …elt
hats, while women displ… …oidered
white blouses, dark skirts and shawls, masses of golden glass beads around their neck, red bead bracelets and cloth headgear which is folded in various significant ways. Most distinctively, both women and men wear their hair in a long single pigtail that is often tied back with a colorful woven band. The traditional costumes are worn daily at home and in the villages, not to impress tourists in the market.

General Information

Though there is no CETUR office in Otavalo, there are several useful travel agents who can arrange visits to weavers' homes in the town, craft villages in the surrounding countryside, as well as horse riding, hiking and visits to ecological reserves. Especially recommended is **Zulaytur** ☎ (06) 921176, Sucre and Colon, where Señor Rodrigo Mora speaks English and is very helpful. Also recommended is nearby **Zulay Diceny Viajes** ☎ (06) 921217, and **Inty Express** ☎ (06) 921436.

For international telephone calls, the **EMETEL office** is on Calderón and Sucre, and if you want to mail a poncho home, the **Post Office** is behind the Municipal on Piedrahita. The **Policía Municipal** happens to be in the same building. For medical emergencies, **Hospital San Luis de Otavalo** is on Sucre, on the northern edge of town.

There is no main bus terminal in Otavalo, though one is about to be constructed. **Buses** north to Ibarra and south to Quito leave from Calderón between Bolívar and Roca regularly. Ask at the local travel agents for information about buses to the smaller villages.

Some gringo travelers who want to learn Spanish while in Ecuador choose to study in Otavalo because it's slightly less expensive and slower paced than in Quito. The Instituto Superior de Español on Sucre 11-10 and Morales is worth checking out. Some of

.. make some money exporting and other textile products they ..t Otavalo.

WHAT TO SEE AND DO

Otavalo's main attraction is its vibrant ***artesanías* market**. On Saturdays one of the squares in the center of town, **Plaza de Ponchos**, as is it is aptly called, is covered with a labyrinth of small shops and stands selling almost every textile and craft item made in Ecuador — ponchos, woolen blankets, woven wall hangings, handknitted sweaters, scarves, gloves, hats, shirts, shawls, embroidered blouses, table cloths, string bags, baskets, ceramics, sandals, leather goods, carvings, beads, buttons, bric-a-brac, and more.

Tourists arrive here by the busload from Quito. Prices are probably a bit lower than in Quito, but you have to bargain. The stallholders will reduce their prices considerably but you must be patient. Use a lot of smiles and laughter and under no circumstances raise your voice or get angry. Walk away if the price is too high, by all means; it just might be lower when you return. Some visitors are surprised that some of the goods are so touristy with bright, garish colors. In fact the Otavalan weavers and textile makers are quite aware of the taste of the majority of their customers, so if you're looking for unusual or antique pieces you will probably be better off going to Quito or to some of the other markets around the country.

There are in fact three markets in Otavalo on Saturdays: the ***artesanías* market** in Plaza de Ponchos from 7 AM until about 6 PM, the **livestock market** on the edge of town at Viejo Colegio Agricultural from 6 AM to 10 AM (be there as early as possible), and the **produce market** which is divided between the new covered market at Plaza Copacabana near the railways station and in Plaza 24 de Mayo. The *artesanías* market has become so popular that not only has it spread physically into the narrow side streets off Plaza de Ponchos, but it has also stretched in time so that there are market stands in the plaza throughout the week. Many people prefer the quieter market days on Wednesdays and Fridays when prices are lower.

As well as a great place for shopping, Otavalo is a photographer's dream. The bold colors and striking designs of the Andean textiles and wall hangings. combined with the elegant costumes and strong faces of the Otavaleños make for powerful images. But it's important to be sensitive to your subjects. If possible, ask permission before you photograph somebody. The concept of *minga*, or reciprocity, is an important concept in *indígena* society. Or if you want to photograph a stallholder, buy something before you ask permission — some give and take is always appreciated. The markets are also good hunting grounds for pickpockets and sneak thieves. Hold on tight to your bags and cameras at all times.

The best way to photograph weavers at work is to take a **guided tour of *indígenas'* homes**. Costing about US$10, tours can be arranged through travel agents (see above). You can buy products straight off the loom and, with permission, photograph the weaving process. Tours of nearby weaving villages are also popular (see below by village names).

If you're in Otavalo for any length of time, and you've shopped until you've dropped, there are a few small museums that might revive your interest. The Museo Arqueológico is attached to Pensión Los Andes on Roca and Montalvo and is free to guests. The Instituto Otavaleño de Antropología is just beyond the Pan-American Highway, on the northern edge of town. It has information in both English and Spanish and is a good introduction to the culture and traditions of the Otavalan *indígenas*. Another insight into the local way of life can be seen at the cockpit on 31 de Octubre and Montalvo, where cockfights take place on Saturday afternoons.

WHERE TO STAY

For such a small town Otavalo has a lot of hotels. Most of the week they are relatively empty but on Friday nights, before the big market day on Saturday, they tend to fill up, so reservations are recommended. One hotel in Otavalo has an almost legendary reputation. It's called **Ali Shungu** ☎ (06) 920750, which means "good heart" in Quichua. Though I have visited the hotel, which is clean and attractive and appears to be excellent, I have not had the opportunity of staying so I cannot personally vouch for all the glowing praise I've heard about it.

Ali Shungu is run and owned by two Americans who fell love with Ecuador about 20 years ago and decided to settle and build their own hotel. Warm, sunny, secure, well-maintained, with 16 rooms, two spacious apartments and a reputation for excellent cuisine, the hotel is in a quiet residential area, just a few blocks from the handicrafts market. It has a lovely garden with views of Volcán Imbabura and folk music on weekends. The hotel runs a shuttle bus service for guests between Quito and Otavalo. A double room is US$36 and an apartment for five is US$108, including tax and service charges. Reservations should be made directly with the hotel as the Ali Shungu doesn't pay agents' commissions. Write to Hotel Ali Shungu, Casilla 34, Otavalo, Ecuador, or E-MAIL alishngu@uio.telconet.net.

Equally highly-praised by guests is the newly opened, ecologically oriented **Casa Mojanda Inn** ☎/FAX (09) 731737, set in 10 hectares (25 acres) of farmland and forested gorge overlooking the sacred mountains of Imbabura and Cotacachi. About 15 minutes by car from Otavalo, the inn has nine guest cottages constructed from adobe, wood and other natural materials. Prices are US$44 per person, including two excellent meals. Dormitory accommodation is US$33 and there's a budget rate of US$12 for a detached hostel in an adobe house up the hill, including breakfast. For reservations ☎/FAX (09) 731737 FAX only 993-6 922969 E-MAIL mojanda@uio.telconet.net. WEBSITE www.casamojanda.com, or write to Casa Mojanda, Apartado Postal 160, Otavalo, Ecuador. Betty and Diego Falconi, who run the inn, arrange excellent village tours, horse riding trips, hikes to the lakes, etc. They are also involved in health and other projects with the local community.

In town there are several good value, more conventional hotels. Popular with the many Colombian tourists, **Hotel El Indio Inn** ☎ (06) 922922 FAX (06) 920325, Calle Bolívar No. 904, is smart, clean and conveniently located, with terrace and restaurant. Double rooms are a little more than US$30, including tax and service charges. At about the same price, **Hotel Coraza** ☎ (06) 921225, Calle Caderón and Sucre, is also new and clean (interestingly, this hotel also describes itself as a distributor of Vicuna blankets). **Hotel Otavalo** ☎ (06) 920416, between Moreno and Montalvo, has large rooms, big beds but erratic water supplies (often a problem in Otavalo). Double rooms with bath are about US$10. Not to be confused with Hotel El Indio Inn, is the also recommended **Hotel El Indio** ☎ (02) 920601, Sucre 12–14, where double rooms are about US$12. There are many hostels to choose from in the budget range. Currently the most popular choice is **Hostal Valle del Almanecer** ☎ (06) 920990 FAX (06) 920216, Roca and Quiroga, which charges about US$5 per person for a shared room and bath in a colonial building. It has a pleasant courtyard and restaurant, is a good place to meet fellow travelers and has mountain bikes for rent. Another popular and very inexpensive budget hostel is **Pensión Los Andes**, on Montalvo, where you can get a bed for about US$3 per night (see above). Although it lacks hot water, the hostel does have its own private archaeological museum!

Tree-lined road at Hacienda Cusín, near Otavalo.

WHERE TO EAT

With so many gringos coming into town for the market, there are several laid back restaurants where you can hang out, meet people and read the experiences of fellow travelers in what are known as "the good, the bad and the ugly" comment books. Oh, and you can also have something to eat and drink. One of the best-known such places used to be an unpretentious little pie shop overlooking Poncho Plaza called Shenandoah. It is still there and you can still get good pies, ice creams and milkshakes, but as Otavalo becomes increasingly popular the competition is growing. Plaza Café, across the street, is another a friendly hangout and it serves good dinners for about US$5. Also on Poncho Plaza is Café Galería, which has atmosphere, music and vegetarian food. Fuente del Mar, on Bolívar 815, is recommended for seafood while Pizza Siciliana, on Sucre and Calderón, is known for tasty, generous pizzas and vegetarian dishes. Pizza Siciliana also has an outlet in the Hotel El Indio Inn. And don't forget the restaurant at Ali Shungu, which is open to non-residents of the hotel.

NIGHTLIFE

It might be said that Otavalo doesn't have much nightlife but if you like live Andean music, salsa dancing, cane alcohol and a raucous atmosphere, what more do you need? There are few *peña* (folkloric music club) bars of which the best known are Peña Amauta, Jaramillo and Salinas, with good local bands; Peña Tucano, Morales and Sucre; and Peña Tuparina, Morales and 31 de Octubre. Peña bars come and go all over Ecuador so ask around to find out about the latest hot spots.

HOW TO GET THERE

There are buses about every 15 minutes to Otavalo from Quito up until about 6 PM. The journey takes about two hours and costs about US$2. Make sure you catch a bus that goes into the center of town rather than continuing on to Ibarra, in which case you will be dropped off on the Pan-American Highway and will have to walk a kilometer (a half mile) into town. Transportes Otavalo and Transportes Los Lagos are recommended. Buses from these companies drop you off near Plaza Copacabana where there is a taxi stand. Buses leave from here for some of the outlying villages. Taxis from Quito to Otavalo should cost about US$40 and take about an hour. The train service between Quito and Otavalo has not been running for several years, but you can take a train to Ibarra, which takes about an hour. The vehicle is actually less a train than an old bus attached to a train chassis.

AROUND OTAVALO

PEGUCHI

The small Andean village of **Peguchi**, less than an hour's walk northeast from Otavalo, is best known for **tapestry weaving**, lovely **waterfalls** and **music**. You can get to the falls by following the railway tracks east of town and heading northwards. Follow the tracks and the cobblestone road until they split. Continue on the road up the hill and to the right into the forest park. If you get lost, ask for *las cascadas* and you'll be directed to the mist-shrouded falls. To get to the village, follow the railway tracks all the way. Near the center of the village you can't easily miss the two galleries of master tapestry weaver and designer, José Cotacachi. José may take you to see some home weaving, but it helps if you speak Spanish. If not, it might be better to join a tour to Peguchi in Otavalo. Several

OPPOSITE: On the road near Peguchi, a weaving village near Otavalo. ABOVE: Children at Peguchi.

groups of well-known Indian musicians come from this village.

Just outside Peguchi is the much-loved and friendly **Hostal Aya Huma** ☎ (06) 922663 FAX (06) 922664, run by a Dutch-Ecuadorian couple, which has a good restaurant, live folk music on Saturdays, locally woven blankets to keep you warm, a garden and quiet surroundings. The hostel also includes Spanish lessons among its offerings. Rooms are from US$7 to US$12 per person. At about the same price, **Peguchi Tio Hostería** ☎/FAX (06) 922619, near the police station, promotes local handicrafts and culture with enthusiasm and is well recommended.

ILLUMÁN

About three kilometers (almost two miles) north of Peguchi, is the weaving community of **Illumán**, makers of tapestries, felt hats and ponchos. The village is also famous for its **traditional healers**, who chase away sickness using ancient rituals and a vast knowledge of local herbs and plants, some of which are now used in Western medicine. People from all over the Sierra come to see the healers of Illumán. One Spanish speaking *gringa* I know came away from a healing session with her clothes covered in spittle and the colored juices of herbs, but cured of her ailment. In the northeast corner of the village plaza, demonstrations of pre-Inca backstrap loom weaving take place at the **Inti Chumbi Co-op**, on the second floor of Conterón family's house. Weavings are on sale.

AGATO

Special demonstrations of traditional weaving also take place in **Agato**, three kilometers (two miles) east of Peguchi. At the **Tahuantinsuyo Weaving Workshop**, Ecuador's most famous weaver, Miguel Andrango, demonstrates backstrap loom techniques using handspun wool and natural dyes. This is of particular interest to those with a special curiosity about weaving. His products, more expensive than those made on the upright loom and colored with chemical dyes, aren't usually for sale at the Otavalo market but can be bought at his workshop and at Hacienda Cusín (see page 92) on weekends. There are buses to Agato from Otavalo and a taxi costs only about US$2.

SAN PABLO LAKE

From Otavalo there are a number of paths leading down to **San Pablo Lake**, just a couple of kilometers southeast of town, which is a popular spot for water sports. If you walk via **El Lechero** (don't ask me why this hill is named "The Milkman"), you get fabulous views of the lake and **Volcán Imbabura**. You can walk or take a bus all the way around the lake, stopping off at one of the hosterías. And you can rent a canoe at **Club de Tiro** on the shore. **Hostería Puerto Lago** offers evening cruises on the lake with music and cocktails.

MOJANDA LAKES

For a more solitary lakeside experience make your way to **Lagunas de Mojanda**, a series of six mountain lakes 18 km (11 miles) south of and 1,200 m (4,000 ft) higher than Otavalo. The largest of these is Laguna Grande de Mojanda, also known as **Caricocha**. The best way to get there is by taxi from town, costing about US$10, and hike back. If you want to stay overnight, bring a sleeping bag and tent because the *refugios* up there aren't usually fit for habitation. If you are interested in riding up to the lakes or trout fishing when you get there, contact a local travel agent, or inquire at **Hacienda Cusín** ☎ (06) 918013 or 918316 or **Casa Mojanda** ☎/FAX (09) 731737.

COTACACHI

Just 15 km (nine miles) north of Otavalo, the small town of **Cotacachi** is the **leather capital** of Ecuador. There are few places in the world where you can get a better deal on a genuine leather jacket, skirt, or handsome travel bag. Market day is Saturday, though dozens of stores are open throughout the week. Curiously, leather goods from Cotacachi is one Ecuadorian product that is not sold in the big market in Otavalo. Another local product is *alpargatas* (sandals) popular with people of the region.

OPPOSITE: Highland landscape TOP near Otavalo. Ibarra, the capital of Imbabura Province BOTTOM is a handsome, old-fashioned town.

In town, the best hotel is **El Mesón de las Flores** ☎ (06) 915009, with double rooms in the region of US$50, while just west of town is the very upmarket **Hostería La Mirage** ☎ (06) 915237 FAX (06) 915065 E-MAIL lamirage @relaischateau.fr, a hacienda-style country hotel complete with a beautiful garden, antiques, fine food, pool and gymnasium. Rooms with half board are about US$150 per person. **Hacienda Pinsaquí** (see HACIENDA LIVING, page 11, in TOP SPOTS) is nearby. Cotacachi isn't known for good budget hotels and restaurants.

LAKE CUICOCHA

Another spectacular mountain lake is **Laguna de Cuicocha**, about 16 km (10 miles) west of Cotacachi town. This deep, blue crater lake with two islands in the middle is a popular recreation area on weekends. Motor boats can be rented to explore the lake, though the islands are off limits because of research projects. A walk around the lake takes about five hours. Be warned: those berries that look like blueberries are something else — and they are poisonous. A round-trip by taxi from Cotacachi costs about US$10. The lake is part of the enormous **Cotacachi-Cayapas Ecological Reserve** that stretches down the western highlands to the tropical lowlands of Esmeraldas Province. Just south of the reserve and about 40 km (25 miles) west of Lake Cuicocha is the remote village of **Apuela**, set in the deep Andean cloud forest. Nearby are the **Nangulvi Thermal Baths**. Basic accommodation available. There are a few buses each day along the scenic but jolting road between Otavalo and Apuela.

FOREST RESERVES

The rich and humid cloud forests, populated by a huge diversity of plants, birds and mammals, are disappearing even faster than the better-known rainforests. Deforestation on the western slopes of the Andes is threatening the survival of mammals such as mountain tapirs, spectacled bears, spider monkeys and pumas. In an attempt to counter this destruction, several adventurous and dedicated individuals have established protected reserves. Their objective is to safeguard the forest from logging, conserve the natural environment and protect endangered species.

Two such ecoactivists are Carlos Zorilla and Sandy Statz whose **Intag Cloud Forest Reserve**, in the vicinity of Apuela, is a model of environmental friendliness. Rustic wooden cabins, solar-generated electricity and homegrown vegetables are indicators of their philosophy. Visitors can see their operation and explore the jungle for themselves at US$45 per person per day, including all meals and guides. For reservations, write to Intag at Casilla 18, Otavalo, Imbabura, Ecuador, giving at least two months notice. **Bosque Nublado de Santo Tomás** is a similar operation in the same area. For information on more of these sorts of ecological enterprises, contact Safari

Tours ☎ (02) 552505 FAX (02) 220426 at Calamá 380 and Jean León Mera, Quito.

IBARRA

For most visitors to Ecuador, Ibarra, the provincial capital of Imbabura, is a stop over en route to somewhere else. Notably, it's the starting point of the antiquated, single-track railway that plunges down the slopes of the Andes to the coastal town of San Lorenzo. The town is also a transit stop on the Pan-American Highway on the way to or from Colombia. But Ibarra is more than a transport hub. Known as the White City, it's a handsome, old-fashioned town of white-walled colonial buildings and peaceful squares filled with flowering trees. Horse-drawn carts still clomp along cobbled streets. Its altitude of 2,210 m (7,366 ft) gives the city a refreshing, comfortable climate and its population of nearly 100,000 creates enough activity without making it too busy. It might not be a great cultural or entertainment center, but Ibarra is a pleasant place to enjoy the slow paced, everyday pleasures of Ecuadorian life.

Background

San Antonio de Ibarra, the city's full name, was founded in 1606 and was named after Miguel de Ibarra, then-President of Quito's Royal Audencia. In its early days it became

The cloud forests on the slopes of the Andes are rapidly disappearing.

the administrative center of the exploitive textile industry. In spite of a massive earthquake in 1868, which killed most of its 6,000 inhabitants and destroyed many of its buildings, Ibarra has retained or rebuilt many of its fine colonial houses. The growing town gradually became, and still is, the main market for the region's agricultural products, such as cotton, sugar cane, coffee, cereals and livestock. It remains a center for textiles and silverware and has a large sugar refinery. Ibarra's population is a mixture of *indígenas*, blacks and *mestizos.*

General Information

The CETUR **Tourist Information** office is on Colón and Olmedo, conveniently near the railway station. This is important because so many travelers need information about the dates and times of trains to San Lorenzo, which nobody seems to know, not even railway officials, if you can find any. Even CETUR might not have the answer, as the hours of the tourist office appear to be as arbitrary as the departure times of the trains. For this and other information, also check with the tour companies **Nevitur Cia Ltda** ☎ (06) 958701, Bolívar and Oviedo or **Turismo Inti Pungo** ☎ (06) 255270, Rocafuerte and Garcia Moreno. Or just ask a taxi driver.

For international **phone calls**, the EMETEL office is on Sucre, a block north of the main square, Parque Pedro Moncayo, while the **Post Office** is on Salinas 6-64, between Oviedo and Moncayo. A recommended **doctor** is Dr. Eduardo Benítez ☎ (06) 955592, Oviedo 8-40. The **Immigration Office** is on Olmedo and Villamar.

What to See and Do

You can see most of the main city sights of Ibarra in a day. To get your bearings, look for the huge **obelisk** near the railway station dedicated to the man who gave the city its name, Miguel de Ibarra. Walk a couple blocks eastwards along Velasco and then three blocks north along Bolívar to the **Parque Pedro Moncayo**, named after a famous journalist and diplomat of the nineteenth century. Some fine buildings, including the city cathedral, whose main interest is its magnificent golden altar and powerful portraits of the twelve apostles, surround the grassy, tree-lined square. Two blocks west of the square is **Parque de la Merced**, as it's usually called, or Parque Dr. Victor Manuel Peñaherra, its official name. A bust of this eminent son of Ibarra, a lawyer and academic, stands in the park. Nearby is the

Basilica La Merced, crowned with a statue of the Virgin. There is also a private archaeological museum on Parque de la Merced with eccentric hours.

WHERE TO STAY AND EAT

Few visitors stay overnight in Ibarra unless they have to get the early train to San Lorenzo the next day. Generally they prefer to stay in Otavalo or one of the nearby country inns or haciendas. If you do take a room, one of the best is **Hotel Ajaví** ✆ (06) 920941 or 955555 or 955221 FAX (06) 955640 or 952485, about a kilometer (just over a half mile) from the town center on the main road from the south. Costing about US$50 per night, this comfortable, modern hotel has a restaurant, bar, pool and sauna. If you just want an inexpensive place to rest your head, try the basic but friendly **Hotel Imbabura** ✆ (06) 950155, Oviedo 9-33 and Narváez. There are also several inexpensive hostels and hotels near the station.

As far as I am aware there is no top class place to eat in Ibarra itself, while the best restaurants are in big hotels out of town. My own favorite is the least expensive of the lot, which is the **open market** near the station. Stand-up stalls and sit-down snack shops cover the complete range of tasty local dishes. The *empanadas* (cheese-filled pastries) are as good as any I've had in Ecuador, and with a big mug of coffee they're just what you need before catching the early train to the coast. Otherwise, **La Estancia**, Garcia Moreno 7-66, is recommended for its rather expensive grills and **El Chagra Restaurante**, just south of Parque La Merced on Olmedo, is the best value budget place in town.

HOW TO GET THERE

There are frequent buses between Ibarra, Otavalo, Quito, Tulcán and other major towns, but the main bus station has been closed for renovation. If it has not yet reopened, most buses will leave from the bus stop near the big obelisk by the railway station. Twice-daily buses for San Lorenzo (7 AM and 10 AM) depart from the stop behind the railway station. Check first to confirm departure points and times.

THE TRAIN TO SAN LORENZO

The train journey down the Andes from Ibarra to San Lorenzo is one of Ecuador's great adventures. It can also be one of its worst nightmares. First, you have to find out if the train is running, and if so, when. In recent years it has been out of action for months at a time because of landslides and breakdowns, and the El Niño floods in 1997 and 1998 which also caused extensive damage. It is possible it will never be repaired because there will be a new road between the two towns. Under normal circumstances there is a train about every other day at 7 AM. Tickets may be on sale the day before departure, but it's more likely you will have to buy one on the day, in which case you should get to the station an hour before the train leaves.

There's usually a crowd of people battling to get to the window to buy a ticket and there's a bigger battle to board the train. Two types of *autoferro* (iron car) make the precarious journey down the mountainside. One is a bus body, the other looks like a moving van, both of which are attached to rail car chassis. The bus version of this ferrovial chimera is used as an occasional passenger train, while the van version serves as a combination cargo and passenger vehicle. I havn't traveled on the former, but getting into the latter by climbing up into the back door is an unholy wrestling match. Once inside, the scrimmage continues for the few seats on the narrow wooden benches along the walls of the truck. Most people have to sit on the floor on their rucksacks or bundles of belongings.

On a recent journey, there were about 60 of us squashed into a dim wagon about eight by three meters (26 by nine feet). We pulled out of the grimy station at 7:30 AM, just a half hour behind schedule. Squinting through the slit windows I could see the early morning sun catching the green flanks of Volcán Cotacachi. Schoolchildren, Otavalan Indians, blacks from the coast and four backpackers shared floor space with sacks of fruit, kitchen pots, chickens, hi-fi

Some of the most beautiful mountain landscapes in Ecuador can be seen around Ibarra.

equipment, straw mats and a dugout canoe. A man in a bright pink T-shirt pulled out a bottle of rum.

The sound of squealing brakes mixed discordantly with the shrieks of kids as if on a ghost train. The biggest thrill is riding on top of the train, which is regularly swept by low slung branches. Passengers on top frequently have to duck or even lie down flat to avoid being pushed over the edge. As the train winds its way around tight bends down the steep slopes, the vegetation becomes thicker and more tropical while the temperature rises. Kids grab twigs and small branches that poke their way through the slats of the slowly descending wagon.

The man in the pink T-shirt is well into his second bottle of rum. He abuses some of passengers so much that at one station he has to be bundled off the train. At this point things turn nasty. Somehow the drunk manages to grab a machete, which he swings about in a dangerous and threatening way. Everybody is screaming. One of the passengers on the roof aims a revolver at the demon drunk with the machete, prepared to shoot if necessary. To everyone's relief, the drunk is eventually disarmed. He's left standing on the tracks, throwing stones towards the back of our disappearing *autoferro*.

In another incident shortly before we get to San Lorenzo, two women get into a huge fight inside the wagon over payment for some food. Hair is pulled, blouses are torn, an ancient, rusty gun is brandished. There's more screaming from the passengers. We clatter into hot and languid San Lorenzo 10 hours after our departure from Ibarra, only three hours late (see MOUNTAIN TRAINING, page 14, in TOP SPOTS).

AROUND IBARRA

There are several pretty towns and villages in the vicinity of Ibarra, which are well worth visiting if you have the time. Of special interest is **San Antonio de Ibarra**, which bears the full name of the city itself and is only two kilometers (a mile and a half) away. San Antonio's reputation for **woodcarving** is known throughout Ecuador and increasingly in other countries. Particularly famous are the realistic carvings of religious figures, old people and nudes, some of which are almost life size. Craftsmen also carve chess sets, furniture, mirror frames, animals, and some modernist pieces. The main square and main street of the village is lined with galleries and workshops, the best known being **Galaría de Arte Luis Potosí**.

Ten kilometers (six miles) south of Ibarra is the attractive village of **La Esperanza**, a good starting point for climbing the daunting **Volcán Imbabura** (4,609 m or 15,360 ft) and the slightly less demanding **Loma Cubilche** (3,836 m or 12,785 ft). Anyone wishing to climb these peaks should seek expert advice before doing so. Esperanza is also a good place to experience a night in a tree house at **Casa Aida**. Ask in the village for directions.

Just four kilometers (two and a half miles) north of Ibarra is the well-known lake, **Lago Yahuarcocha** (Lake of Blood), so-called because of a great battle between the Incas and local Cara Indians, whose bleeding bodies were thrown into the lake, turning the water red. A motor racetrack now circles the lake spoiling its natural setting. Continuing north, you descend into the **Chota Valley** which is inhabited by descendants of slaves who still retain many of their tribal traditions. About 40 km (25 miles) further north at **La Paz** are some thermal springs, waterfalls and a grotto containing a statue of the Virgin. This sacred area is very popular during religious festivals.

North of La Paz is the highland village of **El Ángel** and the access point to the **Páramo del Ángel**, an area of mystical lakes, windswept grasslands and the curious, hairy-leafed, tree-like **frailejón** plant, said to be the biggest plant in the world. If you want to explore this little-visited ecological reserve, ask for the offices of the **Fundación El Ángel** in El Ángel itself. **Fundación Golondrinas** also is also active in conservation work in the area and organizes treks from El Ángel. For details contact Piet Sabbe, Cerro Golondrinas Project Coordinator ✆ (02) 226602 FAX (02) 566076 E-MAIL manteca@uio.satnet.net, or care of La Casa de Eliza, Isabel La Católica 1559, Apartado 17-21-1786, Quito.

TULCÁN

The capital of Carchi Province, Tulcán, just six kilometers (four miles) from the Colombian border, is a transit point for travelers going to and from Colombia. The town was a thriving smuggling center until a free trade agreement in 1992. Now it has become a shopping center for Colombians whose strong currency make goods here less expensive than in their own country. Some drug smuggling goes through the town, giving it a higher than average crime rate and making the streets unsafe at night. It isn't a great town for hotels and restaurants so there's not much point in staying overnight unless you get stuck in transit.

General Information

The CETUR **Tourist Information Office** is on the second floor at Pichincha 467 between Bolívar and Sucre. It should be open each morning and afternoon except Saturday. **Ecco Tur** travel agency is on Sucre 51029. There are **EMETEL** offices for international calls on Olmedo and Ayacucho and at the Terminal Terrestre bus terminal about two kilometers (just over a mile) southwest of the center of town.

What to See and Do

Though Tulcán isn't renowned for its tourist sights, there is one unique and unlikely attraction that is consistently recommended. This is the **topiary garden** in the cemetery two blocks north of the **Parque Ayora**. Fantastic figures carved from cypress bushes create one of the greatest masterpieces of the hedge-clipper's art. The epitaph of Sr. José Franco, the cultivator of the gardens, reads: "In Tulcán, a cemetery so beautiful that it invites one to die."

Where to Stay and Eat

I am not personally familiar with the hotels and restaurants of Tulcán, though I am informed that the one of the best hotels is **Sáenz Internacional** ☎ (06) 981916 on Sucre and Rocafuerte, which costs about US$20 per person per night. In the budget range, **Hotel Alejandra** ☎ (06) 981784, on Sucre and Quito, has been recommended.

How to Get There

Crossing the border from Ecuador into Colombia or vice versa is a simple matter as long as your passport is valid. Both countries give a 90-day tourist visa to almost all nationalities. There are regular buses and mini-buses between Parque Ayora to the border at Rumichaca. The border is open between 6 AM to 9 PM. Money-changing facilities are available but carefully check your transactions. Note that there are occasional customs and immigration checks on the road between Ibarra and Tulcán.

Rackety busses known as rancheros serve some of the most remote Andean villages.

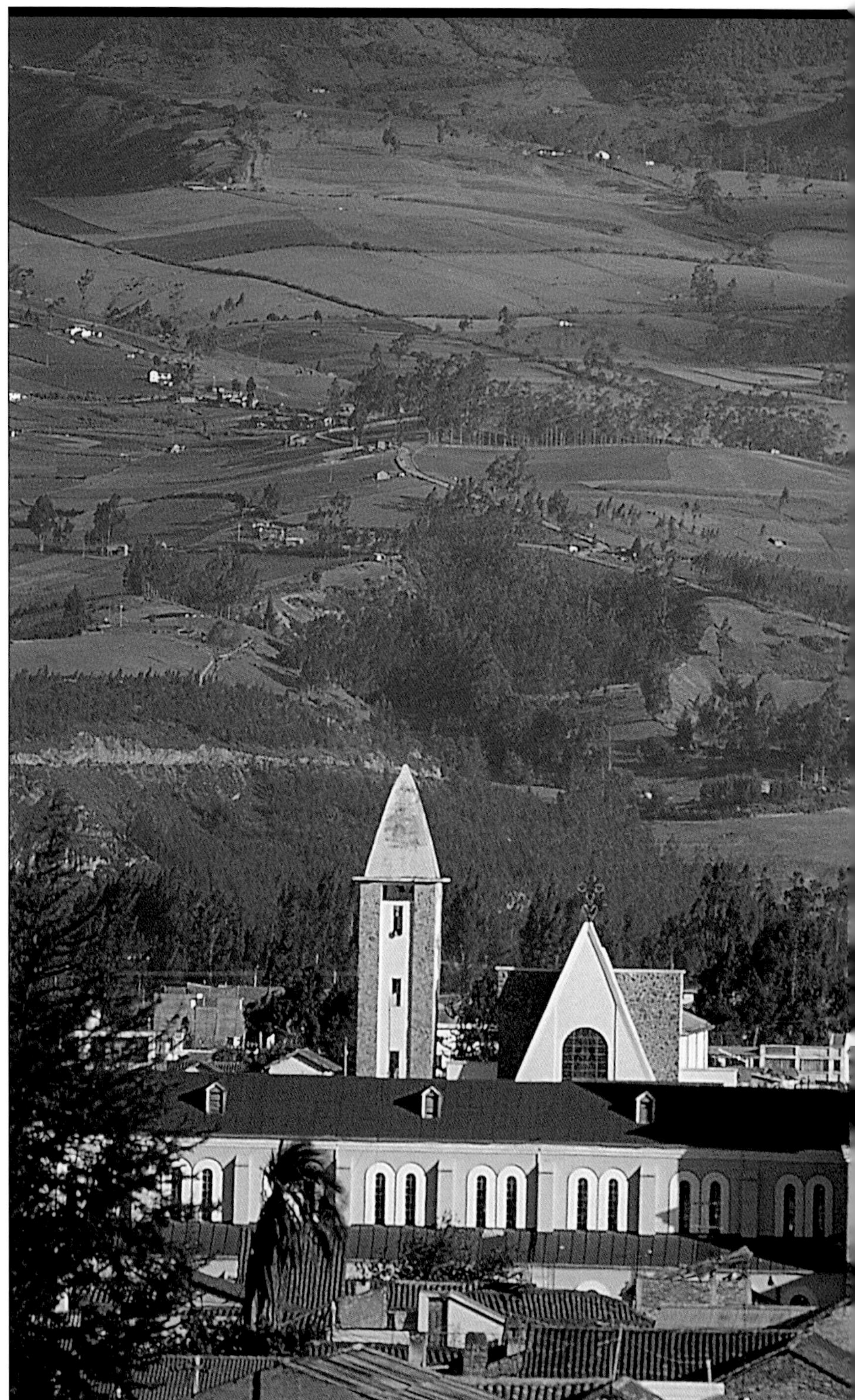

Central Highlands

THE INTREPID GERMAN EXPLORER AND NATURAList, Alexander van Humboldt (1769–1859), climber of many of Ecuador's tallest mountains and holder of the world climbing record for 30 years, named the twin range of mountains running from Quito to Cuenca, the "Avenue of Volcanoes." The description is apt and the name stuck. Travelers going south from Quito by road or rail eagerly strain their eyes and stretch their necks for views of these fabulous mountains. Often they are disappointed, as I have been frequently, because the peaks have a habit of hiding themselves in drifting white clouds. Nevertheless, you will see much stunning scenery in the Central Highlands, along with picturesque colonial towns, feisty festivals and multifarious markets.

LATACUNGA

An unfortunate claim to fame of this highland town, the capital of Cotopaxi Province, is its propensity for catastrophe. In 400 years it has been devastated or destroyed by earthquakes and volcanic eruptions of nearby Volcán Cotopaxi about 10 times, and subsequently rebuilt. The most recent disaster, an earthquake in 1996, left several dead and thousands homeless. Not surprisingly, light gray pumice stone is a favored building material.

The name Latacunga means "God of the Waters" in Quichua though it has also been suggested that it is derived from words meaning "land of my choice" in another Indian language. If the latter is true, perhaps this is why Latacungañyos are so obstinant in living in their disaster-prone town. It is usually said that the danger of another eruption is very small, but an old man who lives nearby told me he had four healthy children, no debts but one major nightmare — that one day Cotopaxi would erupt again and destroy his farm.

Latacunga has some pretty squares and gardens. Otherwise it doesn't offer a great deal to the visitor except for its proximity to natural wonders, remote Andean villages and the nearby market of Saquisilí, which many consider to be the best Indian market in Ecuador (see AROUND LATACUNGA, page 116). In such an eruptive, volatile area it isn't surprising that on a clear day you can see many of Ecuador's tallest volcanic peaks from Latacunga.

WHAT TO SEE AND DO

Most visitors use Latacunga as a base from which to explore the region and most spend little time in the town. Those that do tend to congregate around **Parque Vicente León**, the tourist area of the city. The main municipal buildings are here also, as is the city's **cathedral**, most recently restored in 1973.

There is no CETUR office in town but you can pick up a tourist map from **Metropolitan Touring** on Quito and Guayaquil. A lively, sprawling **market** spreads over several blocks east of **Río Cutuchi**, the big day being Saturday. There is no bus station. Buses to Quito leave from Plaza Chile by the market, buses to nearby villages from a block north of the market, and buses going south on the Pan-American leave from the other side of the river, near the **train station**.

PREVIOUS PAGES: The town of Ríobamba LEFT nestles in the foothills of the Andean mountains. A Local indígena RIGHT from Salasaca, near Baños. OPPOSITE and ABOVE: Colorful flowers and yarn on display at Latacunga market.

If you suffer from cultural withdrawal while in Latacunga your best bet is to visit the **Molinos de Monserrat Museum** of ethnography and art. Near Vela and Salcedo, this Casa de la Cultura is open all day except Sundays and Mondays.

Festivals

An unusual characteristic of the usually macho male Latacungañyos is their love of dressing up as black women. This they do at the **Fiesta de la Mamá Negra**, a raucous occasion of street dancing, heavy drinking, Andean music and fireworks, held each year on September 23 and 24. Another **parade** in honor of the Black Mama takes place two weeks later. And on November 11 Latacunga celebrates its **anniversary of independence** with bullfighting and yet more exuberance.

WHERE TO STAY AND EAT

If your budget can stand it, the best place to stay is at the hacienda **Hostería La Ciénega** ✆ 02) 541337 or 549126, about 20 km (13 miles) north of town (see THE HACIENDA LIFESTYLE, page 91, in ANDEAN HIGHLANDS). In town, the best hotel is probably **Hotel Rodelú** ✆ (03) 800956 FAX (03) 812341, on Quito, near the Parque Vicente. Rooms are about US$20 a night. On the budget end of the scale, **Hotel Estambul** ✆ (03) 800354, on Quevedo and Salcedo, is friendly, safe and helps with travel arrangements.

Foodwise, there are many inexpensive and good value restaurants in town. Look out for **Pollos Gus** on the Pan-American, **La Borgoña**, **El Mashca**, **Pinguino** and **Parrilladas Los Copihues**. The best recommendation is the **Pizzería Rodelu** in the hotel of that name. Most restaurants close early.

AROUND LATACUNGA

Several remote Andean villages are hidden in the mountains above Latacunga. A circuit of what is called the **Latacunga Loop**, which takes in several of these villages and the emerald-blue crater lake of **Quilotoa**, is one of the most beautiful trips in Ecuador. It's an adventurous journey, roads are rough, directions confusing and there are reports of many beggars in the lake area. It's probably

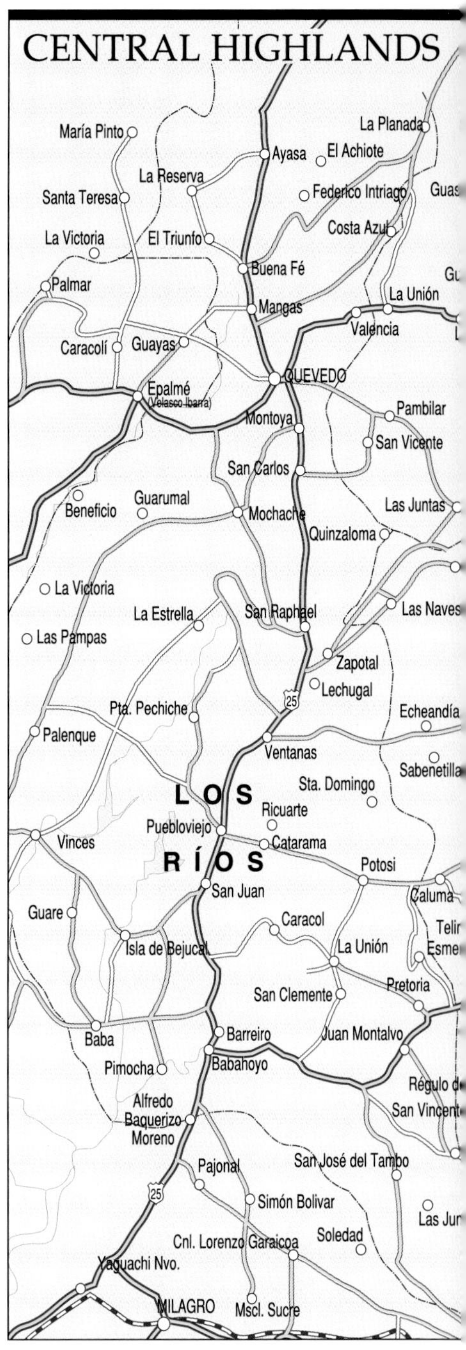

best to go by car with a guide, but you can also take a bus as many of the villages are connected with Latacunga. Check return times carefully before you leave.

About 10 km (six miles) west of Latacunga is the village of **Pujili**, where the

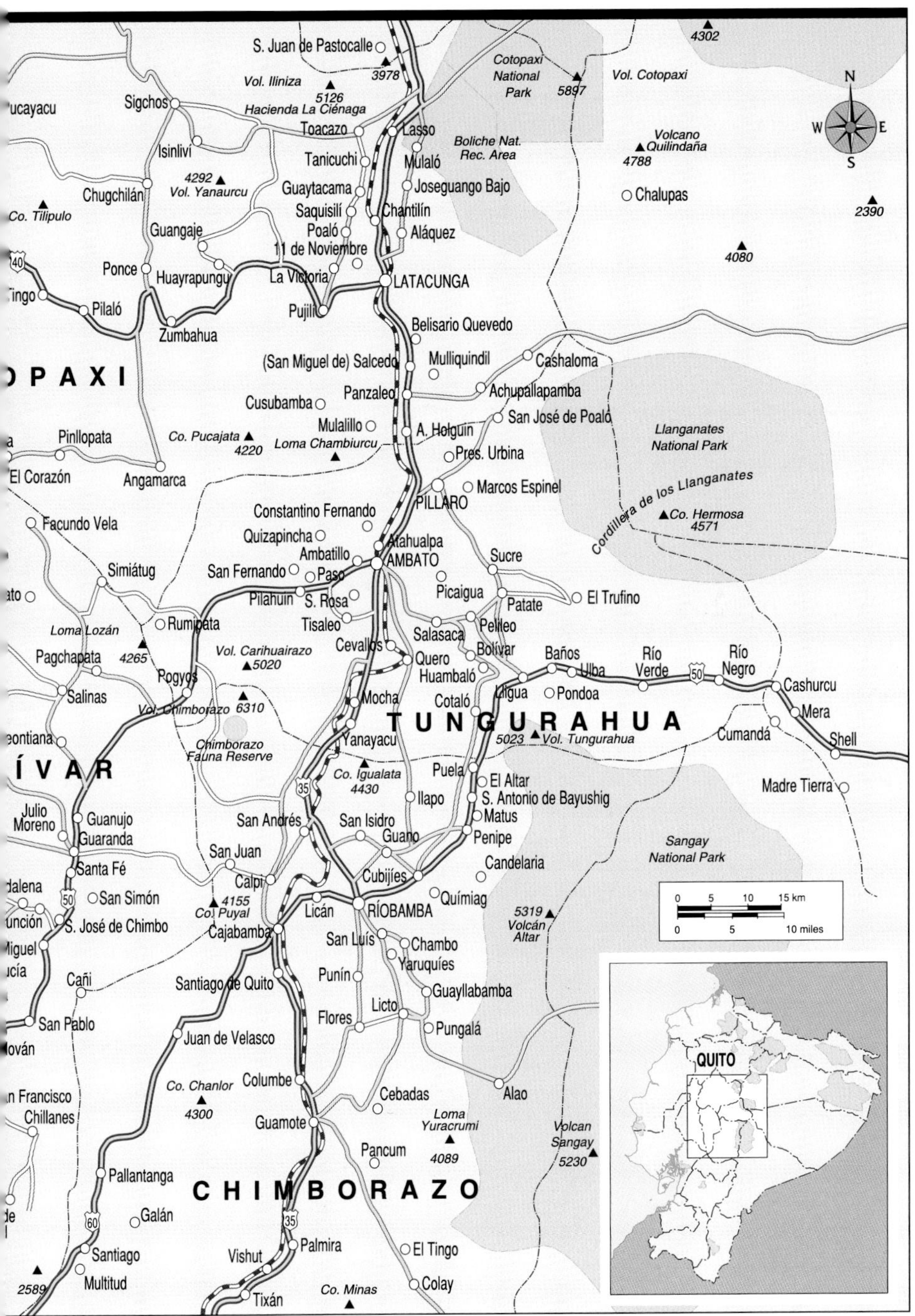

Sunday market is the main attraction. Continuing for another 60 km (37 miles) through grandiose mountain scenery brings you to the small settlement of **Zumbahua**, known for its Saturday market and attendant festivities that include bullfighting and prodigious imbibing of alcohol. Llamas transport goods to market and horses carry home *vaqueros* (cowboys) missing a leg or two. There is some basic accommodation in Zumbahua if you want to join in the pre-market revelries on Friday night.

Southeast of Zumbahua lies the valley of **Tigua**, known as the center of production of detailed and charming **Indian paintings** on sheep's hide or canvass of the sort that are sold on the streets of Quito. This naïve Andean art depicts village life, rural scenes, volcanoes, lamas, festivals, and the myths and dreams of the local *indígenas*. A young Indian girl hardly more than twelve years old tried to sell me such paintings, claiming she had done them herself. Skeptically, I asked her to sketch one of the scenes in my notebook. She did so perfectly. I bought the painting.

About 14km (nine miles) north of Zumbahua you come to **Laguna Quilotoa**. The road is badly signed, so if you are driving you will need to ask for directions. There are also buses to the lake from Latacunga at 10:30 AM on Fridays and Saturdays. The lake isn't visible from the road and you have to climb up to the crater rim before you can look down onto the emerald waters surrounded by steep volcanic slopes. A precipitous path goes down to the water's edge and it takes five or six hours to walk around the lake. Near the crater rim is the small community of **Ponce-Quilotoa**, where travelers can stay at **Cabañas Quilotoa**, run by an artist named Humberto, or at **El Refugio de La Laguna**. Tigua paintings, carved masks and other artifacts are on sale. Warm clothes are needed because it gets chilly at night here.

The best place to stay is the **Black Sheep Inn**, about 20km (12 miles) further north along the road from the lake, near the village of **Chugchilán**. Owned by a couple from Seattle, the Black Sheep is highly praised for its simple, homey atmosphere and its stunning views. Facilities include a book exchange, good information about the area and local Inca ruins, and good food. There is no telephone, and reservations aren't required or even encouraged because nobody is turned away. For US$5 you have a bed for the night and for a bit more you get your own room. If you want to hike around the some of the most beautiful landscapes in Ecuador, this is the place to base yourself.

Continuing north around the Latacunga Loop, you come to the village Sigchos. Don't bother to stay unless you plan to hike in the **Toachi Valley**. Going westwards, the road continues through **Toacazo** and then turns south back towards Latacunga. On the way you can make a side-trip to **Saquisilí**, a small town with a big reputation for its market, one of the best-known in Ecuador. Though interesting textiles are on sale, the market isn't just a showcase of *artesanía*. It is a living, working Andean emporium and a central hub for the web of communities of *indígenas* in the surrounding mountains who come to town on Thursdays to do their trade and meet friends. Visitors are attracted by the colorful costumes of the local people, the main theme being red ponchos and felt pork pie hats.

COTOPAXI NATIONAL PARK

At a height of 5,897m (19,655 ft), the awesome and beautiful **Volcán Cotopaxi** is the tallest continuously active volcano in the world and the second tallest peak in Ecuador after Chimborazo. With its cone of almost perfect proportions, often veiled in swirling mists, it's a mountain of might and mysteries, as well as an object of worship that local *indígenas* believe to be inhabited by powerful spirits.

Seldom quiescent for more than about 15 years, Cotopaxi has erupted many times, devastating the surrounding terrain. Fumaroles smoke in its crater, which is 360m (1,200 ft) deep and 700m (2,333 ft) in diameter at its widest. At night fires sometimes light up the clouds covering the cone reminding the onlooker of the mountain's potential for destruction.

The upper part of Cotopaxi is permanently covered with snow, its flank gray with lava and volcanic ash, while the base stands in the open grassland of the páramo. The wild and desolate area surrounding the mountain, which includes pine forests, several lakes and streams, encompasses the 25,255 hectare (62,514-acre) **Cotopaxi National-Park**.

The most frequently-visited park in the country, Cotopaxi National Park contains campsites, rustic cabañas, a small museum, footpaths, and a basic tourist infrastructure. The entrance fee is about US$10. But because of its size, the park invariably seems deserted, except on some weekends during the dry season from June to August.

The park is one of the last refuges of the endangered **Andean condor** (the name is derived from the Quichua word *cuntur*). With a wingspan up to three meters (10 ft), weight up to 13 kg (28 lb), and length up to 120 cm (almost four feet), *vultur gryphus* is the world's biggest bird of prey. Visitors lucky enough to spot this rare black raptor will note the flashes of white on its wings and the white frill at the base of its neck. Several other rare birds can be seen in the park including various highland **hummingbirds**.

also take a taxi from Latacunga. Many tour companies in Quito run tours to the park.

Some companies in Quito organize tours in which mountain bikes are carried to the park on the top of jeeps. After cycling around the páramo, exploring some Inca ruins and picnicking, the jeep grinds up the mountain as far as the rough road goes, which is to the parking lot at 4,600 m (15,332 ft), just below the *refugio*. Wearing helmets, pads and warm clothes, the mad bikers take off down the mountain. It's not as easy as it might sound because your wheels get trapped in ruts and some of the surface is loose, but it's fantastic fun. You need a good bike with good brakes. **Flying Dutchman Mountain Bike Tours**, which for copyright reasons will be, or has already been, renamed **Biking Dutchman Tours**, pioneered these "uphill by jeep, downhill by bike" adventures and offers very professional service. The one-day Cotopaxi Tour costs US$45. In Quito, the biking Dutchman (Jan Lescrauwaet) can be contacted at ☎ (02) 542806 FAX (02) 449568, Foch 714 and Juan León Mera.

As for mammals, the rare **Andean spectacled bear** makes its home in remote parts of the park, out of sight of visitors. **Pumas** (mountain lions) and **Andean foxes** are sometimes glimpsed, while **llamas** are easy to spot because a captive herd is kept near one of the park entrances. **Wild bulls** munch green grasses and **wild horses** gallop across wide plateaus.

Cotopaxi National Park is excellent place for hiking, cycling and camping. One of the best camping spots is by the shore of **Laguna Limpio Pungo**. Buses from Latacunga and Quito drop you on the Pan-American Highway, by one of the two roads that run up into the park, but then it is a long hike or hitchhike to get into the park itself. Or you can

Ecuador offers plentiful opportunities for mountain biking; speeding down Volcán Cotopaxi is one of the most thrilling trips.

Another way of literally getting a grip on Cotopaxi is to actually climb the mountain. To achieve this you need some climbing experience, fitness, a professional guide, climbing equipment, altitude acclimatization and gritty determination. It isn't a technically difficult climb, but professional advice is advised. Several agencies in Quito offer two-day Cotopaxi climbing packages for about US$150. Make sure the **Ecuadorian Association of Mountain Guides** has approved the guides.

AMBATO

The city of Ambato, destroyed by earthquake in 1949 and subsequently rebuilt, is the fourth-biggest city in Ecuador and the capital of Tungurahua Province. But this rather ugly metropolis with a population well over 100,000, known for its production of cement, shoes, food processing and distilling, doesn't have too much to offer tourists. There's a **Natural History Museum** in the **Colegio Nacional Bolívar** that is filled with stuffed birds and animals and the homes, open to visitors, of the well-known Ecuadorian writers Juan Montalvo (1833–1889) and Juan León Mera (1832–1894). The city is also famous for its exuberant **Fiesta de frutas y flores** during carnival time in February when water throwing, so popular in the rest of the country, is banned. The **Monday market** is reputed to be the biggest in the country though it isn't known for its *artesanía*. For most tourists Ambato is a stopover en route to somewhere else. Travelers from Quito usually pass through to the popular resort of Baños, or they continue southwards along the Pan-American Highway towards Río-bamba and Cuenca.

AROUND AMBATO

The road from Ambato to Baños passes through the small, nondescript village of **Salasaca** that is known for the weaving of *tapices* (tapestries). It is said that the Salasaca Indians were originally *mitmakuna*, people who had been forced to move to Ecuador from Bolivia by the Incas as punishment for revolt. Certainly they have their unique style of dress, with black woven ponchos and wide-brimmed, white felt hats. Some of the words they use for describing the weaving process are said to be similar to those once used in the ancient Inca capital of Cuzco. It is well worth stopping for a while in Salasaca to check out the weavings. Just five kilometers (three miles) further down the road is the little town of **Pelileo**, denim capital of Ecuador, just the place to buy a pair of jeans on Saturday market day.

A few kilometers north of Pelileo, off the main Ambato–Baños road, is the attractive village of **Patate**, reminiscent of the Douro

Valley in Portugal, with its grapevines and views over Río Patate. The **Hotel Turístico Patate** ✆ 70177 is a pleasant place to stay where tours into the little-known **Parque Nacional Llanganates** can be arranged. A cobbled road, with wonderful views down to the patchwork of fields in the valley, leads from Patate to **Hacienda Manteles** ✆/FAX (03) 870123, also a good base for exploring, horse riding, bird watching, hiking and fishing. The hacienda has 1,600 hectares (3,960 acres) of cloud forest, and there are magnificent views of Volcán Tungurahua. The treasure of the Inca leader Atahualpa is said to be buried in the vicinity of the nearby village of El Triunfo on the river Muyo.

BAÑOS

Baños is one of the most popular destinations for tourists and travelers in Ecuador. This small town, nestled in a valley surrounded by steep, green mountains has long been a well-regarded hot spring resort, in recent years it has become a favored stop on the gringo trail. International restaurants, reasonably priced hostels and hotels, several adventure travel agencies, access to both the jungle and the mountains, plenty of nearby attractions and activities, an agreeable climate and some fine shops — all of these make Baños a good spot to hang out for a few days or more in a relaxed atmosphere. Beneath its touristy surface Baños has its own small-town character and charm. One curious local specialty is toffee made from sugar cane, which you can see being pulled in sticky strings from hooks in shop doorways.

BACKGROUND

Extraordinary **paintings** of what appear to be death and disaster in the **Basilica**, dedicated to the **Virgin of the Holy Water**, are a clue to the popularity of Baños with local Catholics. Images of people falling from breaking bridges as they cross ravines, cars toppling from cliffs or villagers fleeing erupting volcanoes are as violent and lurid as Japanese comic books. But there is an important difference. In the Baños paintings nobody gets hurt because at the last moment they are saved by the miraculous intervention of the Virgin of the Holy Water. Like St. Christopher, the Virgin has the power to prevent accidents, which is why many people believe it to be a wise precaution to make offerings and prayers to her image before embarking on a long journey. Also of interest at the Basilica is the adjoining **museum** with the usual display of ecclesiastical costumes, stuffed animals and freak fetuses. One calf's head preserved in formaldehyde has three eyes, two noses and a triple palate, which is reminiscent of some contemporary art.

Also believed to have special powers is the holy water itself that is generated in the bowels of Volcán Tungurahua and emerges in the **Baños de la Virgin** and other outlets. Bathing in and drinking these waters is said to cure various ills and is a major attraction for visitors. The town's location also makes it a gateway between the jungle and the sierra. According to rumor, Baños has long been a transit point for illegal and contraband goods, including drugs.

GENERAL INFORMATION

Although it doesn't have a CETUR tourist office, Baños is a vibrant center of information

because of the proliferation of travel agencies and the number of passing travelers. At least two of the popular cafés, **Café Hood** and **Café Cultura**, keep comment books containing advice about good places to go, agencies to use and guides to avoid. Staff and owners of cafés, restaurants, hostels and hotels can also be good sources of information.

It's not easy to choose between **tour operators** if you want to do a jungle or climbing trip. Most of them are good but there are occasional reports of bad guides, poor food, and inferior equipment. Guides should have a license issued by INEFAN (The Ecuado-

OPPOSITE: Weaver from Salasaca. ABOVE: These woven bands are a specialty of the Cuenca region.

rian Institute of Forestry, Natural Areas and Wildlife) while natural history guides should have a card issued by CETUR. Agencies with a good reputation in Baños include: **Rainforestur**, **Tsanta**, **Vasco**, **Kaniats**, **Julio Verne**, **Aventurandes** and **Marcelio Turismo**. This is not to say that other agencies might not be less expensive or even better because it very much depends on who is your guide on your trip. Jungle trips are about US$45 per day per person and a two-day climbing trip is about US$55, not including a US$10 national park entrance fee. It's a good idea to withhold half the tour fee until completion of the trip.

Mountain biking is a popular activity around Baños. There are many places to rent bikes but check carefully, especially the brakes, tires and gears, before deciding on a bike. The cost for a day's rental is about US$4. Similar precautions have to be taken with **renting horses**. A couple of old nags that a friend and I stupidly committed ourselves to before inspecting had open sores on their backs and were clearly unfit for riding, so we lost our deposit. We would have been better off trying the horses at the German-run **Hostal Isla de Baños** ✆ (03) 740609, which are well looked-after though sometimes overworked. You can also rent good horses by contacting **Ivan** at the **Pizzeria Napolitano** near the Plantas y Blanco Hostal. **Caballos José** and **Angel Aldáz'** horses also have good reputations. They charge about US$5 per hour.

Río Loco (Mad River) ✆ (03) 740332 or 740703 runs **rafting trips** on the Pastaza and Patate rivers which can be booked through Geotours on Maldonado, near the Terminal Terrestre bus terminal. With heaps of water and thundering rapids, followed by sudden stillness and silence, river trips are a great way of exploring the tropical rainforest.

Baños is a small-enough town to get anywhere within a few minutes on foot. People are generally helpful and even without speaking Spanish, gesticulated sign language directions will usually suffice. This is a good place to **learn Spanish** because tuition and living costs are lower than in the capital and it's such a pleasant place. Several schools and private teachers are available. **Pepe Eras** ✆ (03) 740232, **International Spanish School** ✆ (03) 740612, and **Baños Spanish Center** ✆ (03) 740632, are recommended by the South America Explorers Club. Check with Café Hood or Café Cultura for names of other schools and teachers.

The **Terminal Terrestre** bus terminal is on the main highway, on the north side of town, where there is regular bus service to Quito, Ambato and Ríobamba. Transport eastwards and downwards to Puyo and the Amazon basin is more problematic because the road has been under reconstruction for a few years. At the time of writing it is open only from 6 PM on Sundays to 6 AM on Tuesdays, though renovation is is expected to be finished sometime in 1998. Check with local tour operators or with the South America Explorers Club in Quito for its current state of health.

WHAT TO SEE AND DO

It would be a missed opportunity to go to Baños and not experience a hot spring bath. The main baths are the **Baños de la Virgin** by the waterfall near the Palace Hotel at the southeast end of town. There are showers, changing rooms, three pools of varying temperatures, and the cost is minimal. Dress code: a bathing suit. The baths open at 4:30 AM and the earlier you get there the better. A dawn immersion in a hot spring sets you up for the day. Even more pleasant are the baths at **El Salado**, about a mile out of town off the Ambato road. These are less crowded and there are more pools. There's also a cold waterfall to cool off your steamed-up body.

Some people complain that the baths are dirty; it's true that they aren't as immaculate and modern as their counterparts in, say, Japan. But don't be concerned by the slight coloration in the water; it is caused by the water's mineral content. The other complaint from some *gringas* is that they get stared at by the locals, which is all the more reason to go early when fewer people are around.

Want to feel like a kid again, with the warm wind blowing on your face as you speed down a long hill on a bike? Here's the place to do it, from Baños down the **road to Puyo**, a classic bike ride of about 70 km (44 miles), descending from 1,800 m (6,000 ft) to just under 1,000 m (3,333 ft). Though the road is rough in parts and it's not all downhill, there are stunning views of the green flanks of the Andes threaded with silvery waterfalls and dotted with orchids and bromeliads.

The road, which winds through the canyon of the **Pastaza River**, is under repair at the moment (see above) so you have to be careful when you go. If you ride down on Sunday or Monday you can get back up to Baños on a bus in the evening with your bike strapped to the roof. Some of the road is so bad that you may have to carry your bike through thigh-deep mud.

The entire journey to Puyo takes about six to eight hours but you can do a shorter version just to **Río Verde**, about 20 km (12 miles) down from Baños. Here you can leave your bikes in a church, and walk down a trail to the right, just past the church which takes you down into the canyon the Río Pastaza where there's a mighty waterfall, aptly named **El Pailón del Diablo**, the Devil's Cauldron.

Below the canyon is a wooden suspension bridge and a path that leads to **El Otro Lado** (the Other Side), an exquisite house and small herb and vegetable farm with three separate *cabañas* that is totally isolated and surrounded by dense jungle and views of the canyon. In my experience this is one of the most beautiful spots in Ecuador. The house is built in a combination of native style, with a roof of palm leaves and airy, open living spaces. You can stay the night in one of the cabañas for about US$20 per person or have a light meal before heading back. Reservations for El Otro Lado can be made at Café Cultura in Baños ☎ (03) 740419. The bus back to Baños will probably take a couple hours, depending on the state of the road and how much rain there has been.

There are many good walks and horse rides around Baños. A popular excursion is up to the **Bella Vista cross** that overlooks the town, about an hour's steep walking up a path leading off Calle Maldonado. Bring a stick in case of dogs, and it's best to go in a group because robberies have been reported in the area. Other walks include a two-hour climb to **Illuchi** village that gives you great views over the Baños valley and to Volcán Tungurahua.

Just 20 minutes' walk from the town along the Ambato road is the **San Martín Zoo**, a surprisingly large and well-maintained *ecozoológico* with a variety of native

The El Salado baths at Baños are the best at this popular hot spring resort.

animals and birds including jaguars, tapirs, spectacled bears, harpy eagles and condors. Also recommended are the Basilica dedicated to the Virgin of the Holy Water and the adjoining museum (see page 121).

WHERE TO STAY AND EAT

With the large number of hostels and hotels in Baños, visitors usually have the luxury of choice and prices are not generally high. I have not included addresses here because it's easy to get directions at the bus station to where you want to go in this small town. My own favorite is also one of the least expensive in Baños, the aptly and charmingly named **Plantas y Blanco** (Plants and White) ☎/FAX (03) 740044. Outstanding features of this popular hostel are its central location, roof-top terrace with panoramic views and cafeteria for breakfast 24-hour serve-yourself drinks, constant supply of free bananas, clean rooms, fax service, videos and morning steam baths. The facilities might seem five-star but the price is only US$5 per night. In my experience this is the world's best-value accommodation. It's not surprising it is often full.

If money were no object I would be tempted to stay at the **Luna Runtun Resort** ☎ (03) 740882 or 740883 FAX (03) 740376 E-MAIL runtun@tu.pro.ec in the foothills of Volcán Tungurahua overlooking the town. According to the brochure for this swish, new, Swiss-managed resort of chalet-style bungalows this was the favorite spot of the Inca emperor, Huayna Capac, where he "enjoyed lavish dances and voluptuous orgies with his most beautiful and desirable wives before the discovery of America." No voluptuous orgies were on offer when I visited the resort but it does have almost every other facility you can think of, including rooms with fireplaces and private flower-filled terraces, child day care, conference facilities, special programs and excellent food. Double rooms are US$100, plus 20% tax and service charges, including breakfast and dinner.

Back in town there are a number of other recommendable and comfortable hostelries. The **Palace Hotel** ☎ (03) 740740 near the Virgin Falls, is a well-known, old-style establishment. Though some of its many rooms are rather dark, they are quite comfortable. The hotel has its own hot-spring baths, saunas, Jacuzzis, pleasant garden, pool, restaurant and other facilities. Rooms are about US$30 for a double. The nearby **Sangay Hotel** ☎ (03) 740490, is similar. With a more homey atmosphere and less expensive, the German-run **Isla de Baños** ☎ (03) 740609, with lovely gardens, big rooms, bar and restaurant, is a good value. Also reputable is **Café Cultura** ☎ (03) 740419, the predecessor of its sister hotel in Quito, though now under different ownership. Rooms are large and reasonably priced in this lovely converted colonial mansion though bathrooms are usually shared.

Athough many of the restaurants in Baños are of vacation resort mediocrity, there are plenty of good ones. Much favored by the smarter end of the back-packing brigade is the celebrated **Café Hood**, just around the corner from Plantas y Blanco, a vegetarian hangout with good coffee, pancakes, tacos, omelets and a Hindu Plate, along with an alternative atmosphere, book exchange and scrapbooks of useful information for travelers. The American owner, Ray Hood, plans to move to new, larger premises incorporating a small theater. He believes that once the new road to Puyo is open, Baños will boom as an artistic and cultural center.

Others that are frequently recommended include the French-owned but quite expensive **Marianne**, **La Casa Mia** for Italian and local food, **Restaurant y Peña Marqués** (which usually have live Andean music), **Le Petit Restaurant** and **Closerie des Lilas**, both French, **Restaurant El Artesano** with Middle Eastern food (next to Plantas y Blanco), **Regine Café Alemán** whose name reveals its culinary roots, **Café Higuerón** and **Café Cultura**, with a focus on homemade breads and pastries, **Rico Pan**, which is good for breakfasts, **El Jardín**, a place in which to linger awhile, and various competing Italian restaurants, all of quite high standards. Since Baños is a small town your hotel or hostel can tell you how to get to these places.

NIGHTLIFE

Baños might not have a reputation for riproaring nightlife like Guayaquil or even Quito, but it is a town that likes to party. As you walk around in the day you're sure to be offered flyers for a *peña* (folk music event) that evening. And they are worth checking out because Baños attracts some very good Andean music groups. Locations change frequently but the small *peña* bar **Ananitay**, 16 de Diciembre and Espejo, seems to be well-established. On weekends live music starts about 10 PM and goes on until 2 AM. There's a very cheery atmosphere and plenty of dancing with the drink of choice being big jugs of warm *canelazos*, a mixture of *aguardiente* (cane spirit), sugar, and naranjilla (bitter-sweet orange), spiced with cinnamon. The vibrant music and joyful spirit of the evening creates a friendly sociability among locals and gringos.

Near Ananitay is a big, cavernous music bar in the theme of an old sugar cane factory with ancient machinery as part of the decor. The place can be as dead as an abandoned church, but on other occasions it rocks and shakes like dried beans in a maraca. It's called the **Bamboo Bar**, which is confusing because there's another Bamboo Bar, sometimes known as the **Bambooze Bar**, a friendly, popular place with pool tables and good music on the other side of town near Hostal Plantas y Blanco.

Baños may be the smallest town in the world to boast its own (no doubt counterfeit) **Hard Rock Café**, another popular spot with gringos, though it wasn't very inspiring the night I dropped in. Other bars and discos worth checking out for a night on the town are **Peña La Burbuja**, **Illusions Peña Bar** and **Agoyán**, all of which are best on weekends.

For another sort of evening entertainment, the **Centro Cultural Baños** screens well-selected, cultish video movies most nights at 8:30 PM in a tiny theater on the street that runs down the east side of the Basilica. The man who runs the show and sells tickets is, naturally, the ubiquitous Ray Hood of Café Hood.

How to Get There

Baños is a popular place for a weekend break from Quito. Most people come by bus or with their own transport. Buses run frequently, though you might have to change in Ambato. There are also plenty of buses com-

In Ríobamba's Moldanado Park stands this statue of Pedro Moldonaldo, an Ecuadorian geographer who was a member of the French team that surveyed Ecuador in the eighteenth century.

ing up the Pan-American Highway from the south, in which case you might have to change at Ríobamba. If you are coming from Puyo in the Oriente, be aware that at the time of writing the road was open from Sunday evening until early Tuesday morning.

SANGAY NATIONAL PARK

The vast and inaccessible Sangay National Park stretches like a huge blanket of dense vegetation over the eastern flanks of the Andes, from just south of Baños to almost as far as Macas in the south. The park's terrain and wildlife exemplify the diversity, wildness and impenetrability of huge areas of the relatively small country of Ecuador. Most of the steep, thickly-vegetated slopes span altitudes of more than 4,000 m (13,330 ft) over a horizontal distance of just a few kilometers as the condor flies. If the park were ironed flat its surface area would be far greater than its 272,000 hectares (673,267 acres). Its mountain forests are too thick and inhospitable for human habitation, but they are home to many strange and rare creatures — spectacled bears, mountain tapirs, ocelots, porcupines, jaguarundis (wild cats) — some of which are unknown anywhere else on earth. Few humans penetrate this wilderness because the slopes are too steep, the jungle is too thick and no roads lead to its deepest secrets.

The park, too gentle a word for such a hostile patch of land, is also the footplate for three of the 10-tallest mountains in Ecuador: Tungurahua (5,016 m or 16,718 ft), El Altar (5,319 m or 17,728 ft), and the still active and dangerous-to-climb Volcán Sangay (5,230 m or 17,432 ft). None of them are easy to climb, though Tungurahua is the least difficult, El Altar the most technically challenging and Sangay, because of constant volcanic activity, is probably the most dangerous (see RECOMMENDED READING, page 262, for mountain climbing guidebooks with information about these and other Ecuadorian mountains).

Exploration of Sangay National Park is beyond the scope of this book, but for those who want to do so the national parks' administrative body, INEFAN, is very helpful. The organization provides information about the park, advice about guides, and even free transport to the three entrances to the Sangay National Park: Alao, Pondoa and Candelaria. INEFAN can be contacted in Ríobamba (see GENERAL INFORMATION, below) or at the INEFAN main office ☎ (02) 548924, at the Ministry of Agriculture and Ranching, Eighth Floor, Amazonas and Eloy Alfaro, Quito.

RÍOBAMBA

The capital of Chimborazo Province and agricultural center of the region, with a population of more than 100,000, Ríobamba, at an elevation of 2,700 m (9,000 ft), is a pleasant country town that comes alive during market day on Saturday. Small-scale industries include ceramics, cement, textiles, shoe manufacturing, food processing and native artifacts. The town lies just south of Volcán Chimborazo and if the weather is right there are fine views of Ecuador's tallest mountain (once thought to be the tallest peak in the world) as well as Carihuairaso, Tungurahua and Altar. Although not a popular tourist destination, Ríobamba is a good base for exploring the region and a departure point for a thrilling train ride down to Guayaquil.

BACKGROUND

In pre-Inca days the Peruhá tribes settled the Chimbo region. After the Inca conquest, in typical Inca manner, many of these tribes were forced south while people from the south, were moved north to replace them. As a result there is a great mixture of *indígenas* in the region who wear a variety of traditional costumes and hats.

In 1534, the Spanish took over an Inca site where the modern town of Cajabamba is located, 19 km (12 miles) south of present-day Ríobamba. Eleven years later a Spaniard, Pedro de Cieza de León, on an epic 17-year horseback journey from Colombia to Bolivia, praised the lodgings at Ríobamba and wrote of "beautiful fair fields, whose climate, vegetation, flowers and other features resemble those of Spain."

In 1797, a huge landslide devastated the town, killing hundreds of inhabitants. The survivors moved the city to its present location, bringing their cathedral with them, which they rebuilt brick by brick. In 1830, the first Ecuadorian constitutional congress met at Ríobamba and proclaimed the republic. Several surviving buildings, including the old cathedral, many in need of restoration and repair, are sad memorials to the city's previous capital status.

GENERAL INFORMATION

The helpful CETUR **tourist office** ☎ (03) 960217, 10 de Agosto 25-33, half a block from the main plaza, Parque Sucre, is open most weekdays from 8:30 AM to 5 PM with a break for lunch. For information about Sangay National Park, **INEFAN** ☎ (03) 963779, is located in the Ministry of Agriculture on Avenida 9 de Octubre near Duchicela. Several travel agents and guides in town are helpful with expeditions and climbing. **Expediciones Andinas** is on Argentinos 38-60 and Zambrano, **Andes Climbing and Trekking** is Colón 22-21 and the **Asociación de Andismo de Chimborazo** is on Chile 33-21 and Francia.

For phoning and sending and receiving faxes, **EMETEL** is on Tarqui and Velos and the **Post Office** is on Avenida de Agosto and Espejo.

There are two main bus stations. Buses for Baños and the Oriente leave from the **Terminal Oriental** on Avenida Espejo and Luz Elisa Borja, while all other long-distance buses depart from **Terminal Terrestre** on León Borja, just over a kilometer northwest of the town center. A few blocks south of Terminal Terrestre there is an area from where buses depart for many local towns, while buses to Guano leave from the north of town on Rocafuerte and New York.

There is only one **train station,** on Avenida 10 de Agosto and Carabobo. There is only one line, which goes north to Ambato and Quito and south to Alausi, Bucay and Guayaquil. There are very few trains. In fact there were no trains at all for 10 years after the El Niño storms of 1982 and 1983 while repairs were made to the tracks. There are about five trains a week to Guayaquil and two to Quito since operations have resumed. This less-than-hectic timetable is nevertheless subject to change. The latest information is that trains leave Ríobamba at 6 AM every day of the week except Tuesdays and Thursdays. The Quito trains run twice a week on Saturdays and Sundays, departing at 9 AM. The most exciting and scenic section of this remarkable **mountain railway** is between Alausi and Bucay, known as the **Devil's Nose** because of its steep gradient. Some

Ríobamba's old colonial cathedral overlooks Moldanado Park.

people take the train only between these two towns, and complete the rest of their journey by bus. Riding on the roof of the train and ducking overhanging branches, is a travel experience that is not to be forgotten.

WHAT TO SEE AND DO

A gold "monstrance" encrusted with pearls and diamonds is the greatest and best-known treasure to be seen in Ríobamba. A monstrance? My dictionary defines it as an "ornamental receptacle in which the consecrated Host is exposed in Roman Catholic churches for the adoration of the people." The beauty of the object itself defies the ugliness of its appellation and it is well worth seeing if you have time to visit the religious art museum, **Convento de la Conceptión** on Argentinos and Larrea, which has been well-restored by the Banco Central and contains a fine collection of gold artifacts, jewelry and religious art.

But the main attraction of Ríobamba, as in so many of other Sierra towns, is its **market**. Each Saturday the streets and squares of the city fill up with stallholders and hawkers selling a wide range of household goods and food products, as well as local crafts and artifacts. Souvenires such as shawls, ponchos and woven belts can be found around Parque de la Concepción, at the intersection of Orozco and Colón. Woven bags made from *cabuya* fiber, known as **shigra**, are local specialties, as are baskets and mats woven from reeds from the shores of nearby Lake Colta.

Ríobamba is also an important center for the **tagua nut** trade. This is a palm nut, about the size of a small hen's egg, that is relatively soft when taken from the fruit and easily carved. After being exposed to air and light for a while it becomes as hard as ivory. The tagua, which comes from the lowland rainforest, is used to make buttons, carved ornaments and even chess sets. Tagua products make great souvenirs because they are so small and easy to carry. Chess sets cost from about US$20. Since the commercial use of tagua nuts are seen as an alternative to cutting down the rainforest, any purchase you make will be an act of environmental friendliness. To see craftsmen carving the nuts, and a good selection of tagua products, go visit the **Tagua Shop** on León Borja 35-17 and Uruguay.

Ríobamba is known in Ecuador as the "Sultan of the Andes," perhaps because of its wide avenues, imposing buildings and many beautiful parks. On a fine evening, from **Parque 21 de Abril,** also known as **La Loma de Quito**, the panoramic views of the city and its surrounding peaks are magnificent.

WHERE TO STAY AND EAT

Ríobamba has more than its share of large, inexpensive, run-down hotels with antiquated plumbing, bare light bulbs and holes in the

sheets. But don't despair. There's also a quota of clean, bright, modern hostelries that meet the expectations of today's tourists. At the top of the range, at about US$40 per night for a single, is the **Abras-pungo** ☎ (03) 940820, about three kilometers (almost two miles) out of town on the road to Guano, a new hacienda-style hotel with a restaurant and bar. Similarly-priced and also out of town, about 15km (nine miles) north of the city, is the restored hacienda, **Hostería La Andaluza** ☎ (02) 904223 FAX (03) 904234, which has an excellent restaurant and has been described as the best hotel in Chimborazo Province. **Hostería El Troje** ☎ (03) 960826, four kilometers (two and a half miles) down the road to Chambo, is in the same ballpark.

In town, no hotel has established an undisputed reputation for quality and style. In the center, **Hostal Montecarlo** ☎ (03) 960557, 10 de Agosto 25-41, is clean and comfortable at about US$25 for a single and US$30 for a double, with phones in the room and a restaurant. **Hotel Whymper** ☎ (03) 964575, Miguel Angel León and Primera Constituyente, has big rooms, some of them with views. **Hotel Imperial** ☎ (03) 960429, Rocafuerte and 10 de Agosto, right in the center of town, is clean, friendly, popular, sometimes noisy and inexpensive. Luggage can be stored and the hotel arranges good value tours to Chimborazo.

One advantage of Hotel Imperial is that it is just a few steps from one of the best restaurant-bars in town, **El Delirio,** situated in the house once occupied by the Great Liberator, Simón Bolívar. It is said that Bolívar wrote a famous epic poem in this house about the failure of his dream, his personal delirium. If this powerful historical association isn't enough, the food is excellent and garden enchanting. Very close by is the **Bambario Café and Bar,** which is warm, gringo-friendly and well-stocked with advice about tours. Also recommended are **El Mesón de Inéz,** Orozco and Morales, **Cabaña Montecarlo**, 10 de Agosto 25-45, and the charmingly-named **Chifa Joy Sing,** on Guayaquil near the station, for an inexpensive but satisfying Chinese meal.

NIGHTLIFE

Not many travelers come to Ríobamba for its nightlife. But if you happen to be in town and that's what you want, there's a reasonable amount of action around the eastern end of León Borja, especially on weekends. On the *peña* beat, names to look out for are **El Faraon, Ureja Guardea** and **Media Luna.** For *discotecas*, try **Casablanca** and **Gems Shop**. For salsa on weekends check out the **Unicornio** on Pichincha and Villarroel.

AROUND RÍOBAMBA

The major trip from Ríobamba is to **Chimborazo,** 6,310 m (2,1031 ft), known to the local *indígenas* as Taita (father) Chimborazo, which is paired with Mama Tungurahua. First climbed by the English mountaineer, Edward Whymper in 1880, the Big Ice Cube attracts numerous mountaineers during peak climbing season in December and from June to September. Only serious and experienced mountaineers should attempt this peak. Full ice and snow climbing equipment, and a good guide, are required. It is easy enough, however, to reach the first *refugio* at 4,800 m (16,000 ft) by car or jeep from Ríobamba, though acclimatization is necessary. Then it's about an hour's slow climb to the second refuge at 5,000 m (16,665 ft) where the views are stunning. Here you can stay the night for about US$10 if you have a warm sleeping bag. Climbs to the summit begin around midnight and take about 10 hours, with four hours for the return trip. The Imperial and other hotels arrange reasonably-priced day trips to the refugios for small groups (about US$15 per person) while a serious climb can be arranged with **Alta Montaña** ☎ (03) 963964 in Ríobamba, or with the agencies listed under GENERAL INFORMATION above.

For the less energetic, there are plenty of other attractions in Ríobamba. Journeys to **neighboring villages** on local buses provide an insight into the traditional Andean way of life, and a backdrop of superb scenery. Rug making is a specialty of the village of **Guano** where there are various other items for sale in its numerous craft shops. Santa **Teresita** has its own thermal baths and **Guamote** is a pretty town with a busy Saturday market. **Laguna de Colta** is very beautiful and sometimes you can see local *indígenas* gliding through the reeds on bamboo rafts.

Known as "vegetable ivory," tagua nuts, which come from a rainforest palm, are used for making buttons and a variety of decorative objects.

Southern Highlands

TRAVELING SOUTH DOWN THE SPIKY, mountainous spine of Ecuador, a slow change takes place. After the climax of Chimborazo, the peaks become lower and the mountain ranges flatten and spread. You feel you are leaving Quito, far, far away and the pace of life becomes increasingly *tranquilo*. Until the early sixties there were no paved roads linking Cuenca, the third-largest city in Ecuador and the central hub of the region, to Quito and the coast. Many communities are still isolated for lack of proper roads, creating a sense that some of the beautiful hills and valleys are in a deep sleep. Vilcabamba, known as the Valley of Eternal Youth because of the longevity of its inhabitants, was cut of from the rest of the country until only a few years ago. Now this beautiful valley is slowly becoming a destination of choice for cognoscenti travelers. More than in the rest of the country, there is a strong sense here of the Inca past. At Ingapirca, once a major stronghold and now the most important Inca ruin in Ecuador, the spirit of the Incas still hangs in the air.

CUENCA

Considered the most beautiful city in the country, Cuenca likes to call itself the Athens of Ecuador. But its narrow, cobbled streets, houses with wrought iron balconies, flower-filled patios and many fine old churches are more reminiscent, to my mind, of ancient hill towns like Ronda and Córdova of Andalucía in southern Spain. The city is proud of its colonial-style architecture, its many churches and its artistic and intellectual heritage. The University of Cuenca is rated as one of the best in Ecuador and Latin America, and at the same time the city is something of a colony of artists and artisans. Cuenca is also the biggest production center of the misnamed "panama" hat. If you enjoy exploring back street markets, looking into old churches, museums and craft shops, sitting around in patio cafés and watching the world go by, then Cuenca is for you.

BACKGROUND

The Cuenca area was inhabited by Cañari Indians who put up a long and fierce fight against the Incas moving up from the south in the fifteenth century. Under the command of the Tupac Inca Yupanqui, the Incas eventually prevailed and built themselves a splendid city called Tomebamba in an area the Cañaris called "Guapondelig," which means "plain as vast as the sky." The city was designed as a northern version of the magnificent Inca city of Cuzco. Reports spoke of buildings set with precious stones and emeralds, and sun temples covered with sheets of the finest gold. Sadly, Tomebamba was a short-lived accomplishment. Before the Spanish conquistadors' invasion the Incas destroyed their own creation. Today, not much remains of the Inca city aside from a few excavated walls by the River Tomebamba.

In April 1557, the Spanish founded the city of Cuenca to the northeast of the ruins of the Inca city, in an area known as Paucarbamba, which in the Quichua language means "plain of flowers." It was a well-chosen site with fertile soil watered by four rivers and a pleasant, spring-like climate. In typical fashion, the Spanish at once began building the cathedral on the west side of the main plaza, Parque Caldederón. As the city grew, and more buildings were constructed workers sometimes unearthed Inca artifacts. In 1980 excavations by the river, undertaken by the Banco Central, uncovered Inca tombs and skeletons, and silver and gold relics.

GENERAL INFORMATION

The CETUR **tourist office** at Hermano Miguel and Presidente Córdova supplies maps of the city, but not much more. More useful information about Cuenca and the environs is available from some of the tour companies. The small **Expediciones Apullacta** ☎ (07) 837815, Luis Cordero 940, is particularly helpful and can arrange reasonably-priced individual or group tours anywhere in the region. **Ecotrek** ☎ (07) 642531 FAX (07) 835387, at Larga 7-108 and Luis Cordero,

PREVIOUS PAGES: Wide fertile valley LEFT in the Southern Highlands; the surrounding mountains are slightly less high than in the north. A lady selling reed mats RIGHT in Cuenca. OPPOSITE: The Museo de las Conceptas in Cuenca has an impressive display of religious art and artifacts

THE SOUTHERN HIGHLANDS
CAÑAR
AZUAY
ZAMORA
LOJA
CHINCHIPE
PERÚ
La Troncal
Zhud
Tambo
Huangra
3755
San Carlos
Pto. Inca
4163
Rivera
Va. Nueva
Taday
4770
(Santiago de) Méndez
Naranjal
4633
Biblián
Patu
Déleg
Azogues
Sta. Rosa
Patuca
El Cajas Nat. Rec. Area
Solano
Sta. Teresita
Yunganza
4445
Bulcay
Chauca
Angos
CUENCA
4088
Indanza
Limón (Gral. Leonidas Plaza Gutiérrez)
4137
Sígsig
Principal
Cumbe
Ludo
Los Tayos Cave
Chorrohuaycu
Serrag
3419
3480
Girón
Granadillos
Asunción
3527
Tinajilla Pass
Kalaglaz
San Luis
Tucumbatza
Sta. Isabel
Nabón
Bermejos
Cord. del Cóndor
Corraleja
Amazonas
Gualaquiza
Chilla
Oña
Bomboiza
Banderas
Manú
Chupilones
3044
Maijie
Cordillera Cordoncillo
Las Peñas
Huertas
Saraguro
La Paz
El Panguí
Numbaime
3830
Chicaña
Salatí
El Ari
Quimi
Yantzaza
El Cisne
Piantza
El Cisna Sanctuary
2844
Zumbi
Catamayo
LOJA
Soñaderos
Guayzimi
3022
Zamora
Jumbué
Pachicutza
Podocarpus National Park
Changaimina
Vilcabamba
3720
Cariamanga
0 5 10 15 km
0 5 10 miles
El Ingenio
Loyola
Chaco
QUITO
Valladolic
Amazula
Sta. Ana
3466
Palanda
S.Fco. de Vengel
2200
N
W
E
S
Isimanchi
Zumba
Chito
La Chonta
35
45
80

has a good reputation for more adventurous climbing and jungle trips, and arranges encounters with shamans. **Metropolitan Touring** ☎ (02) 831185 is at Sucre 6-62 and Borrero.

For international phone calls and fax services, **EMETEL** is on Benigno Malo between Córdova and Sucre, while the **Post Office** is on Gran Colombia (the main shopping street) and Borrero.

The Terminal Terrestre **bus terminal** is one kilometer (just over a half mile) northeast of the town center, and five minutes' walk from the **airport.** Buses go to all major cities, and planes go to Quito and Guayaquil.

WHAT TO SEE AND DO

With its historical interest and good shopping, there's plenty to do in Cuenca, except perhaps at night if the bars and discos aren't your cup of tea. The city is a big mouthful of culture, and if you don't want to suffer from intellectual indigestion by trying to see too many things in too short a time, your best bet is to be ruthlessly selective.

Start in the central plaza of the Old City, **Parque Calderón**, where you can sit on a park bench and absorb the atmosphere of the city. The *Cholos Cuencanos* (local *indígenas)* saunter by in their wide skirts and white or colored panama hats, neatly dressed old Cuencan gentleman sit reading newspapers and shoeshine boys proffer their services. Overlooking the square are the pink marble façades and magnificent sky-blue domes of the **Catedral de la Immaculada Concepción** (New Cathedral). The domes are the finest features of the cathedral, but because of design miscalculations when construction began in the 1880s, they were too heavy for the building, so the bells still haven't been hung. Take a look inside the cathedral with its fine stained glass and the marvelous play of light in its vast interior. The New Cathedral was built because the Old Cathedral, **Iglesia de Sagrario** (on the other side of the square but rarely open to the public) had become too small for the burgeoning congregation of Cuencan Catholics.

Visiting Cuenca's 30-odd fine churches could keep you occupied for weeks, but if you only have time to see one other religious wonder it should be the **Museo de las Conceptas**, housed in the infirmary of the Convent of the Immaculate Conception on Hermano Miguel 6-33. The chapel contains a beautiful, but lurid, display of crucifixes created by local artist Gaspar Sangurima, considered to be the Father of Arts and Crafts in Cuenca.

It might be said that arts, crafts and religion, in reverse order, are what Cuenca is all about. Certainly there are enough churches and museums to back up such a theory. If you want to see contemporary Cuencan art,

try the **Casa de Cultura**, near the Old Cathedral. On the second floor there is usually an exhibition of local artists, and paintings are on sale. About seven blocks west on Sucre is the **Museo de Arte Moderno**, which also has several works by local artists.

For artifacts relating to regional Inca and pre-Inca civilizations, go to the **Museo del Banco Central**, just out of the center of town, at the Tomebamba archaeological site on Larga and Huayna Cápac. Also well recommended is the **Museo de las Culturas Aborígenes** ☎ (07) 811706 on Avenida 10 de Agosto 4-70. If you call ahead you can get a

Cuenca's main plaza, Parque Calderón, is dominated by the "new" cathedral built a century ago.

guided tour in English, French or Spanish of this huge private collection of pre-Columbian art.

Some say Cuenca is the best place in Ecuador for **shopping**. And it's true that prices seem as good, if not better, than elsewhere in the country and there's plenty of choice. Around **Gran Colombia** and roads leading off it, you will find many shops selling *ikat* weavings, woolen sweaters, leather goods, carvings, basketwork, antiques, jewelry, filigree work, silver and gold items, precious stones, paintings, sculpture, pottery, ceramic tiles, candelabra, cameras, camping equipment, panama hats, and much more.

You can also visit a **panama hat factory** where the finishing stages are carried out, the main work on the hats having been done in the weavers' homes. Ask CETUR, or one of the tour companies for details. The two **main markets** are around the **Church Of San Francisco** and **Plaza Rotary**, which are best for craft items. Stands are open most days of the week, but the main market day is Thursday.

WHERE TO STAY

Cuenca has a good reputation for its hotels and hostels, from the top to bottom of the range. But it is a good idea to ask for discount because printed rates are often higher than what the hotel is prepared to charge, depending on the season, of course. As is common in Ecuador, locals pay less (legally) than foreign tourists.

Always highly praised for character and friendliness is **Hotel Crespo** ☎ (07) 827857 FAX (07) 835387, by Río Tomebamba, Larga 7-93 and Cordero. Rooms with high ceilings and river views are about US$65 for a double. Slightly more expensive is the swish **Hotel El Dorado** ☎ (07) 831390 FAX (07) 831663 in the

center of town. Swishest of all is the Swiss-run **Hotel Oro Verde** ☎ (07) 831200 FAX (07) 832849, on Ordóñez Lazo on the northwest outskirts.

In the mid-range category, the **Posada del Sol** ☎ (07) 838695, Bolívar and Mariana Cueva; **Hostal Chordeleg** ☎ (07) 824611 FAX (07) 822536 Gran Colombia and Torres; and **Hostal Caribe Inn** ☎/FAX (07) 822710 Gran Colombia and Padre Aguirre, have been recommended.

If you are traveling independently for pleasure rather than business, the less-expensive hotels, and hostels with common living areas and shared kitchen facilities, are often more fun and are better places to meet fellow denizens of the road of all ages, nationalities and backgrounds. One such place in Cuenca is the **Macondo Hostal** ☎ (07) 840697 FAX (07) 833593. Tarqui 11-64 and Lamar, in a beautiful old colonial-style house with a garden. The rooms are pretty and very clean, with shared or private baths, around US$10 for single and US$14 for a double. Book ahead if possible. The Swiss-owned **El Cafecito** ☎ (07) 827341, sister to its namesake in Quito, on Honorato Vásquez and Luis Cordero, which charges about US$5 for a shared room and not much more for a private room with bath overlooking the garden, is also recommended.

One Hostería, about an hour by road from Cuenca, that has been highly recommended is **Hostería Uzhupud** ☎ (07) 250339 FAX (07) 806521, a Spanish-style complex of several buildings with nice terraces, gardens, views and a large pool. Although reasonably expensive, they also have less-expensive accommodation for students and children.

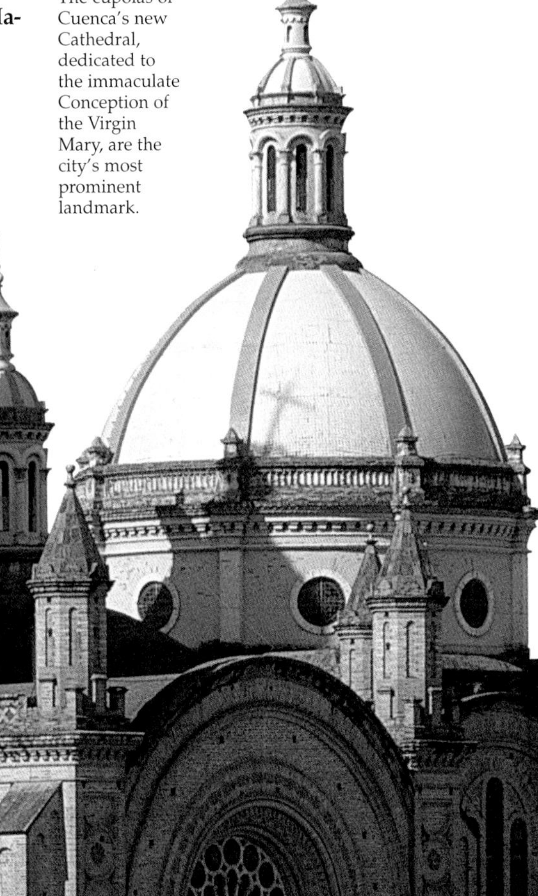

The cupolas of Cuenca's new Cathedral, dedicated to the immaculate Conception of the Virgin Mary, are the city's most prominent landmark.

Where to Eat

La Cantina Bar & Restaurant, on Córdova and Borrero, has a beautiful restaurant with excellent food, often accompanied by live music. **El Jardín,** in the same vicinity, has a reputation for food of the highest international standards with prices almost to match, while my favorite, **Villa Rosa,** Gran Colombia 12-22, is excellent in every way, and is worth experiencing even if just for a bowl of soup and a basket of bread. Good standard budget fare in a garden setting is served at **El Cafecito**. For local food at reasonable prices, **El Refugio** on Gran Colombia is safe and tasty. In spite of the Spanish feel to the town there's almost nothing resembling a cozy *tapas* bar, but plenty of pizza shops. I have to say I picked up a stomach bug after eating at one of Cuenca's better-known pizza places, so I'm loath to recommend any. If you have a taste for ice cream and cakes, **Heladería Holandesa** on Benigno Malo 9-45 is a popular choice.

Nightlife

Despite its sedate image and the impression that everyone is in bed by 10 PM in Cuenca, there are a number of hot nightspots in the city if you can dig them out. For a night on the town you could do worse than head to the **Piccadilly Pub**, on Borrero and Córdova, where pictures of red London buses on the wall and pints of beer give visiting Brits a dose of nostalgia. The pub has a pool table in the back and lively music. Ask the barman or fellow customers about clubs and discos. Chances are you'll be told of bars on Ordóñez Lazo near the Hotel Oro Verde. **Saxon** might be mentioned and **La Morada del Cantor** will be recommended for good *peñas*. If you don't have any luck at the Piccadilly, try **La Cantina** across the road. There's a cool disco called **UBU** in town. Ask around for the location.

AROUND CUENCA

Driving north from Cuenca on the Pan-American Highway you soon arrive in **Cañar Province**. You'll notice that the hats of the local *indígenas* here are no longer the straw panamas favored by the *Cholos Cuencanos*. Instead, the Cañari Indians wear white felt hats with a wide, turned-up brim or plain old felt *trilbies* with a narrow brim and an indented crown.

Nothing to do with hats, of course, but on the whole the Cañaris are a proud but rather sad community. In spite of fierce resistance they were subjugated by the Incas, many of them being forced to move south as *mitmakuna*. Then, after they fought on the side of the Spanish, they were sent to work in gold and silver mines by their colonial masters. Six hundred years ago the Cañaris dominated what is now southern Ecuador. Today they are reduced to some 40,000 people scratching a subsistence herding cattle in the highlands of Cañar Province.

Continuing north, the road passes through the old colonial town of **Azogues**, the provincial capital, named after the Spanish word for mercury which was mined in the area. A few kilometers further is the mountain village of **Biblián**, which is overlooked by a vertiginous church, **La Madona del Rocio**, built high into the cliffs above the village.

Coming by car it's another 20 km (12 miles) or more along the road, which hardly merits the designation of Highway, before you turn off to the right into a patchwork quilt of pastel greens, browns and yellows spread over wide, sweeping valleys and smooth round hills. This is the approach to the **ruins of Ingapirca**, an Inca fort, temple, or observatory, or perhaps all three. In spite of extensive archaeological research, nobody has figured out the function of this massive stone complex that commands the brow of a hill and dominates the valleys for miles around.

Ingapirca might not be as impressive as some Inca sites in Peru, but it is the best Ecuador has. Some find the ruins boring while others, like myself, find it a moving experience to see and touch the beautifully-cut stones, fitted together so accurately and without mortar by craftsmen of a vanished civilization. There are good walks in the area around the ruins and you can visit a rock formation, known as the

Face of the Inca. If possible, combine a trip to the ruins with a visit to the Friday market at the nearby village of **Ingapirca** where Cañari cowboys in sheepskin chaps loll drunkenly on their horses while the women, all of them hatted and wearing traditional costume, quietly shop for potatoes, *cuy* (guinea pig) and shining aluminum pots and pans.

Visits with Ingapirca can be arranged by any travel agent in Cuenca and there's also a direct bus that leaves the Terminal Terrestre at 9 AM and 10 AM and returns at 1 PM and 3 PM, which costs about US$1.50. Check the times as they may well change.

Many of the villages around Cuenca excel in the crafts and are well-known for their **markets**. The small village of **Chordeleg**, which can be reached in about two hours by bus from Cuenca, changing at **Gualaceo**, is well-known for its filigree jewelry. As well as jewelry stores and a busy Sunday market, the village boasts a small ethnographic museum with information about local handicrafts, including explanations of how the *ikat* process works. Not far away are the villages of **Bulcay** and **Bulzhun**, known for backstrap weaving of *macanas* (*ikat* shawls).

About 30 km (19 miles) west of Cuenca is the **Cajas National Recreation Area**, a striking landscape of more than 200 lakes and countless ponds lying placidly under barren cliffs. This under-explored, high-altitude natural marvel, where temperatures drop below freezing at night and which can be cold and rainy in the afternoon, is for the adventurous, well-prepared and well-insulated hiker. On a clear morning the views are spectacular. The park is home to the highest growing tree in the world, the diminutive **quinoa tree**, as well as many rare species of plants, birds and animals. **Fishing** is said to be good on **Lake Toreadora**. For more information contact one of the tour agencies in Quito listed under GENERAL INFORMATION, above. Ecotrek is connected with the new **Huagrahuma Páramo ecolodge** on the edge of the park. There are buses from Cuenca to El Cajas every day except Thursday leaving from San Sebastián church at about 6 AM, which return at 3 PM.

ABOVE: The backstreets of Cuenca are a treasure trove of small shops.

The Deep South

GUYAQUIL AND THE SOUTH
N
W
E
S
Montecristi
PORTOVIEJO
El Progreso
Epalmé (Velasco Ibarra)
La Pila
Colón
San Jacinto
Beneficio
Guarumal
Membrillal
La Victoria
Manantiales
Sangan
Sucre
La Estrella
Pto. de Cayo
JIPIJAPA
Las Pampas
Salaite
Joaz
Balzar
América
Machalilla
Julcuy
Cerritos
Virgínia
Vinces
Pto. Lopez
San Gabriel
Salango
La Paz
Machalilla National Park
Palestina
Macul
Puerto Rico
Pedro Pablo Gómez
Guare
Cascol
La Rinconada
Sta. Lucía
Dos Rios
La Cadena
Sta. Clara
Gral Vernaza
San José
R. Mangla
Limonal
Olón
Pedro Carbo
Baba
834
Sabaneta
Pimocha
Manglaralto
Daule
Las Piedras
La Victoria
Valdivia
San Pedro
Salanguillo
Pablo Iguana
Ayangue
Tarifa
Corozo
Palmar
GUAYAS
Yaguachi Nvo.
Co. Verde
403
Buijó
San Pablo
Aguadita
GUAYAQUIL
Casiguana
Pta. Sta. Elena
265
Durán
SALINAS
LA LIBERTAD
Chongón
Delia
Km 26
Sta. Elena
Azúcar
Pta. Carnero
Zapotal
Cerecita
El Consuelo
Taura
Anconcito
Atahualpa
San Isidro
La Esperanza
Sucre
El Real
Caimito
Pta. de Piedras
Churete
Chanduy
Tugaduaja
San Lorenzo
Engunga
San Juan
Pto. Roma
Isla Escalante
Pto. Inca
Pta. de Piedras
San Antonio
Isla Mondragón
Engabao
El Morro
Playas (Gral. Villamil)
Posorja
Pto. Naranjal
San Pablo
Data de Posorja
Bajada
Puná
La Resbalosa
Campo Alegre
Río Hondo
La Victoria
Golfo de Guayaquil
Isla Puná
La Joya
Balao
Asunción
Pto. Grande
227
Tenguel
Pta. Arenas
Pta. Carnero
Pagua
Bajo Alto
Isla Santa Clara (El Muerto)
Sta. Cruz
Jambelí
MACHALA
Progreso
Patococha
La Caña
PASAJE
QUITO
El Retiro
Buenavista
Bellavista
Pitahaya
SANTA ROSA
Chilla
Huaquillas
San José
Chacras
ARENILLAS
Torota
Carcabón
Saracay
Piedras
Palmales
Piñas
La Bocana
Balsas
TUMBES
Los Amarillos
Chaguarpa
Cordillera Larga
PERÚ
Olmedo
Mercadillo
Casanga
Cazaderos
Celica
Guachanamá
607
Algorrobillo
El Empalme
0
20
40
60 km
10
30
40miles

THE PAN-AMERICAN HIGHWAY GOING SOUTH from Cuenca passes through spectacular scenery as it climbs to the **Tinajilla Pass** at 3,527m (11,755 ft), and through the páramo of **Gañadel**. There are no trees, nor houses — just scrub, grassland and barren, desolate, empty mountains. With virtually no other vehicles on this bumpy, potholed highway the driver swings the bus around bends at hair-raising speeds, with cliffs to one side and steep precipices to the other. At one point, I looked down on a valley filled with a white lake of clouds.

After three hours we stop in the pretty main square of the small town of **Saraguro**. An attractive, smartly dressed young woman wearing a black bowler hat, snow-white blouse, wide black skirt and black woolen shawl closed with a large silver pin, holding a small child, climbs down from the bus. She is one of the Saraguro *indígenas*, said to be descended from the Inca tribes who settled this area. Many of them are quite wealthy and well educated.

The shawl pin, or ***tupu***, is a characteristic Saraguro accessory, as are **filigree earrings**, both of which are family treasures passed down from generation to generation. This traditional jewelry can be bought in some of the small shops in town. The **Inca ruins** in the area are overgrown and hard to find.

LOJA

For most travelers Loja is a place to change buses and head on down to Vilcabamba, the almost legendary destination of the gringo explorer. But should you get stuck, or choose to stay a while, Loja is a pleasant enough old colonial town with two universities, a law school and a conservatory. But there isn't a great deal to grab the attention of the tourist. If you haven't seen enough colonial art by this stage of your travels, you could visit the **Convento de las Conceptas**, but you do have to get a permit from the Bishop of Loja to see the collection. The **Banco Central** also has a local **branch museum** in Loja. As expected, there are also a number of fine churches in town.

PREVIOUS PAGES: Loja Province in the south LEFT is one of the least-visited region of Ecuador. An old woman from Vilcabamba RIGHT, a town known for the longevity of its inhabitants.

More likely you might need practical facilities, such as the **EMETEL** telephone office on Eguiguren, a block east of Parque Central. For travel services, such as for flights to Quito or Guayaquil, try **Hidaltur** on Bolívar 10-33, or **Delgado Travel** at Sucre and Colón. If you're heading for Peru, there's a **Peruvian Consulate** on Sucre 10-56. The **TAME office** is on 24 de Mayo across the Río Zamora. **La Tola airport** is 30 km (19 miles) west of Loja town at **Catamayo**. Buses to Vilcabamba leave from the **Terminal Terrestre**, where the bus from Cuenca gets in. And if you have to stay the night, there are many good value hostels and hotels available.

VILCABAMBA

Vilcabamba is one of those places that has achieved a reputation almost entirely by word of mouth. Among young backpackers and aging hippies, most of the talk is about the hallucinogenic juice of the **San Pedro cactus plant** grown in the area, but Vilcabamba is also famous for **longevity** of its inhabitants. Whether the town's two best-known characteristics are connected is a subject of speculation.

Many who travel to Vilcabamba have also heard of **Madre Tierra** ✆(07) 580269, a friendly ecolodge that has expanded over the years in the hills just out of town. Starting as the private home of a Canadian-Ecuadorian couple who used to put up friends and friends of friends, it has grown in the past years into a complex of *cabañas,* complete with restaurant, swimming pool, bar and health spa.

This was my destination one glorious, crimson-skied evening when the bus from Loja crested the hill overlooking the valley of Vilcabamba, a great bowl of checkered fields surrounded by smoothly sloping mountains, a Shangri-La of the Andes. An Australian psychiatrist, her son and I climbed from the bus, about a kilometer from the town. A group of young Israeli backpackers, who were getting on board, showed us the way to Madre Tierra.

As soon as we arrived I knew this was the place I had been searching for after weeks of hard traveling around Ecuador. All travelers need a break from the road from time to time. This was the Ecuadorian equivalent of the motel on the prairie in Nevada where you hole up for a week or two, or the little pub on the edge of Dartmoor where you go to write your book. The atmosphere spelled out "relax" in big bold letters.

Three seamless days passed in a mood of perfect indolence and pleasure. Madre Tierra is a place where you can't help but meet people. I spent a lot of time with the two Australians, a German doctor and two German girls I met earlier in my travels on the train journey to San Lorenzo. We went riding, had massages and mud baths, sat out on the balcony looking at the stars. We went into town and checked out the bars. We sat around campfires, drinking beer and telling stories. Doctor Klaus spoke about colonic irrigation (also available at Madre Tierra) and told us about his experiences with the shamans in the jungle.

The accommodation? I slept in a very small, somewhat damp single room in a bamboo hut thatched with leaves. Klaus and the young Australian had a big hut to themselves, about a 20 minutes' walk into the woods. The Australian psychiatrist had a room to herself overlooking the pool. The two German girls stayed in the main house. The cost? About US$15 per night per person, including breakfast and an excellent dinner. Renting horses, massages and mud baths are extra.

One morning I sat down for breakfast on the open terrace overlooking the valley with Jaime Mendoza, owner of Madre Tierra. He spoke in glowing terms of the charms and healthfulness of Vilcabamba and the longevity of its inhabitants. The altitude of about 1,500 m (5,000 ft) creates the perfect pressure for your health, in particular your heart, he explained, and the year-round temperature of between 17°C (63°F) minimum and 26°C (79°F) maximum is ideal. Furthermore, the water, which comes from the watershed in ancient forests in the nearby Podocarpus National Park, is laced with gelatins that destroy toxins in your body.

On average only one person in 1,470,000 lives to be a hundred, Jamie explained, but a study in Vilcabamba showed that out of a population of 3,000, as many as 64 people were over 100 years old. When I pointed out that some studies disputed such figures, he dismissed them with a wave of his hand. Who knows? Whatever the truth about the longevity of the inhabitants of Vilcabamba, it is certainly a very pleasant place to be. Many are the stories of people who come here for a few days and stay for years.

WHERE TO STAY AND EAT

Aside from **Madre Tierra** (see above), there are a number of other pleasant and reasonable places to stay in and around Vilcabamba. **Cabañas Río Yambala**, or Charlie's Cabins as they are sometimes called, have a very good reputation. Quiet and secluded, they are about four kilometers (just over two miles) southeast of town (take a taxi from the main square) and cost around US$5 per person per night. There is a restaurant and cooking facilities, and the owners, Charlie and Sarah, arrange horse riding and camping trips to the Podocarpus National Park. Only slightly more expensive, but a very good value, **Cabañas El Paradíso** ✆ (07) 963649, on the same road as Madre Tierra but a little nearer town, are clean, comfortable and, curiously, have their own pyramid for energizing sessions. A night in the pyramid costs about US$10. Nearby and more upmarket is **Hostería de Vilcabamba** ✆ (07) 580271 FAX (07) 580273, an attractive and well-appointed hotel with swimming pool, sauna and hydro-massage included in a price of about US$25 for a double room. The best budget place in town is **Olivia Toledo's rooms**, a block from the main square and costing only three or four dollars per night. Also in the center of town, the **Hidden Garden** FAX (07) 580281 E-MAIL zetpeter@lo.pro.ec, is a fun place to stay in the US$5 price range, including a garden and pool. A useful contact in Vilcabamba is **Pablo** of **Pablo's Money Exchange**, across the road from the Terminal Terrestre, who aside from changing money and traveler's checks, performs various services for travelers.

Vilcabamba's climate, altitude and pure water are said to account for the health and longevity of its residents.

PODOCARPUS NATIONAL PARK

Wild, remote and in many parts unexplored, **Podocarpus National Park's** 141,400 hectares (350,000 acres) of pristine Andean forest is thought to predate the Ice Age and is of supreme importance to science. More than 550 **species of birds** have been recorded, perhaps more than in any other area in the world. Endemic species are common because of the unusual ecosystem created by the meeting of Amazonian and Andean weather patterns. Several threatened species depend on Podocarpus for their survival. The park is also the original source of quinine: the **cinchona tree**. Natural quinine extracted from the bark of the tree is the only remedy 100% effective against all strains of malaria.

"Have you been to the edge…? Gavilan Takes You Higher." These are the words that New Zealander Gavin Moore of **Caballos Gavilan** FAX (07) 673186 (Vilcabamba) uses on his photocopied flyer to entice customers to come on his unusual and exciting horseback adventures into the tropical cloud forest. "Magical, misty and mystical," his brochure continues, "the unique and almost undiscovered area around Podocarpus National Park is fast becoming world famous. Unspoiled wilderness, pure water and a primeval forest combine to make this one of the most perfect places on the planet." A three-day, Indiana Jones-style jaunt in the jungle with Moore, including horses, food and lodging, costs around US$80.

You can also get information about the park from **INEFAN** at Azuay, between Olmedo and Bolívar in Loja, at the **Acroiris Foundation** nature conservation organization, also in Loja, at Lauro Guerrero and Mercadillo, or at the **Cajanuma ranger station** inside the park itself. The entrance fee to the park is about US$10 and a taxi from Loja costs about the same. The ***refugio*** at the station has good facilities but if you want to go up to the **highland lakes**, a one-day hike, you'll need camping equipment.

Acroiris (which means rainbow) also has information about **ecological issues** affecting the park, such as encroachment by gold miners. In 1995, some 500 colonists entered into the park and started mining for gold. After schoolchildren in the Loja area sent a mountain of protest letters to then-President Duran, the miners were forced to leave. The battle between conservationists and miners in Podocarpus is not an issue that is easily solved. Recently miners vandalized an INEFAN *refugio*, and in another tussle a conservationist was shot.

The indígenas of the small town of Saraguro are thought to be descended from Inca tribes who settled the area.

Sprite

Amazonia

NOBODY KNOWS HOW MANY SPECIES OF PLANTS and animals live in the tropical rainforests. Conservative estimates suggest a figure of about 30 million species. But as they continue to probe this mysterious and largely unexplored realm, some scientists believe that the figure could be as high as 80 million or more, and that rainforests could account for more than half of life forms on earth.

Roughly speaking, species already accounted for in the rainforest include 80,000 trees; 3,000 land vertebrates; 2,000 fresh-water fish; almost half the world's 8,500 species of birds; 1,200 different kinds of butterflies. Among these diverse life forms, many of them endemic to the region, and some of them endangered, there are all sorts of weird and wonderful creatures: a monkey small enough to sit in the palm of your hand (pigmy marmoset); the world's largest rodent (capybara); the world's biggest snake (anaconda); and the world's noisiest animal (the howler monkey, whose voice can carry as far as 10 miles).

Some of our favorite foods come from the Amazon: chocolate (cacao), cinnamon, cola, ginger, cashews, black pepper, cayenne pepper, avocado, eggplant, sugarcane, vanilla and figs. Many medicinal plants have been found in the rainforest, such as quinine for malaria and *curare*, used by Amazonian hunters to paralyze prey, and in western medicine as a muscle relaxant during operations and for Parkinson's disease. Hallucinogenic plants, such as *ayahuasca*, used by shamans in religious and curing rituals, are being studied in the west for possible medical and psychiatric use. Many more such herbs from the rainforest medicine chest are bound to be discovered in the future, as long as miners, loggers and farmers don't destroy it.

The above facts are important because they indicate how vital the Amazonian rainforest is to our planet. But they don't tell us how important the rainforest is in human terms. The guardians of this natural cornucopia are the indigenous inhabitants themselves. In the Amazon basin, some 200 tribal groups guard a priceless biological heritage contained in an area of about five million sq km (almost two million square miles) of tropical forest. Over a period of about 10,000 years, generations of these peoples have lived on the wettest place on earth, which has an average rainfall of 25 cm (100 inches) a year. They know the rainforest. They know its plants, its birds, its animals, its rivers, its rhythms. They have not destroyed it because this jungle is their home where they have learned to live full and meaningful lives in an environment that gives them everything they need. They are the true masters of the rainforest.

The rainforest is also important for people who visit, like you and me. While we may marvel at the richness and beauty of its na-

ture, at the same time it is completely alien to us. We can try to make some connection with this strange world, by swimming in a river, walking in the rainforest or spending a night in hut in the jungle. Even if we share no common language, we can sit with people who rely totally on this natural world, who don't separate the physical from the spiritual, whose way of life as jungle nomads contrasts sharply with our own material concepts of materialism and possession. In the rainforest we can travel back in time to a world of hunt-

PREVIOUS PAGES: The dugout canoe LEFT is the traditional form of transport in the rainforest. A Cofán Indian RIGHT from the Cuyabeno Wildlife Reserve. OPPOSITE: All rivers in Ecuador's Oriente eventually flow into the Amazon. ABOVE: Cocoa beans, one of many products of the rainforest.

ing and gathering, a world in which our species has lived for 99% of its time on earth. We in the West have forgotten that life, but the people of the rainforest haven't.

In the Ecuadorian part of the Amazon basin there are many such indigenous peoples, the biggest groups being the Siona-Sequoia, Cofán, Huaorani, Quichua, Shuar and Achuar. Some of them have only recently been in contact with people outside their forest environment, and it is thought that there are still small groups that continue to be totally isolated. Others, however, have either been in touch with the world outside for years and have adapted to it, or have been destroyed by its alien diseases.

Many Amazon peoples don't like visitors, who come as miners, colonists, travelers, tourists, photographers, travel writers, anthropologists, botanists, priests or policemen. But some realize they cannot remain isolated forever, and that tourism is a lesser evil than the logging and mining that destroys their forests. But wherever you go in the rainforest, it is wise to do so with a sensitivity and a respect to the peoples whose home it has been for thousands of years.

OPPOSITE: The Amazonian rainforest TOP is one of the wettest places on earth with an annual rainfall of 25 cm (100 inches). Cacao plantations BOTTOM produce edible seeds from which cocoa and chocolate are made.

Northern Oriente

IF YOUR TIME IS LIMITED AND IT'S WITHIN YOUR budget, the easiest way to see something of the Oriente, as Ecuador's Amazon basin is usually called, is to buy a package tour from a reputable operator, either in your own country or in Quito. This way all arrangements will be made for you. You will be flown from Quito to Lago Agrio, Coca, Tena, Shell (near Puyo) or Macas, and then it will probably be a rough road ride for a while, and then a motor-driven dugout canoe to the lodge where you are staying. In this way you will experience the rainforest but won't suffer too much hardship.

Alternatively, you can fly in independently and arrange a tour when you get to one of the gateway towns, all of which have hotels, tourist facilities and agents who can arrange jungle trips that are less expensive than they would be if you arranged them at home or in Quito. In this way you will probably save some money but it will take more time. The least expensive way is to go by bus.

Of the four main land routes into the Oriente, the shortest is from Quito over the Papallacta Pass down to Baeza. From this old colonial, but somewhat by-passed, town you can head on to Lago Agrio or Tena. But the bus journey is long, bumpy and uncomfortable, and many people who go out by bus under their own steam decide to fly back.

PAPALLACTA

About 80 km (50 miles) over the Eastern Cordillera from Quito, and in a pleasant setting on the rim of the Amazon basin, the cloud forest town of Papallacta is a convenient stopping point on the way to or from the Oriente. The town is also a destination in itself, particularly for Quiteños staying the weekend, its chief attraction being its very hot springs. The main baths are the Termas de Papallacta, a one-kilometer (half-mile) uphill hike from the main Quito-Baeza road, where there are about half dozen pools ranging from very hot to very cold. Though the water isn't clear, because of the mineral content, the complex has recently been refurbished and the pools are clean. Changing facilities are available and the cost is about US$2.50. One a clear day there are beautiful views from the baths of Volcán Antisana.

If you're stopping off at Papallacta on your way down to the Oriente by bus, it's best to do so on a weekday to avoid crowds. It is even more alluring on your way back up from the rainforest, when you can relax and soak away your aches and pains from your jungle-weary, bus-jolted body. Buses between Baeza and Quito can drop you off at the beginning of the path up to the *baños*.

WHERE TO STAY AND EAT

There are some new, but rather expensive, cabañas and rooms at the pools themselves suitable for families. The restaurant at the pools, **Café Canela**, is good and the trout is recommended. Less expensive accommodation can be found in the village down the hill at **Hotel Quito**, the backpacker's choice, or at **Residencial El Viajero**.

THE ROAD TO LAGO AGRIO

The road from Papallacta to Lago Agrio bypasses the main town of Baeza before continuing northeast along the Río Quijos. For most of the way it follows the trans-Ecuadorian oil pipeline, along which oil is pumped from the oil fields deep in the Oriente, up and over the Andes and down to the Pacific

PREVIOUS PAGES: Cofán dwelling LEFT in the Cuyabeno Wildlife Reserve. Jungle predator, the Jaguar RIGHT is the largest species of cat. OPPOSITE: Cofán house in the jungle. ABOVE: Oil companies are drilling or surveying much of Ecuador's rainforest.

coast. The pipeline and the road itself were cut through the jungle after oil was discovered north of Lago Agrio in the late 1960s. Settlements of colonists and small coffee farms are now strung along the twin thoroughfare, and much of the primary rainforest has been cut down.

About two hours out of Baeza on the right is a path leading down to the 145-m (483-ft) San Rafael Falls, the highest falls in Ecuador. Bus drivers should know where to stop if you ask for Las Cascadas. After about half an hour's walk, passing a lodge where you can stay the night, you come to a ridge with a great view of the misty falls. The bird watching here is as almost as impressive as the mighty falls themselves. Look out for a cross in memory of a Canadian photographer who fell to his death in the area in 1988. It might deter you from a risky climb to the foot of the falls that is steep, slippery and treacherous.

A bit further east on the other side of the main road is the hard-to-find head of the trail to Volcán Reventador, a relatively small mountain by Ecuadorian standards (3,562 m or 11,872 ft), but nevertheless a two- to four-day hike to the peak. Take a guide if you plan to climb this recently active volcano because it's easy to get lost.

Continuing the bus route west for another four hours, you come to the oil town of Nueva Loja, better known as Lago Agrio, a nickname coined by American oil men, from the Spanish words for the oil town of Sour Lake in Texas. Though many of the roads are now paved, rubber boots and muddy streets, bars and brothels, are the defining characteristics of Ecuador's biggest oil town. Jungle trips can be arranged here, but if you want to see pristine primary forest this probably isn't the best place for it. Lago Agrio is where to observe the interaction between multinational oil operations and ancient lifestyles of indigenous Amazon peoples, as prospecting and drilling destroys their lives, their traditions, their habitats and their homelands.

General Information

The INEFAN (national parks administration) office ☎ (06) 830129, on Manabí and 10 de Agosto is open mornings and afternoons from Monday to Friday. If you want to explore the area this is a good place to start. Among other things they should be able to tell you which agencies are licensed to operate in the nearby Cuyabeno Wildlife Reserve, so you can avoid those cowboy outfits who sometimes get turned out of the reserve. There is an EMETEL office on Avenida Quito, the town's main street, and Orellana. The TAME office is on 9 de Octubre and Manabí, and the airport is just five kilometers (three miles), east of the city center, an inexpensive yellow-truck taxi ride away. Most buses leave from Avenida Quito. The capital itself is a bone-shaking 10 hours back up the Andes.

Where to Stay and Eat

Lago Agrio's shortage of good hotels is evidence that it is not a tourist town. Most people come here to work and aren't too fussy where they rest their weary heads. The best place is the overpriced **El Cofán** ☎ (06) 830009, on Avenida Quito, at about US$50 for a double. **Hostal Gran Lago**, a kilometer (just over a half mile) west of town, is also said to be good. Most budget travelers opt for **Hotel D'Mario** ☎ (06) 830172 FAX (06) 830456, at about US$10 per night for a clean and comfortable room. Its downstairs restaurant serves generous pizzas, fried chicken and other popular gringo food. For a more upmarket experience try the restaurant at the El Cofán.

AROUND LAGO AGRIO

Just 20 km (12 miles) east of Lago Agrio is western tip of the 606,000-hectare (1.5 million-acre) Cuyabeno Wildlife Reserve, founded in 1979 to protect the rainforest from encroachment by oil companies and settlers. The area is considered to be one of the most important areas of natural beauty and ecological diversity in the Amazon basin. Its dense primary jungle forest is home to various Indian groups, including the Cofán, Siona, Sequoia and Shuar. There is also abundant bird life and myriad rare and exotic plants and creatures, from pink dolphins, caiman, electric eels, manatees and anacondas to jaguars, tapirs, agoutis, peccaries, armadillos and tortoises.

Unfortunately, despite its protected status, oil companies have ravished much of the region. Wells have been drilled, roads built, forests cut down, and millions of gallons of raw crude oil have been spilled into its rivers, creeks, swamps and lagoons. During the last 17 years, spills from the trans-Ecuadorian pipeline, which Texaco built in 1972, totaled 72 million liters (16 million gallons), half again more than was spilled in the *Exxon Valdez* accident. Spills such as these contribute to high rates of malnutrition and health problems among the local *indígenas*, including birth defects and neurological disorders. Indian organizations and conservation groups continue fighting to save the rainforest from more destruction (see THE GRINGO CHIEF, next page).

Despite massive damage, vast areas of the Cuyabeno and its surroundings are untouched and unspoiled, so that visitors to the park may see no evidence of the environmental spoilage and contamination. Local people play a increasingly active part in tourism, and there are number of lodges and camps where visitors can experience the rainforest in all its pristine beauty. To an extent, ecotourism is seen as a viable and less-destructive alternative to the petrodollar.

Many companies organize tours in the area. In Quito, **Native Life Travels** ℂ (02) 550836 FAX (02) 569741, J Pinto 446 and Amazonas, run by *indígenas* from Cuyabeno, have a good reputation and their prices are reasonable. **Nuevo Mundo Expeditions** ℂ (02) 552617 FAX (02) 565261, also in Quito, have a reputation of being ecologically sensitive and organize tours to the Cuyabeno River Lodge. Metropolitan Touring runs excellent camps on the shores of Lakes Iripari and Imuya outside the reserve. The same company also operates an enormous, flat-bottomed riverboat, the *Flotel Orellana*, which cruises Río Aguarico near the Peruvian border. This is the ultimate way of exploring the jungle in style and comfort. Shore trips, guides, canoe rides, lectures and good food are all included in the price. For more information on this well-recommended jungle cruise contact **Metropolitan Touring** ℂ (02) 463680 or 464780 FAX (02) 464702; in Quito they're at República de El Salvador 970. Their postal address is PO Box 17-12-0310, Quito. Several tour companies in Lago Agrio organize less expensive tours to Cuyabeno Wildlife Reserve and the surrounding area.

The Flotel Orellana carries tourists in luxury accommodation deep into the rainforest — the most comfortable way of exploring the Amazon without getting bitten.

THE GRINGO CHIEF

It's been used in more than a few headlines in the past, and there's no other nickname for him: "The Gringo Chief." His name is Randy Borman, American-born, son of missionaries working in the Oriente, and brought up with a blowpipe in his mouth. When his parents left Ecuador, Randy stayed on in the jungle. He is a missionary himself, but not in the conventional sense. Randy's mission is to slow the destruction of the rainforest and protect its wildlife and the cultural identity of the people among whom he was raised, the Cofán Indians. He speaks Cofán, his wife is Cofán and he lives with a community of Cofáns who have elected him as their chief.

When life became impossible in the Cofán village of Dureno near Lago Agrio — hunting lands cut to pieces because of deforestation — Randy and a group of Cofáns moved deeper into the jungle. They settled miles down the Río Aguarico at a spot called Zabalo near the Peruvian border. According to latest information, Randy still lives there in traditional Cofán style. He takes adventures tour groups into the jungle. He hunts wild pigs with a lance. He cuts his own dugout canoes from forest trees. And he defends the Cofáns against cultural extinction. Like David against Goliath, he fights the good fight against slayers of the rainforest and its wildlife.

Among other events in the course of his skirmishes in the jungle, Randy and his "braves" have destroyed an unmanned drilling platform built illegally on Cofán land and kidnapped a 23-man seismic testing crew for trespassing. He has also helped with law suits in the United States against oil companies. Thanks to people like Randy, the Cofáns and other Indian groups, oil companies in Ecuador are being forced to admit that the rainforest isn't a vacant land, where they can do whatever they like. Oil companies are now required by the Ecuadorian government to take out "clean-up insurance" to cover spills and other contamination. The destructive, but profitable, oil boom is destined to end when Ecuador's oil reserves run out in a couple of decades.

For information about visiting the Cofán community in Zabalo contact **Wilderness Travel** ✆ (510) 558-2488 FAX (510) 558-2489 E-MAIL info@wildernesstravel.com, 1102 Ninth Street, Berkley, CA 94710, USA.

COCA

The jungle town of Coca is no place for sightseeing, nor is it a destination of choice for most travelers. The river port's *raison d'être* is as a transport hub where you hop off a plane and jump into a boat going down-river, or stay no longer than it takes to arrange an expedition into the interior. Like Lago Agrio, it is a field base for oil workers. The town has no aesthetic merits, unless unpaved streets, muddy in rain and dusty when dry, and dilapidated, shanty-style buildings are your idea of civic beauty. One unimpressed writer described Coca as a "gritty, dirty, riverside pit."

The town owes its importance to its strategic location at the confluence of Río Coca with Río Napo. If you were able to continue on far enough down river, across the border into Peru (which isn't legal), you would come to where the Napo joins Río Marañon and turns into the Amazon. From there the world's mightiest river flows for some 3,200 km (2,000 miles) across South American to the Atlantic Ocean. Such was the incredible journey of Francisco de Orellana, who in 1542 made the first documented voyage down the Amazon. For this reason the official, but seldom-used name of Coca is Puerto Francisco de Orellana.

GENERAL INFORMATION

Foreigners arriving in or leaving Coca by river are required to show passports at the Capitaña by the landing dock. For those on group tours this will most likely be taken care of by the agency, as will down-river transport by motorized canoe. For independent travelers, boats usually leave around 8 AM Mondays (and sometimes Thursdays) and return on Sundays (and sometimes Wednesdays).

Most buses leave from the new Terminal Terrestre on the north side of town, but some leave from the center. Check carefully. There are buses to Quito (10 to 12 hours),

Ambato, Santa Domingo, Tena and Lago Agrio. The airport is just outside town on the road to Lago Agrio. There are two TAME flights most days to Quito that take about 45 minutes. Flights are regularly full, so confirm your reservation. There are also irregular air force flights to Oriente airstrips.

Other useful facilities in Coca include an EMETEL office, a post office, and an INEFAN office for rainforest information and where entrance fees are paid for protected nature reserves. There is no CETUR tourist office, but there are a number of private agencies. Amazon Jungle Adventures and Emerald Forest Expeditions are recommended, as are Selva Tour, Ejarsytur and Yuturi. If you want to visit a Huaorani village, it is important that you go with a guide who is registered to make visits. Some Huaorani settlements prefer not to have visitors.

WHERE TO STAY AND EAT

The best hotel in Coca is **Hostería La Misión** ☎ (06) 553674 FAX (06) 564675, on the riverfront, costing about US$35 for a double room with air conditioning. Facilities include a restaurant, bar and swimming pool with river views. In the center of town, **Hotel El Auca** ☎ (06) 880127 or 880600, is a popular choice. With a restaurant and big garden, it costs about US$20 for a double. A little less expensive and quieter is the **Hotel Oasis** ☎ (06) 880174, on the waterfront. The restaurants at La Misión and El Auca are probably the best in town. For a beer and a burger go to the US-run Papa Dan's on the riverfront and for jungle food, such as capybara, the world's largest rodent, try El Buho. After your meal, the Krakatoa Bar is good for a few beers.

JUNGLE LODGES BEYOND COCA

Downstream from Coca on Río Napo there are a number of well-equipped lodges tastefully constructed in native style, while incorporating modern features. Most visitors staying at these places pay for their tours in advance in their country or in Quito.

Best-known of these resorts is the American-owned **La Selva Jungle Lodge**, winner of a ecotourism award in 1992, about three hours by fast private launch from Coca. In a wonderful spot overlooking Lake Garzacocha, the lodge is considered of the best of its kind in Ecuador. Facilities include comfortable rooms, good food, a butterfly farm, a small research station and two bird watching towers. Kerosene lighting ensures that the magical jungle sounds at night aren't drowned out by an electric generator. Canoe trips and jungle treks with knowledgeable guides are part of the package, and camping in the rainforest can be arranged.

A vital question with all such lodges is: how good is the wildlife in the area? Most reports tell of abundant birdlife around La Selva with more than 500 species, including the rare zigzag heron. However, one recent field report filed with the South America Explorers Club said there was very little wildlife in the jungle around the lodge, although there was an incredible diversity of plant life. "In our walks we saw very few birds, only a few monkeys and nothing that walked on the ground that wasn't an insect or spider." The writer also complained that that in the four-day, US$700 package, the first and last days were spent traveling to and from Quito. It is

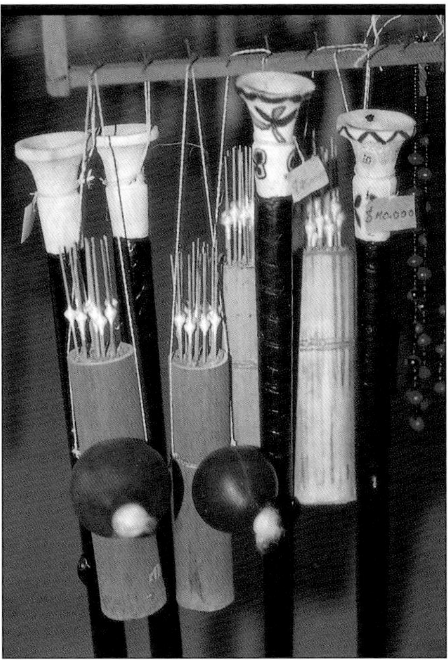

Blowpipe darts in quiver; the traditional hunting weapon of the rainforest is still used by local tribes, and played with by tourists.

fair to say, however, that many visitors are extremely satisfied with their experiences at La Selva. For more information call ((02) 554686 or 550995 FAX (02) 563814 or 567297, or write to PO Box 635, Sucursal 12 de Octubre, Quito.

About 10km (six miles) upriver from La Selva is the equally comfortable and well-run native-style cabaña complex, the Swiss-owned **Sacha Lodge**, where comforts of a first-class hotel have been brought into the heart of the jungle to the shores of a blackwater lagoon. Facilities and activities are much the same as La Selva, one small difference being that Sacha has electric lights and hot water baths. Local people work at both lodges, but visits to *indígena* communities are not part of the program to avoid what could be artificial, perhaps even embarrassing encounters. For further information contact Explorer Tours ((02) 522220 FAX (02) 508872, Reina Victoria 1235 and Lizardo García, Casilla Postal 1608, Quito.

A scenic five-hour journey by motorized canoe down the Río Napo from Coca, **Yuturi Lodge**, is the most remote of the upmarket cabaña complexes. Facilities aren't as luxurious as the two upriver lodges, but activities include exciting nighttime caiman watching and visits to a local *indígena* community. At around US$500 for a four-day, high season package from Quito, prices are lower than La Selva and Sacha. For more information contact Yuturi Jungle Adventure ((02) 544166 FAX (02) 522133, Amazonas 1022 and Pinto, Quito. Or check with Hotel Oasis in Coca.

Less expensively, there are a number of more-basic facilities along the tributaries of the Río Napo offering good jungle experiences. **Primavera lodge**, a converted hacienda is only an hour downriver from Coca (it was closed at writing, so check on its current situation). Activities include a visit to **Isla de Los Monos** (Monkey Island) and the **Pompeya Museum** of indigenous artifacts. Prices are around US$30 per person per night. For more information contact Primavera ((02) 565999 FAX (02) 525774 at Pasaje José Trevinio 114 and Avenida 12 de Octubre, Quito.

The *patrón* of Primavera, Otto Rodríquez, also owns some hidden-away cabañas on the spectacular **Pañacocha Lagoon** on the north side of the Napo, beyond La Selva, where guests can enjoy wilderness hiking and paddling canoes through jungle backwaters. Information and prices are the same as for Primavera. In the same area, local guide Julio Jarrín runs a rustic cabaña complex in a spectacular setting on the banks of the **Pañayacu River**. For lack of showers, baths are taken in the river. Prices are reasonable. For more information contact Ejarsytur Cía. Ltda. ((06) 88025, Calle Antigua Misión, Coca.

At the lowest end of the price scale, but near the top in terms of ecotourism, **Cabañas Limoncocha**, in a beautiful setting only an hour by boat from Coca, is run by AIL (Indigenous Association of Limoncocha). The complex belonged to the upmarket Metropolitan Touring group before they moved their operations to the Aguarico River because of mining activity. But now that those activities have abated, wildlife is returning and the local Quichua community is running the show. For more information contact AIL, at CONFENIAE ((02) 220326 FAX (02) 543973, Avenida 6 de Diciembre 159, Quito. Or ask travel agents in Coca for César Cerda, the ecotourism coordinator of the project.

The last village in Ecuador before the Río Napo enters Peru is **Nuevo Rocafuerte**. However you need a military permit to enter the area, and it isn't legal to cross into Peru. If you find yourself in the area you can probably stay at the local mission, but there is no restaurant in town. Another reason not to go is that the local Huaorani have had enough trouble with oil companies to have to cope with tourists as well.

THE HUAORANI RESERVE

The traditional home and hunting grounds of the Huaorani rainforest people have been in the Napo area for millennia. In the past few years, however, their land and lifestyle have been damaged and mightily disturbed by the petrochemical and tourist industries. The Huaorani reacted by imposing tolls for the use of their rivers, and entrance fees to their communities, most of which are now part of the Huaorani Reserve south of Coca. Sometimes they demand gifts, which oil companies usually pay because it helps them in obtain concessions.

In his book on the impact of tourism on the Huaorani people, *Crisis Under the Canopy,* Canadian writer Randy Smith says tourist guides have complained that "the Huaorani are becoming less interesting to tourists as they become more "civilized," leaving nudity and other traditional ways behind." This assertion crystallizes the dilemma of tourism for *indígena* peoples. The implication is that *indígenas* can benefit from tourism only if they retain traditional ways so they can be viewed like creatures in a zoo. No wonder Huaorani are skeptical about tourist visits.

Yet in the same book, Smith goes on to say that in a survey of 18 Huaorani communities that he conducted in 1992, 14 reacted favorably to the idea of being involved in ecotourism projects. Quoting this survey in his book, *The Ecotourist's Guide to the Ecuadorian Amazon*, Rolf Wesche points out that the tendency is for each Huaorani community to establish separate arrangements with individual guides. Smith advises visitors to use a guide that has good relations with the communities, or a tour company that is partially Huao-owned. Coca-based guides that the author recommends are Juan Enomenga, author Randy Smith, Julio Jarrín and Tseremp Ernesto Juanka. Travelers with a particular interest in entering the reserve are advised to ask around for these guides in Coca.

Travelers who want to visit the Huaoranis, and are sensitive to their situation can write to **Amazon Jungle Tours**, PO Box 17-21-1066, Quito, or inquire at Papa Dan's Bar by the river in Coca. **Tropic Ecological Adventures** runs a program with the Huaorani, where visitors spend a few nights in Huaorani territory and experience their way of life. Andy Drumm, the founder of Tropic, is a Fellow of Britain's Royal Geographical Society, an advisor to the Huaorani people and works with Moi Enomenga, who was featured in the acclaimed 1995 book *Savages* by Joe Kane. For more information contact Tropic ✆ (02) 225907 FAX (02) 560746 E-MAIL tropic@uio.satnet.sat, Avenida República 307 and Almagro, Edificio "Taurus," Dpto. 1-A, Quito.

The rainforest is a cornucopia of medicinal plants, many of them yet to be discovered.

Central Oriente

TENA

The small town of Tena (population 15,000) is the capital of Napo Province, the biggest but most sparsely-populated of Ecuador's provinces. The town is situated among low-lying hills, green valleys and fast-flowing rivers where agriculture spreads along road corridors, but tracts of thick forest still carpet riverbanks and hillsides. Founded by the Spanish in 1560 at the strategic junction of Río Tena and Río Pano, the town was an important colonial center in the Ecuadorian Amazon for trade and Christian proselytizing. Only about six hours by bus from Quito, Tena is one of the most accessible destinations in the Oriente and increasingly a base for many types of jungle adventures.

While missionaries go into the jungle to convert the natives, young backpackers go in search of spiritual knowledge and simple life in natural surroundings. When they return from jungle trips and Quichua villages, they enthuse about rafting down rivers, showering under waterfalls, exploring caves, tracking down ancient rock inscriptions, sleeping in jungle huts, spotting rare species of wildlife and medicinal plants, panning for gold, entering blowpipe shooting competitions, sampling exotic foods and participating in shamanic ceremonies. Above all they speak about the friendliness and amazing knowledge of plants and animals of their Quichua hosts. One friend of mine was shown how to roll a wound-up vine leaf over his legs and arms to pull out the hairs, as the people in the *campamento* (camp) where he was staying thought he would look more attractive without body hair.

GENERAL INFORMATION

There's a none-too-useful CETUR **Tourist Office** by the market, near the **airport** north of town, which tends to be open Monday to Fridays in the mornings and afternoons. As usual in Ecuador, you get better information by chatting with travel agents and fellow travelers. **Flight destinations** are limited to Coca and Puyo, though a planned route to Quito might be in operation now. The Terminal Terrestre **bus terminal** is just southeast of town, on the road to Puerto Napo. Bus destinations include Baeza, Quito, Ambato, Lago Agrio, Coca (a grueling, seven-hour, bone-shaking ride) and Puyo. For telephone calls, **EMETEL** is at Olmedo and Montalvo. The **Correo** (Post Office) is two blocks south on the main plaza.

WHAT TO SEE AND DO

Though a pleasant town, Tena isn't an architectural gem, nor are there many attractions aside from socializing with locals and fellow travelers. Most people come to Tena to **explore the jungle** or **pan for gold** in the rivers, and they prefer to stay in *cabaña* complexes outside of town. Several agencies in town can help with these activities, though don't expect to get rich quick with gold; a few grains are all you're likely to find.

A good starting point for organizing a budget jungle trip is **FOIN** (Federación de Organizaciones Indígenas) who represent many Quichua communities in the upper Napo area. Operating under the name **RICANCIE** (the acronym for their ecotourism and cultural network) programs have been developed in reaction to the exploitation of outside tourist operators coming into their villages. There are a number of programs from camping in the jungle to taking part in spiritual ceremonies with a shaman. Accommodation is usually in traditional Quichua *cabañas*, and it is possible to visit several indian communities. Sharing your culture by dancing or singing with your hosts, and helping with communal work may be part of the program. Inquiries should be made care of Tarquino Tapuy, RICANCIE ✆/FAX (06) 886614, Bellavista Baja, Calle Atahualpa and 9 de Octubre 435, Casilla 243, Tena, Napo. Prices are between US$35 and US$50 per day, depending on the size of the group. It helps if you speak Spanish, but there are some English-speaking guides.

"Jungle Trip in Tena, English-speaking Guide." This is the headline of an account of

PREVIOUS PAGES: The languid tranquillity of the jungle LEFT hides thousands of species of living creatures, such as this parakeet RIGHT. OPPOSITE: Panning for gold is an ancient practice in this gold-rich land.

a jungle trip made by an experienced traveler. "I can't think of anyone I would rather be in the jungle with than Olmedo and Oswaldo. As guides they are the best a extremely knowledgeable about the flora and fauna, giving fascinating insights into the secrets of the jungle...." Travelers in Ecuador were passing this account from hand to hand like a treasure map. Those who did go exploring with Olmedo and Oswaldo (his son) Cerda were extremely satisfied. Prices in 1997 were only US$20 per person per day. To find these **all-star guides**, go to the Cerda family house at 9 de Octubre 356, Barrio Bella Vista Baja, 10 minutes from the bus station, or ask at the agencies and hotels in town.

Another highly-recommended agency for jungle tours is **Amarongachi Tours**, which operates out of their own hotel, **Traveler's Lodging Amarongachi** ☎ (06) 886372, 15 de Noviembre 432. The company arranges jungle stays or accommodation at their own **Shangri-La Cabañas**, on a cliff overlooking the Río Anzu. It has established joint ventures with **Quichua communities**, most of which are along the Río Jatunyacu, southwest of Talag.

Local Quichua *cabaña* complexes are popular with budget travelers, not only because prices are reasonable, but also because the visitor will have a more intimate contact with people in villages. Upmarket resorts aren't common in the area, though the cabaña complex of **Hacienda Chaupi-Shungo**, overlooking the junction of the Misahuallí and Inchillaqui rivers, a kilometer (just over a half mile) southwest of Archidona, has been described as one of the best-kept secrets of the Tena region. At about US$30 per day including meals, the friendly and tranquil hacienda is popular with honeymooners and others in search of total relaxation.

At the other end of the tranquillity scale, for **whitewater rafting** and **kayaking** through spectacular jungle scenery, great things are said about **Ríos Ecuador**. Highly experienced guides run trips for all levels of skill and experience, some of them through giant rapids and roller coaster waves. Based on worldwide experience, the company believes that the Upper Napo and Río Misahuallí offer some of the best and most exciting kayaking and rafting in the world. Chief instructor Genner Coronel is one of the country's top kayakers and has competed all over the world. Rates are from about US$50 per day to US$300 and up for a full, five-day kayaking course. For more informations, contact Ríos Ecuador at ☎ (02) 553727

E-MAIL kayak@riosecua.ecx.ec at Apartado Postal 17-07-9762, Quito, or go to their headquarters in Tena inside the Hostal Camba Huasi building, across the street from the south side of the bus terminal.

Another stop on the Tena adventure trail is climbing the 3,900 m (13,000 ft) **Volcán Sumaco**, a five- to six-day round trip involving hacking your way with a machete through the jungle wilderness of **Parque Nacional Sumaco-Galeras**, one of the newest and least-known national parks. Contact one of the climbing agencies in Quito for more information.

Ancient and curious **rock inscriptions**, known as petroglyphs, are a unique attraction in the Tena region. In spite of years of research their origin or significance has not been explained. It is believed they were carved for traditional rites. There's a good guide to these mysterious markings in *The Ecotourist's Guide to the Ecuadorian Amazon*, available in Quito bookstores. Though the book gives their locations, most of the petroglyphs are buried under vegetation and you will need a guide to find them. It also gives tentative interpretations of the ideographs such as, "looks like a spider, or a frog, but is in fact a jaguar," or, "spirit that blends itself with a light ray."

The Tena area is also known for its numerous and magnificent **limestone caves**, many of which haven't been explored, or even discovered yet. The most famous are the gigantic **Cuevas de Jumandi**, about four kilometers (two and a half miles) north of the village of Archidona, which is 10 km (six miles) north of Tena. To get around the caves you need a reliable, strong flashlight, rubber boots and a hat. The hat not only protects you from low-slung **stalactites**, but also from the resident **vampire bats** whose radar navigation systems don't detect human hair.

WHERE TO STAY AND EAT

Most of the accommodation in Tena is basic and inexpensive. The afore-mentioned **Travelers' Lodging Amarongachi** ✆ (06) 886372, on 15 de Noviembre, two blocks north of the bus station, is highly-rated and popular, costing around US$15 for a double. Some of the rooms have balconies, and there's a view from the rooftop patio. With about the same rates, **Hostal Villa Belén** ✆ (06) 886228, on the Baeza road near the airport is a clean, modern hotel within an old hacienda with a garden and restaurant. More upmarket, but still not too expensive is **Hostal Los Yutzos**, with a garden and beautiful views of the river at the southeast end of town. In the same price range are **Hotel Turismo Amazónica** in the center of town, and **Hotel Internacional El Mol**, near the airport. There are several budget hostels in town, though many suffer from common Oriente problems — lack of constant water supplies and inadequate plumbing.

The restaurants in most of these hotels are the best in Tena, the one at **Villa Belén** being particularly worth trying. **Cositas Ricas**, next to the Amarongachi, is a favorite haunt of travelers. Their vegetarian fare is carefully prepared and the varieties of juices are a feature. In the budget range, the restaurant at **Residencial Enmita**, on Simón Bolívar south of the airport, is also good.

Tena isn't famous for nightlife, but those with an ear to the ground will hear some salsa beats on weekends at **La Gallera**, **Tattoo's** and **El Rodeo** down by the river.

MISAHUALLÍ

Misahuallí is either an over-touristy village, surrounded by despoiled rainforest and depleted wildlife, or a charming river port, conveniently situated for jungle excursions. Both views are valid. True, jungle tourism makes the place tick. Several agencies, guides, restaurants and a variety of accommodations cater to a steady stream of tourists and travelers who want to experience the thrills and adventures of the rainforest. Like Tena, Misahuallí is reasonably accessible from Quito and tour prices, if you shop around, are less expensive than in Quito.

Much of the primary forest in the area has been cut down for agriculture, destroying the natural habitat of large mammals such as jaguars, tapirs, monkeys, capybaras and ocelots. But on high escarpments, and in deep ravines that are inaccessible to the set-

Exploring the jungle can be a test of one's powers of adaptation, as well as a journey into mankind's past.

tlers, there are large tracts of virgin forest abundantly populated by birds, butterflies, insects and plants and flowers. The further east you go away from the settled areas, the more prolific the wildlife. As for charm, it is also true that Misahuallí does have its attractions, with its picturesque location at the confluence of Río Napo and Río Misahuallí, its surrounding network of meandering waterways, river beaches, rapids, waterfalls and panning for gold along the shores of the Napo. In addition, there are several fine ecolodges down river, as well as a number of Quichua communities that welcome guests.

GENERAL INFORMATION

With a population of only about 4,000, Misahuallí isn't well endowed with urban amenities. On the Pununo road there's an **EMETEL telephone office**, with only two lines, and there are a few **shops** where you get basic supplies. There's also a **doctor** at the end of the Tena road who runs the **pharmacy** near the main plaza.

For accommodation, Misahuallí is no Saint-Tropez. A good, clean choice is the helpful **Hotel Albergue Español** FAX (06) 584912, by the river, at about US$10 per person per night. With about the same rates, and also clean and helpful is **Hostal Dayuma Lodge**, owned by Douglas Clarke. **El Paisano** (also known as Paleface Inn) on the Pununo road about 100 m (330 ft) from the central plaza, is popular with backpackers, has a garden restaurant with vegetarian food and hammocks. For jungle lodges, see below.

The best restaurants are in the hotels listed above. Beyond these, there are the usual *comedores* serving standard *desayuno* (breakfast), *almuerzo* (lunch) and *merienda* (dinner).

There are plenty of **travel agencies** and **guides** in Misahuallí, though some are relocating up to Coca where jungle tourism is expanding. But finding the right jungle tour may take two or three days if you want to save money by joining a group.

One of the key factors in choosing a tour is the guide. If possible, meet the guide who will be taking you through the jungle to see if you get along with each other, whether he or she is knowledgeable about the things that interest you and, most importantly, how well you share a common language. Also ask to see the **guide's license**, as there are many stories of people being cheated by unlicensed guides. And check the terms of the agreement carefully to see what you have and have not paid for. Rubber boots, for instance, an essential item, might not be included in the deal. The usual rates for guides is between US$25 and US$50 per day, half of which you should pay at the end of the trip. Before leaving downriver you must show your passport and register its number at the port captain's office on the waterfront.

Operators might seem charming and plausible when you talk to them in their offices, but when it comes to equipment, food, routes and other facilities they might be a bit shaky. One trick is for guides to say they'll take you to their home village, but once there they have nothing to do with you. They've simply used your tour as a way to visit their family. Untrustworthy operators, it seems, will go to any lengths to win your confidence, even falsely using the name of a well-known guide. The best way to find a guide is by **word of mouth**. Talk to other travelers and read the comment books kept in some of hotels and cafés. The South America Explorers Club in Quito is also a source of recommendations.

JUNGLE LODGES

There are at least seven major jungle lodges downriver from Misahuallí, and several budget cabaña complexes. The closest, **Misahuallí Jungle Lodge**, a 100-m (330-ft) canoe ride from the town to the other side of the river, mostly caters to groups but also welcomes drop-in travelers. A three-day, two-night trip from Quito, including full board and jungle excursions, costs around US$200. Overnight stays are negotiable.

Eight kilometers (five miles) downriver is the famous **Jatun Sacha** (Big Forest) **Biological Reserve**, a 2,000-hectare (5,000-acre) tropical wet forest, one of the most biologically-diverse tropical areas on earth. No less than 532 bird species have been recorded in the reserve along with 863 butterflies and more than 2,500 plant species. Scientific staff and student researchers from Ecuador and overseas help with reforestation and agroforestry projects as well in the Amazon Plant Conservation Center. Although the reserve and some of its facilities are open to the public, non-scientists aren't usually allowed to stay in the reserve's residential *cabañas*. Instead, they are directed to the luxurious and spectacular **Cabañas Aliñahui** (Beautiful View) nearby, which is managed by the non-profit Jatun Sacha Foundation. For more information contact the foundation at Casilla 17-12-867, Quito, or the Jatun Sacha Foundation ☎/FAX (02) 441592 E-MAIL jatsacha@jsacha.ecx.ec.

Continuing down river for about 10km (six miles) you come to the large and lavish **Casa del Suizo** on a bluff overlooking the river. This is about as good as you can get in rainforest luxury. At about US$200 for a three-day package you get a full range of activities, including rafting and a visit to the **AmaZOOnica** animal rescue center, as well as comfortable cabañas, great food and landscaped tropical gardens. Explorer Tours ☎ (02) 522220 FAX (02) 508872, Reina Victoria 1235 and Lizardo Garcia, PO Box 1608, Quito provides information and makes reservations.

Other jungle lodges further downriver are the rustic but comfortable **Cabañas Anaconda**, **Dayuma Lodge** (at the confluence of the Puni and Arajuno rivers), and **Hotel Jaguar**, one of the oldest tourist facilities on the Napo, built in 1969. Inquire with Quito travel agents for more information on these lodges. The more-remote **Yachana Lodge**, in the village of Mondañam is halfway between Misahuallí and Coca on the Río Napo. The lodge a program of the non-profit organization **FUNEDESIN** to work with indigenous groups. In a reciprocal arrangement, local people learn about things like bee keeping, while tourists learn about medicinal plants. For more information contact FUNEDESIN ☎ (02) 541862 E-MAIL dtm @pi.pro.ec. at Andrade Marín 188 and Diego de Almargo, Casilla 17-17-92, Quito.

For an authentic experience staying in a Quichua community contact **RICANCIE** in Tena as detailed above under TENA, WHAT TO SEE AND DO. The indigenous organization works with several Misahuallí communities, including **Capirona**, the first in the scheme, and the model for subsequent communities. I have not visited Capirona but I have heard glowing reports of it. The *Ecotourist's Guide* says, "The Capirona tourism program emphasizes the presentation of Quichua culture, through traditional local foods, Quichua folk tales, pottery-making, blowgun demonstrations and jungle hikes highlighting medicinal plants and places associated with legends."

How to Get There

The easiest and quickest way to get to and from Misahuallí is by bus. Buses depart several times a day from the main plaza to Tena, where there are onward connections. Buses also leave from Tena to the small downriver village of Ahuano, beyond Misahuallí on the north bank of the Napo. But the bus has to take the road on the south bank to La Punta (not marked on many maps), and passengers cross to Ahuano by dugout canoe. This is the best way to get to Casa del Suizo unless the lodge has already arranged transport.

A more romantic and exciting way to travel up and down the Río Napo is by boat. There is usually a passenger boat from Misahuallí to downriver settlements in the morning, that costs about US$3. Passage in your own boat costs about 10 times more. Motorized dugout canoes make the six-hour journey between Coca and Misahuallí once or twice a week, but their schedules depend on demand and river conditions. Ask around the port to find out which boats are leaving and when.

Pink dolphins can sometimes be spotted breaking the surface of placid rivers in Ecuador's Amazonian forests.

PUYO

As capital of Pastaza Province and with a population of 20,000, the town of Puyo is one of the most important trade centers in the Oriente. But the town's significance to travelers and tourists is as a jumping-off point for trips deeper into the *selva* (wet forest). Flights from Quito and small airstrips in the jungle go through the airport, Shell, named after the oil company that built it. Shell is about 10km (six miles) west of Puyo near Mera on the Baños road.

Travelers mostly stay overnight in Puyo if they are waiting for a connecting flight or for a bus going back up into the highlands. At the time of writing the road from Puyo to Baños was only open from 6 PM Sunday to 6 AM Tuesday, so if you return from a jungle trip outside of this window and want to get to Baños, you'll have time to kill in Puyo. If you do get stuck in Puyo don't expect too much activity. Though human settlements existed here for many thousands of years, the town has not adapted to gringo travelers. On the whole, you are better off in Baños. When the improved Baños road is open, expected in 1998, Puyo's value as a gateway to the Oriente will be greatly enhanced.

GENERAL INFORMATION

The **Terminal Terrestre bus terminal** is on the west side of town, though after 6 PM most buses go into the center. Buses leave for the main Oriente towns as well as Guayaquil, Ambato and Quito. On days when the Baños road isn't open, buses going west have to go through Tena. Basic utilities include an **EMETEL** telephone office, a block west of the market and a **Post Office**, a block south of the main plaza.

WHAT TO SEE AND DO

When you've finished writing postcards, take a stroll northwards up Avenida 9 de Octubre for about a half hour until you get to a rope bridge over Río Puyo. Cross the bridge into the grandly named **Parque Pedagógico Etno-Botánico Omarere**. Here you will find a botanical garden with medicinal plants and some traditional Quechua homes, one of which is home to a real, living shaman. You can also swim in the river by the park.

If you are interested in supporting alternative jungle technologies and protecting the indigenous rainforest peoples' way of life, contact **Spirit of Water** ☎ (03) 883618 FAX (03) 883021, Apartado 16-01-709, Puyo, Provincia Pastaza. The Achuar independent organization, OINAE FAX (03) 883827, is at Ceslao Marín 583 and 27 de Febrero, Puyo.

Puyo isn't a tourist town like Tena or Misahuallí, so there are few travel agents. Most people heading off for the deep jungle have already made travel arrangements in Quito or Guayaquil. One agency which has been recommended is **Amazonia Touring** ☎ (03) 883219 FAX (03) 883064, 9 de Octubre and Atahualpa.

WHERE TO STAY AND EAT

At the top end of the scale, **Hostería Turingia** ☎ (03) 885180 FAX (03) 885384, on Orelana and Villamil, has clean *cabañas* in a tropical garden and a good restaurant. The travelers' choice is the clean and friendly **Hotel Europa Internacional** ☎ (03) 885228 FAX (03) 885384, on Avenida 9 de Octubre between Atahualpa and Orellana, which also has a budget restaurant downstairs. Aside from dining at these two hotels, **El Mesón Europa**, near the bus station, has a good reputation and just for its jazzy name it's worth trying **Cha-Cha-Cha Pollo a la Braya** near the Turingia.

KAPAWI ECOLOGICAL RESERVE

Our 200-km (125-mile) flight in a five-seat light aircraft from Shell to the airstrip near the Peruvian border would take 45 minutes. Spread below us, the jungle canopy seemedlike an unbroken sea of green broccoli coiled with meandering brown rivers. From time to time we looked down at a scattering of huts in a clearing in the jungle. Then our droning Cessna plunged into a billowing mass of clouds, its small windows became

OPPOSITE: A flash of bright color in the green canopy draws the attention of a tourist.

sheets of opaque white paper and I wondered how our radar-less pilot was going to find his way out of this bubble of blindness.

Below us was one of the most remote, unspoiled, and most pristine part of the Ecuadorian Amazon basin, so far untouched by logging or oil drilling. When oilmen came to make a survey here a few weeks earlier, the local Achuar promptly kidnapped them. The Achuar have a reputation for violence; revenge is part of their culture. But they released the oilmen unharmed, warning them never to return.

The Achuar are the most isolated of all Ecuadorian *indígenas*; their first contact with the outside world was as recent as the late 1970s. In that hot, wet wilderness there is one Achuar per square kilometer. They live in small, nomadic family communities. Every few years, when the soil is no longer fertile in their settlement, they move deeper into the jungle to slash and burn another plot for manioc gardens. As hunters, gatherers and fishermen, they are highly self-sufficient, but in our market economy they earn as little as US$70 per year.

The Cessna bumped to a halt on the red earth strip. Heaving backpacks, we clambered down a muddy path through thick foliage to a fast-flowing river the color of an old copper coin. A dugout canoe powered by an outboard motor sped us upriver to the wooden landing stage for Kapawi Lodge. A small delegation of Achuar in sarongs and white shirts greeted us with trays of seasonal palm hearts. According to Achuar calendar, based on the movements of the Pleiades and the star Aldabaran, this was the season *Uwi juarmau*, fruit time of the chonta palm.

Completed in 1996 after two years of construction, Kapawi Lodge is state-of-the-art ecotourism. The architecture and building materials for the cluster of buildings, perched on stilts along the shore of a lake, are entirely in Achuar tradition, using wood, palm leaves and twine. The long walkways connecting the individual huts are all made of materials from the rainforest. There's nary a nail in the place. But there are also many twentieth century conveniences in this luxury, environmentally-friendly biosphere in the middle of the the most remote rainforest: solar energy, biodegradable soaps, and specially-made bags for shower water which are spread outside to heat in the sun. Also in evidence are electric lights, mosquito screens, kitchen utensils, computers, radios, walkie-talkies, refrigerators, and outboard motors.

But the most ecotouristic element of this project is the role of the local Achuar. CANODROS SA of Guayaquil, the company that built and owns the lodge, has agreed to pay the local community US$2,000 a month for the use of the land, which they will return after 15 years, along with the lodge itself. CANODROS SA pledged it will train the Achuar during this period, and the majority of the employees will be Achuar.

For the tourist, Kapawi offers magic and mystery, not to mention sweat, fear, and out of body experiences. The magic comes when you paddle a canoe through a glassy lagoon listening to the jungle all around you: pipes and whistles, trills and drones, the jabbering of monkeys, the odd plop of fish and the soft *kuala-kuala* of the paddle in the water. There's magic, too, when you trek though shady glades under giant kapok trees and watch a troop of leaf-cutter ants going about their business, or when you sit back on your balcony, beverage in hand, overlooking the dark lake listening to the high wine of jungle insects and the deep croak of frogs.

The mystery is all around you, too. What is that sound? What is this creepy creature? How do you see the spirits of the jungle, in which Achuar believe: the anaconda, the pink dolphin and the Harpy Eagle? What happens if you drink the hallucinogenic concoction they call *nataam* (scientific name: *banisteriopsis*).

I asked this last question of the managers at Kapawi who had tried nataam, for research purposes, of course. "I turned into a vine," he said. "and my body started growing leaves. Then a huge anaconda, that became a string of DNA molecules, wrapped me up. I was being pulled down into the underworld, but I resisted and forced myself to wake up. I was really scared. I rushed out of the house and bathed in the river. Somebody came out to try to calm me down. I went back to bed and had visions of my own death. I saw my body lying in a coffin."

"For about a month after that I felt death was sitting on my shoulder. I felt it following me down jungle paths and I would turn around to look behind me. Paradoxically, I felt very good to be alive, each minute of the day."

The second time the manager took *nataam* with the shaman he did not resist the feeling of being tempted in the underworld. "I just let go and had the most beautiful experience, but the shaman told me not to tell anyone about it afterwards."

This same manager arranged for me and another guest to spend a night at a shaman's house. Wachikiat, an Achuar guide, piloted the canoe up the Pastaza River and accompanied us to the settlement in the jungle. During the afternoon we sat for hours on a little wooden bench drinking *nijiamanch*, a slightly acidic, yeasty, milky-white broth, made by one of the wives of the shaman by chewing up manioc and spitting it into a big, earthenware pot where it ferments for a few days. It is said that this "beer," or *chicha* as it's called by the Quichuas, tastes of the woman who makes it. As practiced beer drinkers, we had no trouble quaffing it down from bowls continually refilled by the shaman's first wife. Following Achuar custom, we carefully avoided looking her in the eye as she served us.

But we chickened out on the opportunity to sample *nataam*. While the shaman, whose creased face looked like a deflated leather football, sat in the back of the thatched hut singing songs to himself, we fixed up mosquito nets on a bamboo platform in a nearby hut and watched little kids playing with a jaguar kitten. Before crawling under our nets in the early evening, Wachikiat told us — or rather mimed — how he had twice fought a jaguar in the jungle without a weapon. We went to sleep to the sound of the shaman's song.

I awoke at 3 AM. In the dark the women of the house were already making a fire to for the "tea." This is the most important time of the day for the Achuar. Before dawn, the members of the community drink huge quantities of a brew made from some sort of leaf, which tastes quite pleasant, while at the same time making you want to vomit. While drinking tea people discuss their dreams of the previous night and decide what to do that day. Having gulped the tea at great speed and belched a bit, they walk out of the hut and throw up in the bushes. This literally out-of-body experience is considered to be a way of cleansing the stomach. If, like me, you are unable to regurgitate the liquid you end up feeling ill the rest of the day.

Because there was no shared language, there was almost no verbal communication between us gringos and the Achuars throughout our stay. But after we left in our canoe Wachikiat told us that the shaman said he had enjoyed our visit and we were welcome to return. Next time I'll try *nataam*.

For more information on Kapawi Ecological Reserve contact CANODROS SA ☎ (04) 285711 or 280164 FAX (04) 287651 E-MAIL ecotourism@canodros.com.ec WEB SITE http://mia.lac.net/canodros or write to Luis Urdaneta 1418 and Avenida del Ejercito, PO Box 8442, Guayaquil, Ecuador.

Forms of life that you may never have seen or imagined are on display in limitless variety in the rainforest.

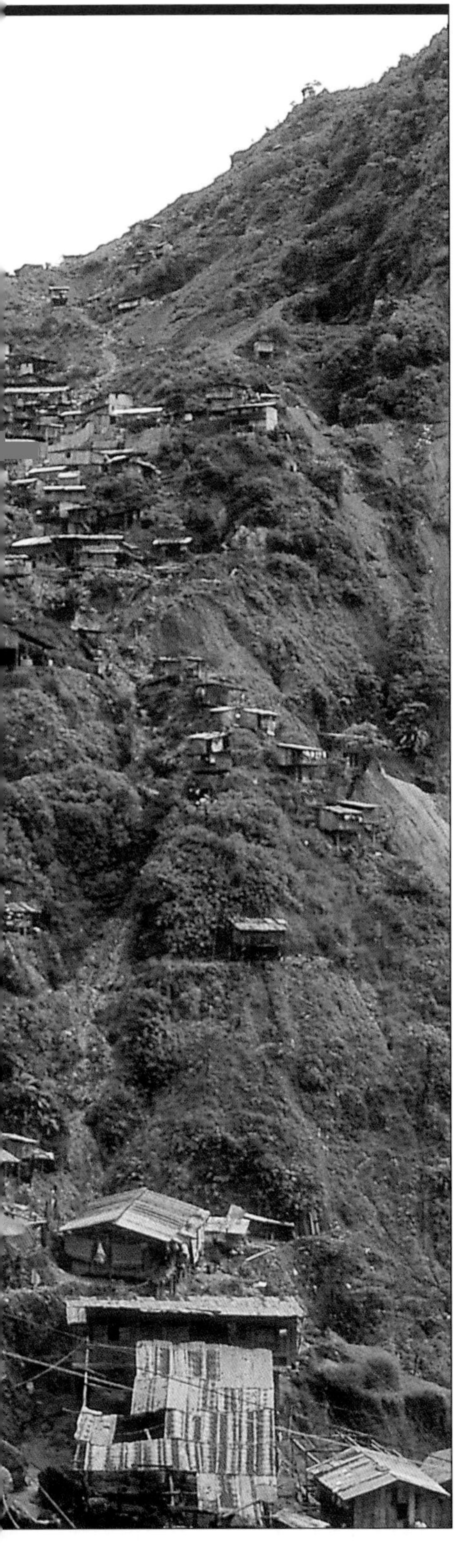

Southern Oriente

FROM PUYO, THE SOUTHERN ORIENTE HIGHWAY bumps and rattles along the eastern foothills of the Andes. Through the open sides of lurching *rancheros* passengers look out at deteriorating concrete towns, cattle ranches, sugar cane fields, coffee plantations and dense, tangled vegetation. Inca gold came from some areas in the Southern Oriente, and gold is still mined in technologically primitive open-sky operations and by ever-hopeful individuals and families. The southern part of the Oriente isn't as popular with tourists as the areas to the north. But for those who like to travel way off-the-beaten track there is the advantage of visiting places where the rare gringo is greeted with more than usual friendliness. The town of Sucúa, south of Macas, is the headquarters of the Shuar Indian federation, from where tours can be arranged to Shuar territory near the Peruvian border.

Ecuador's southeast border with Peru has been a sore spot ever since the 1942 treaty between the two countries. Ecuador claims this was an unfair treaty that allowed Peru to expropriate territories which rightly belong to Ecuador. From time to time there are border skirmishes. In 1995, an incident escalated into a heavy fighting with many more casualties than either side was prepared to admit. Many people were evacuated from the strategically-located town of Macas.

MACAS

The capital of Morona-Santiago province, Macas is an old Spanish town that had been a trading and missionary post for some 400 years. But with a fast-growing population of 15,000 and more and more new buildings, the town is acquiring a modern face and is becoming important as a tourist center. At present Macas can only be reached from the north or south on Route 45, the southern Oriente highway, or by plane. But a new road down the Sierra is under construction from Guamote on the Pan-American Highway. The project will give an added boost to Macas, though there has been a lot of criticism because the road will pass through Sangay National Park threatening the habitats of endangered species like the Mountain Tapir, of which only some 2,000 survive.

In line with the town's new image there is a large and relatively new **Terminal Terrestre bus station**, an **airport** with flights to and from Quito, a quite new main **plaza** and a **cathedral** that was completed in 1992. For international phone calls, the **EMETEL** office is on Avenida 24 de Mayo between Cuenca and Sucre. With double rooms around US$20 per night, the clean, modern high-rise **Peñón del Oriente** ✆ (07) 700124 FAX (07) 700450, on Domingo Comin 837

and Amazonas, is everybody's nomination for best-value hotel in town. **Hostal Esmeralda** ✆ (07) 700160, near the airport, is also clean, modern and very good value. Recommended restaurants are **La Randimpa** for Cuban food and music, and **Alonde Ivan** for tropical atmosphere and *ceviche*.

TOURS FROM MACAS

Though not as popular as a base for jungle exploration as Coca or Misahuallí, the vast Amazon basin stretches out east of Macas, with all its potential for adventure. Visits to local **Shuar communities** can be arranged, as well as horseback riding, whitewater rafting, fishing and treks to remote caves, hot springs and waterfalls.

PREVIOUS PAGES: Shacks huddled on the hillside LEFT are home to miners seeking their fortune in the gold mines of Nambija, near Zamora. A handful of gold RIGHT can make a man rich for life. OPPOSITE: Modern mining technology has yet to replace human workhorses. ABOVE: Tools of the miner's trade.

At **Miazal**, for example, 50km (31miles) southeast of Macas over the Cutucu Mountain Range, a hot spring bubbles from the earth and flows from a rock in a naturally **hot waterfall**, while next to it is a **cold waterfall** of pure mountain water. Where else can you find natural hot and cold waterfalls side by side in the middle of a tropical rainforest? There's no road to Miazal and it is a tough 50-km (31-mile) hike from Macas that takes a few days. Instead, visitors come by light aircraft and stay in the simple, but comfortable, Shuar-style **Miazal Lodge**. In the nearby Shuar community visitors learn about the way of life of a people who live in close contact with their natural world.

In the vicinity of Miazal there are caves which are inhabited by colonies of the extraordinary **Oilbird**. These huge, nocturnal, fruit-eating creatures live more like bats than birds and use a form of sonar navigation in the form of audible clicks which keeps them from crashing into the walls in the pitch-black caves. Oilbirds have long been prized by the indians because of their fatty flesh that they boil down into oil and use for cooking and lighting. The best-known Oilbird cave is **Cueva de los Tayos**, near Santiago between Méndez and Morona, but you'll need a guide to find them.

For more information about trips from Macas, including to the Sangay National Park (see page 126 in CENTRAL HIGHLANDS) contact **Ikiaam** ("jungle" in Shuar) ☎ (07) 700457, near the Terminal Terrestre in Macas, and run by helpful and knowledgeable Shuar guides. **ETSA** ☎ (07) 700550, which is inside the Terminal Terrestre building, is also recommended as a reliable Shuar agent, as is **Tuntiak** ☎ (07) 700185, in front of the Peñón del Oriente. **Ecotrek** ☎ (07) 841927 FAX (07) 835387 E-MAIL ecotrek@az.pro.ec, at Larga 7-108 and Luis Cordero in Cuenca arranges trips to Miazal.

SOUTH TO ZAMORA

The Oriente Highway continues south from Macas to the small town of **Sucúa**, a major center of Shuar Indians (also known as Jivaro) who are best known for their erstwhile habit of cutting off and shrinking the heads of their enemies. You can get infor-

mation about Shuar culture and shop for handicrafts, but because of missionaries you won't see any *tsantsas* (shrunken heads) in the town's **Shuar Cultural Center**. The best place to see *tsantsas* is at the Municipal Museum in Guayaquil. Sucúa is also the location of the headquarters of the **Shuar Federation**, from whom you have to obtain permission to visit Shuar villages.

Carrying on southwards you pass through the small towns of **Méndéz** and **Limón**. Unless you have some personal business, or you're on the run from the CIA, there's not much incentive to stop in either. From Limón you can either travel on south, or branch off west on a spectacular road over the mountains to **Cuenca**. The narrow, unpaved roads in this area aren't

always passable because of landslides, floods or other disasters, especially during the rainy months of April to June, so be prepared for delays.

The next town down the spectacular, bone-shaking road is **Gualaquiza**, about four hours from Limón. Its remoteness and its scenic setting in the hills are the town's main attractions, as well as nearby unexplored **Inca ruins**, deserted **caves** and the **Salesian Mission** of **Bomboiza**. Further on, the village of **Yantzaza** is said to be one of the fastest-growing towns in Zamora Chinchipe Province, because of mining activity. Nearby is the Wild West, gold-rush town of **Nambija**, once a source of Inca gold, which you are unlikely to visit unless you want to risk life for a false vision of sudden riches.

If you have made your way all the way down the Southern Oriente Highway by bus, you will be greatly relieved to reach the town of **Zamora**. There might not be much to do in this quiet provincial capital, but at least you shower or bathe away aches and pains from your stiff and shaken frame. The best hotel is the **Internacional Torres**, though **Hotel Maguna** is comfortable and popular. From Zamora, take the scenic road up into the Sierra to **Loja**. From there you have a choice of heading off elsewhere by bus or plane or by making your way to **Vilcabamba** (see page 144 in THE DEEP SOUTH) for some well-earned rest and recuperation.

The streets of Nambija are not the safest in Ecuador.

The Pacific Coast

REINA DEL MAR

THOUGH BETTER KNOWN FOR ITS ANDEAN MOUNTAINS, Amazonian rainforest and the unique Galápagos Islands, Ecuador has a long, varied and fascinating coastline that until recently was underrated. Stretching some 1,500 km (937 miles) from the border with Colombia to Peru in the south, the Pacific coast embraces long stretches of deserted beaches, with warm swimming waters, working fishing villages, luxury vacation resorts, ecolodges, mangrove swamps, and steamy ports, surfing beaches, wildlife sanctuaries and environmentally damaging shrimp farms.

At present there is no continuous road down the coast, which means that many areas are isolated and rarely visited. My trip along the coast in a Land Rover, from San Lorenzo to Guayaquil, included several sections where we had to drive along the sand for lack of a road. Other times, the owner and driver of the "buggy," Frankie Malinson (the American-Ecuadorian owner of Savage World Tours in Quito) had to make a long inland detour, while I continued down the coast by boat. The journey was further complicated because *La Costa* had recently been hit by storms that closed roads, destroyed bridges and even battered and shut the well-known Alandaluz Ecological Resort and Tourist Center. It was a journey of adventure, discovery, fun, and in places, perhaps, a touch of danger. Some areas of the coast aren't for the faint hearted.

Current road-building programs are starting to open up much of the coast, making it much more accessible. A coastal road to the northern border is almost finished, and will bring increasing numbers of Colombian tourists. In one sense, now is the time to visit the unspoiled Ecuadorian coastline, while it is still relatively undeveloped. On the other hand, development is bringing with it badly needed infrastructure, accessibility and tourist facilities.

Though it has no precise inland demarcation, Ecuador's coastal region generates the major part of the country's industrial and agricultural wealth, and is home to roughly half its population. But no love is lost between the coast and the sierra. Coastal people call those from the sierra *burros* (donkeys), while *serranos* say people from the costa are *monos* (monkeys). Whatever these differences, many agree that *La Costa* is a state of being, a state of mind and a place where people like to party and stay out late. Certainly it is where Ecuadorian vacationers go to relax and have fun.

SAN LORENZO

Ecuador's most-northern coastal town is linked to Ibarra in the highlands by the extraordinary *autoferro* railway that takes most of a day to descend from an altitude of 2,210 m (7,370 ft) to the coastal plains (see page 109 in NORTHERN HIGHLANDS). A rough road that also links the two towns is gradually being upgraded and will eventually supersede the railway, which was badly damaged by the El Niño floods in 1997 and 1998.

Whichever way you come, you may be mildly surprised when you arrive in this hot, tropical coastal town, where the streets are mostly unpaved, full of pot holes and sprouting weeds. Most houses are ramshackle and the inhabitants, most of whom are black, have a languid, easy-going air and never seem to be in much hurry. San Lorenzo isn't striking for its affluence or energy, especially during the heat of the day. Come nightfall, however, when the air gets cooler, people saunter in the streets, sit in the park chatting with their friends, or just stand around watching the world go by. A salsa beat or marimba riff fills the air. "Walk and learn," they say here. "Walk and know."

BACKGROUND

San Lorenzo dates back to the sixteenth century, when a slave boat from Africa was wrecked off the coast. The escaped slaves, or maroons as they were called, established themselves around this estuary of islands and mangrove swamps. In their early days, the maroons allied with the freebooting British pirates, including Sir Francis Drake, were harassing Spanish galleons. The British supplied them with guns and cannon for use against their colonial masters, while the maroons gave the British food and a haven.

PREVIOUS PAGES: Coconut palm LEFT at a hostería near Río Verde on the coast of Esmeraldas Province. A natural abundance of the fruit RIGHT made Ecuador the original banana republic. OPPOSITE: A lonesome fisherman sings Latin-style blues near Chanduy.

THE PACIFIC COAST

0 2 4 6 80 km
0 1 2 3 4 5

QUITO

N
W E
S

COLOMB
Isla Palma Real
San Pedro
Mataje
Limones (Valdéz)
San Lorenzo
La Tola
Tambillo
Isla la Tola
Tobar Dono
Las Peñas
Borbón
Cayapas Mataje Nat. Park
Carondelet
Awa Indian Preserve
Río Verde
Colope
Lagaro
Steve's Lodge
ESMERALDAS
Montalvo
Urbina
Alto Tambo
Atacames
Vuelta Larga
Súa
Pta. Galera
Tonsupa
Playón
Lita
Quingüe
Galera
Chinca
Río Esmeraldas
R. Santiago
2070
Caimita
ESMARALDAS
Guada
Tongorachi
Bislí
Muisne
R. Muisne
Montañas de Mache
Cube
546
Cotocachi-Cayapas Ecological Reserve
Ensenada de Mompiche
Montañas de Chindul
Chucaple
Portete
4535
El Cuerval
Bolívar
2112
Isla de Cojimíes
Daule
25
Malimpia
4939
Cojimíes
Cupa
Quinindé (Rosa Zárate)
IMBABURA
Hotel Coco Solo
Salima
Pueblo Nvo.
Cañaveral
El Limón
La Cieba
Beche
775
La Unión
Pedernales
Maquipucuna Biological Reserve
Pululahua Geobotanical Reserve
Pta. Pedernales
Pto. Quito
La Independencia
Equator Monument
Otón
La Vigencita
Tabuga
Atahualpa
PICHINCHA
S. Jacinto de Búa
25
Punta Ballena
QUITO
Novillo
Matal
Pitagua
Sumo
La Delicia
Rio Guajalito Reserve
Jama
Pta. Venado
Maicito
SANTO DOMINGO DE LOS COLORADOS
Cauque
El Carmen
S. Raphael
Muyoya
Covento
30
Sandía
Pta. Alta
Sangolquí
Cabo Pasado
Flavio Alfaro
25
30
Río Mariano
Canoa
Yescas
Mte. Nuevo
2215
Pasochoa Forest Res.
Aloag
Aloasí
Boca de Briceño
MANABÍ
266
Patricia Pilar
Calupiña
San Vicente
Doblones
El Mirador
Chaupi
35
Bahía de Caráquez
Boyacá
Ricuarte
Los Angeles
Cotopaxi National Park
Chone estuary
543
Guadual Gde.
Pta. Charapotó
Chone
El Mate
Camarones
Boliche Nat. Rec. Area
San Clemente
Chugchilán
Ayasa
Charapotó
Canuta
Santa Teresa
Guasaganda
Crucita
Cañitas
Calceta
Chantilín
Bahía de Manta
Palmar
Mangas
La Unión
Guayacán
Rocafuerte
LATACUNGA
MANTA
Tingo
Pujilí
Guayas
40
Cabo San Lorenzo
Montecristi
Pichincha
Puelblo Nuevo
San Lorenzo
40
QUEVEDO
COTOPAXI
Pambilar
La Pila
PORTOVIEJO
4220
Santa Rosa
Co. Pucajata
L
Beneficio
Pinllopata
Río de Caña
Mapasingue
San Carlos
PÍLLARO
Pta. Canoa
Isla de la Plata
San José
Membrillal
San Jacinto
El Salto
Guarumal
AMBATO
Pta. S. José
21
Motete
Sucre
San Raphael
TUNGURAH
Pto. de Cayo
Balzar
Zapotal
Chimbor
JIPIJAPA
La Reyesa
Pondoa
Pta. Pedernales
Olmedo
Salinas
Salaite
Cotaló
Machalilla
Cerritos
Ventanas
Julcuy
La Unión
BOLÍVAR
Pta. Los Frailes
LOS RÍOS
Agua Blanca
Colimes
La Paz
Pto. Lopez
El Altar
Calpi
Machalilla National Park
Penipe
25
Guaranda
Alandaluz Ecological Tourist Centre
9
RIOBAMBA
Cascol
50
Palestina
Cajabamba
San José
Pretoria
Balzapamba
San Luís
La Cadena
Olón
Dos Rios
Limonal
Barreiro
N
San Pablo
Cañitas
Montañita
Sabanilla
Licto
Daule
Pimocha
Babahoyo
Juan Montalvo
Manglaralto
Hu
Columbe
Valdivia
Isidro Ayora
La Victoria
Alao
Pablo Iguara
60
Guamote
San Pedro
Tarifa
Guangalá
25
Palmar
GUAYAS
Simón Bolivar
35
Monteverde
Santiago
Carrizal
Río Seco
21
Vishut
El Tingo
Pascuales
Buijó
San Pablo
MILAGRO
Colay
Aguadita
Durán
GUAYAQUIL
Pta. Sta. Elena
Bucay
1
Bellavista
Naranjito
Pitishi
Alausí
5050
SALINAS
LA LIBERTAD
70
Chongón
Delia
Km 26
Pta. Carnero
Sacachum
Cerecita
Daular
Taura
El Triunfo
Chunchi
Compud
Chanduy
La Esperanza
25
El Real
Caimito
70
La Troncal
Llagos
4493
Tugaduaja
Churete
Zhud
San Juan
Sabana Gde.
Manglares Churute Ecolo
CAÑAR
Engunga
3755
San Antonio
San Antonio
Ingapirca
Cañar
S. Lorenzo
Va. Nueva
Rivera
Engabao
4163
Amalzuna
El Morro
35
Log
Luz María
Taday
Playas
Posorja
Agua Piedra
La Resbalosa
4633
Azogues
Patu
Paute
Palmas
Puná
Chapurco
Pta. Arenas
Checa
Chi
Isla Puná
Solano
La Victoria
El Cajas National Recreation Area
Sevilla de Oro
Golfo de Guayaquil
Yungan
Balao
25
CUENCA
Baños
45
Chordolog
4088
Pto. Grande
Tenguel
AZUAY
Indanza
Cumbe
Sígsig
Pta. Carnero
Pta. Arenas
Pan de Azúc
80
S. Juan Bosco
Cordillera Boliche
Girón
3480
Gima
Isla Santa Clara (El Muerto)
MACHALA
La Ramada
Granadillos
Pta. de Jambeli
El Tablón
Chigüinda
Sta. Isabel
80
PASAJE
35
Amazonas
El Rosario

Cut off by inland forests and high mountains, the community of African ex-pats retained its cultural traditions and independence. Some of these survive in the form of Marimba music and the summoning of spirits with macumba voodoo. Its only lifeline being the sea, the community remained cut off from the rest of the country until the construction of the *autoferro* railway to Ibarra in the 1959 enabling export of agricultural products to the Sierra. With the completion of the road linking Colombia in the north, and the big city of Esmeraldas to the south, San Lorenzo will benefit from more traffic. Locals say that in 20 years it will become a real city, but at the same time San Lorenzo may loose some of its languid charm.

GENERAL INFORMATION

Gringos getting off trains, buses or boats are usually met by youths offering to find them hotels, introduce them to restaurants or even supply them with drugs. Be careful, and certainly don't fall for the drug scam. Another group, posing as plain-clothed policemen, will accost and threaten to arrest the travelers who have brought marihuana from the first group of youths. A pay-off is usually the only way out. As for hotels and restaurants, you won't lose much by accepting the offer of these self-appointed guides. It's easy enough to choose your own hotel because almost all are equally gruesome. The best of the bad lot is the **San Carlos**, a short walk down from the railway station, which is relatively new and clean, but don't count on steady supply of water of any temperature or clarity, nor functioning toilets. But at US$5 per night, what can you expect? At least the rooms have fans and mosquito nets.

For restaurants, probably your best bet is to follow one of your self-proclaimed guides, who of course will want a tip if you approve of their suggestion. Otherwise check out **La Estancia**, **La Red** or **Conchita**. There's excellent dining in San Lorenzo so it's worth looking around. Crabs, clams, conches, shrimps, oysters, crawfish and even turtle can be on the menu, all fresh as a flapping fish.

San Lorenzo doesn't have many facilities of use to tourists. There is no CETUR tourist office, though there is an **EMETEL office** on the other side of the wide street from the San Carlos. I was able to make a call to Japan from there.

WHAT TO SEE AND DO

The good news is the **marimba music**. The bad news is that you are unlikely to hear any unless you're in town on a Friday or Saturday night, or during a fiesta. Ask around. It's a small town and if something is happening everyone knows. There's also a famous marimba school, where if you are lucky you might hear some marimba being played. Videotape of marimba competitions are on display.

I spoke with Jackson, better known as El Potente (the Powerful One), because of his ability to play for hours nonstop. At 23 years old, he is a top miramba player. El Potente told me how the marimba came to San Lorenzo from Africa with the first castaways. The music is very similar to African marimba music, but there are subtle differences, he said. For example, resonators used on African marimbas are made of gourds, but in San Lorenzo they use bamboo. The most interesting experience in San Lorenzo is to see and hear this culture for yourself.

Another option is to take a boat across the estuary, and up the mangrove-banked Río Santiago to the small, impoverished riverside village of **La Tolita** which has is a small museum and an archaeological site. More than 2,000 years ago shamans and chieftains of the Tolita culture were buried here in *tolitas* (small mounds), and people from far away came to worship and trade. Few travelers make this journey despite the Tolita culture's noteriety, mostly because of the extraordinary Tolita gold and platinum jewelry found at this site, some of which can be seen in the Museo Nacional del Banco Central del Ecuador, the Central Bank Museum in Quito. The magnificent Sun God mask that is the bank's logo was found at La Tolita (for information on La Tolita see page 187 in THE PACIFIC COAST). Seeing these exhibits make you realize that the advanced gold and platinum working techniques used by craftsmen in the mangrove swamps of Tolita two millennia ago were not discovered in the western hemisphere until the nineteenth century.

Regrettably, there's not much to be seen in La Tolita except for the one-room museum attached to the school, where there are a number of burial jars. The bones of the dead were broken so the bodies could be squeezed into these less-than-life-size urns. When excavated, some of the urns also contained gold and platinum jewelry, serpent figures and figurines representing supernatural spirits to help the dead in afterlife. No gold artifacts are displayed at La Tolita because most of them have drifted away to big museums or private collections. One of the villagers, Antonio, can show you pits where archaeologists have been digging but when I was there they were full of rainwater. Antonio has his own collection of Tolita figurines that he sells to visitors.

If you are interested in exploring the San Lorenzo area, check with **Excursions El Refugio** near the EMETEL office. They organize various tours in motorized dugout canoes including swimming trips to the deserted **island of San Pedro**. Also ask here about trips to **Borbón** and further up river to **Steve's Lodge** at the junction of the Cayapas and Onzole rivers, owned by Hungarian Stephan Tarjany. And find out about visits to the **Cotacachi-Cayapas Ecological Reserve**.

How to Get There

Most travelers come down to San Lorenzo from Ibarra by bus or train and then continue on down the coast. Motorized dugouts leave from the San Lorenzo waterfront to **La Tola**, from where you can travel on to **Esmeraldas** by bus or ranchero. Check with the Capitanía on the waterfront for boat departure times. Early-morning boats to La Tola will connect you with a bus that will get you to Esmeraldas the same day. Alternatively, there is boat service to Borbón on the Cayapas River, from where there are buses and *rancheros* to Esmeraldas. There are also boats to Tumaco in Colombia, though this is not an established tourist route and is said to be frequented by drug smugglers.

LIMONES

Most boats heading to La Tola go by way of the small island town of **Limones**, the next port down the coast from San Lorenzo. Arriving by motorized dugout, with mango forests on either side of the wide delta, your first glimpse of the town is a row of gray, sun-bleached shacks standing on stilts over the water. After disembarking at the wooden jetty, you pick your way though unpaved back streets with duckboards over stagnant, mosquito-breeding pools of water. Outside almost every meager house lies a dugout canoe, equivalent to a car in roadless Limones. Few gringos visit this dreamy town that looks like a location in a novel by Gabriel Garcia Márquez. Dark-skinned kids follow you, laughing and pointing, delighted by the arrival of strangers.

Limones, a town of some 8,000 people, has seen better days. At one time it was an important port for timber trade, where logs floated upriver from the forests were cut and loaded onto freighters. Now most of this is handled in Borbón, on the mainland. Although we saw mountains of shrimp by the waterfront, people say fishing isn't as good as it used to be. Without jobs, young people drift off to bigger cities like Esmeraldas and Guayaquil down the coast.

In an effort to address some of the social and economic problems of this poor community, the privately-funded **Fundación CIDESA** has set up a project in Limones working with local groups.

CIDESA can arrange visits to mangrove forests, beaches and other places of interest in the vicinity. If you plan to visit CIDESA it's best to write in advance to PO Box 172150, Quito, or ✆(02) 226303 or 527119, locally (06) 789143 E-MAIL cidesa2@cidesa.org.ec. Limones offers a fascinating glimpse of life the Pacific coast of Ecuador. But the hotel scene isn't one of the town's great assets. Aside from a bed at US$5 per night, the best hotel in town, **Hotel Mauricio Real** ✆(06) 789155, has nothing to commend it, not even running water.

THE ROAD TO ESMERALDAS

Frankie Malinson and I rejoined his buggy where he had left it at La Tola. We headed out of the dog-eared town and down the coast. Our first stop was the **Majagual Mangrove Reserve**, where we clumped in our boots along walkways over oozing black mud, and peered up in awe at what are thought to be the tallest and oldest mangrove trees in the world, 60m (200 ft) high and 1,000 years old. This ancient, perfectly intact mangrove ecosystem is home to three-toed tree sloths, anteaters, ocelots, green iguanas, capybaras, small jaguars, parrots, herons, kingfishers, woodpeckers, storks, pelicans and the deadly poisonous fer-de-lance snakes. But you have to be patient to see these creatures; all we spotted were a few birds, numerous butterflies and a number of crabs scurrying into black holes in the mud.

Back at the research station, we sampled a rare and exquisite liqueur made by soaking the roots of black mangrove in a bottle of *aguardiente*. After years of maturation, the blood-red spirit has the smoothness of a fine cognac and the energy and health-giving properties of ginseng, but if you drink too you might hallucinate. In the silence of the swampy, prehistoric forest wilderness, I would not have been surprised to see a pterodactyl flapping overhead, or a dinosaur lumbering through the mud.

Two German women who joined us on our travels were riding on top of the Land Rover. Driving down **Las Peñas beach**, a wide expanse of sand cut by streams, they were sprayed head-to-foot with wet sand and mud, and the buggy looked as if it been driven through a river up to its windows, as indeed it had. The Ecuador coast is excellent for four-wheel driving.

We stopped at the beach of **Bocana de Lagarto** (Mouth of the Alligator) for a swim and some beers. Lying in a hammock in the shade of a coconut palm, I chatted with a lady who thought Great Britain was in Asia and wanted me to marry her daughter. Gringos are rare in this area and tourism is yet to make an impact. We usually think of tropical beaches as places where you lie in the sun and swim in the sea. But Bocana de Lagarto is a working fishing community, where men pull their boats up the sand by hand and mend their nets in the sun. Aside from us, there wasn't a tourist in sight for miles and miles of palm-fringed beaches and rolling breakers.

We lunched for about US$3 each on delicious fish soup, fresh prawns, rice and coconut milk at a restaurant with no name, opposite the dance hall in the dirt-poor village of **Montalvo**, just in from the coast. Outside, a skinny horse carrying a cowboy wearing a straw hat ambled down the street. "It's the Wild West out here," said Frankie. "Life is monotonous on the range, out on horseback, herding cattle, chopping sugar cane, bringing in sacks, loading and offloading trucks. Coastal farmers, called *Montuvios*, are usually mixed-race black and Indian, or *negros de monte*, blacks of the mountain."

Approaching **Esmeraldas**, capital of the province with a population of 250,000, we tuned in to local radio 96.3 FM, and heard fast-talking DJs playing up-beat salsa. "It's a funky, popping place," said Frankie, "Good discos, good nightlife, but if you don't know your way around you might feel the hair rising on the back of your neck. Aside from the nightlife, there's not much for tourists in Esmeraldas but street gangs, poverty and slums." This doesn't seem to deter city slickers who fly into General Rivadeneira Airport from Quito for partying weekends in nearby Atacames. We by-passed the provincial capital and headed for that well-known caravansary on the gringo trail just 25km (16miles) to the south, the nearby beach resort of **Atacames**.

ATACAMES

A row of round straw huts stretches along the big beach at Atacames. Each has an identical framework with a palm-thatched roof, a circular bar inside, bamboo furniture and open walls to let in the warm night air. Hammocks are strung between palm trees or poles in the sand. The huts belong to municipal authorities who lease them to operators of discos, clubs, bars and restaurants. Most feature loud Latin music and exotic cocktails made from cane liqueur and umpteen different Ecuadorian fruits. Try a Green Lady, a Forbidden Lover or a Coco Loco, the latter being a mixture of coconut water, cane spirit, grenadine and lemon served in a huge coconut shell with a straw. Too many of these will indeed make you *loco*.

Walking out onto the wide beach on a clear night, big white waves roll up the

sand, while behind you the beach bars form a necklace of colored lights. Sexy, swinging salsa mingles with the booming song of the sea. Atacames is a party town, a place to let your hair down. "Carnival on the beach here is out of control," says Frankie. "People taking their clothes off, throwing water and eggs at each other. It's wild. If you like salsa, samba, reggae, rock, techno, jungle or just plain rock 'n' roll, this is the place to be."

But keep close to the bar areas if you go out on the beach at night. Muggings and rapes happen in Atacames from time to time, even in daylight. Not long before our visit an American professor and a female student were held up at gunpoint during the day on the beach while the girl was raped. Also, avoid Atacames during holiday weekends and fiestas unless you want to be washed away in the crowds of Quito party people.

If you're interested in a wild Atacames weekend, get there by Thursday evening, or make reservations in advance. There's lots of mediocre and overpriced accommodation that fill up quickly. **Villas Ocro Iris** ☎ (06) 731069, (02) 525544, has cabins on the beach four around US$40 for a double, depending on season. At about the same price, the big, modern **Le Castell** ☎ (06) 731542, is also a convenient base for nighttime activities. For a cheaper deal on the beach, try **Hostal Chavalito** ☎ (06) 731113. Many of the hotels are spread along the

Malecón (embankment), the road that runs behind the row of beach bars. Many travelers head for this strip and check out what's available.

The same goes for food. Though Atacames is better-known for liquid than solid consumption, there are several reasonably-good food stands and restaurants on the Malecón. Beef kebabs cooked over charcoal, fresh *ceviche*, hot dogs and hamburgers are standard beachside fare. There are several good **food stands** in the market near Discoteca Paradiso and **Marcos Restaurant** is good for ham-and-egg breakfasts. When you've partied out in Atacames, head down the coast for some rest.

SOUTH TO MUISNE

Tonsupa and **Súa** lie respectively just north and south of Atacames, like two younger twin brothers who haven't learned to party with the adults. Tonsupa is upmarket with condos and timeshares while Súa retains some fishing village charm, with pelicans and boats lying at anchor in its placid bay. Both are good places to relax in relative peace, and buses regularly run between Esmeraldas and these two smaller towns.

In Tonsupa, the beachfront **Cabaña Turística Doña Emerita** ☎ (06) 710407, is recommended, while in Súa stay in the hillside cabañas of **Hotel Chagra Ramos** ☎ (06) 731006.

Small and exclusive, the town of **Same** (pronounced sah-may), which faces a long, palm-fringed beach overlooked by some big modern condominiums and Florida-style beach houses, is one of the best places to be in in this vicinity.

Probably the best meal we had on the coast was at the whimsical **Seaflower** restaurant and hotel ☎(06) 861789, run by Margarita Lehmann, a German sculptor who has a great love for seashells and a gift for cooking fresh seafood meals. Her *cazuela* (mixed seafood stew) is highly recommended, as is her homemade sauerkraut and smoked pork chops. Though not cheap by Ecuadorian standards, the meal was excellent value by European or North American standards. Entertainment was provided by a frisky golden lion tamarin playing games on the terrace with a cat and a dog, and jumping up onto our table to steal bread. Seaflower's three small rooms are attractive and reasonably priced. Next door, **La Terraza** ☎ (06) 544507, also has a good restaurant and well-equipped cabañas. Same is well-recommended for a honeymoon, or a few days of therapeutic idleness.

Tonchigüe is the last little town on the coastal road going south from Same before it turns inland towards Muisne. Just beyond the town a rough ranch road leads out to the **Galera headland**, one of the most remote and dramatic parts of the Ecuadorian coastline. Out here there are isolated beaches, cliffs, coves, caves, tunnels, forests and one or two small settlements only accessible from the sea.

Twenty years ago a young Canadian adventurer, Judith Barrett, drove around the beaches in a jeep at low tide looking for a place to camp. She and her companion found a forested gully leading down to a small beach, where they camped for a month with only wild animals and birds for company. It was an idyllic, Robinson Crusoe experience, and Judith vowed she would return and set up her own wilderness retreat. Eighteen years later she had saved enough money to buy the land.

Today, three years after the purchase, **Playa Escondida** (Hidden Beach) is one of the most magical ecorefuges on the coast. A handful of rustic cabins and a camping ground look out over big billowing trees and the sea. An observation platform, where you can sleep overnight is under construction in the semi-tropical forest. Wildlife here includes parrots, seabirds, anteaters, guantas, foxes, iguanas and wild cats. Ebony and kapok trees grow here. Judith says that giant turtles regularly come to Playa Escondida because they have to find an inlet in the rocky coastline, just as she and her friend two decades earlier. "Sometimes when we are eating dinner a turtle will come right outside the restaurant," she says, "We get to see her lay her eggs."

Cabins at Playa Escondida are US$8 per person per night, and camping is US$5. A full meal service is US$10–20 per day. For information and reservations call ☎ LOCAL (09)

Atacames is a rowdy, partying beach town.

733368 or write to Casilla 789A, Sucursal 3, Quito. You will need your own vehicle to get there, or you can rent a pick-up truck or hire a taxi at Tonchique for the 20-km, (13-mile) one-hour, rough-road journey.

The road to **Muisne** can be dangerous at night. Gangs from Esmeraldas put up barricades and hold up buses, especially on paydays. As we drove down the dark, unlit road we saw the occasional kerosene lamp illuminating a group of Montuvios standing around a wayside pool table, but no barricades. Frankie parked the buggy in a friend's garage in **Salto**, near the ferry to Muisne Island. A short crossing over the Río Muisne brought us to the island's quay, where young men on tricycle rickshaws offered us rides up the one-kilometer (half-mile) dirt road to the beach.

There are no cars in Muisne, bikes and horses being the popular form of transport. Under bright stars and a big moon, the beach was wide and long with great rollers crashing on the sand in front of a scattering of beach bars and inexpensive hostels. Muisne makes no pretenses at being an up-market resort. We checked in at **Hotel Calade** ☎ (05) 480279, a basic backpackers' joint with mosquito nets and showers, which suited us fine and US$5 a night had no ill effects on our budget. The rest of the evening passed by at the **Habana Club** beach bar drinking *Cuba Libres* (rum and coke) and listening to reggae.

NORTHERN MANABÍ

Early the next morning, after an exhilarating hammering in the big white breakers, I was back at the ferry quay, stepping into an open-top motorized canoe to continue down the coast to **Cojimíes**, just over the border between the provinces of Esmeraldas and Manabí. Louis, a Filipino accountant based in Los Angeles accompanied me, while Frankie had to drive his Land Rover round a five-hour inland loop to join us at **Pedernales**. Coming out of the estuary, our canoe was stopped by a launch with an armed and scruffy-uniformed Ecuadorian who insisted on checking our passports and baggage. I don't know what he was looking for but his a cap, emblazoned with the words "US Navy," made him look more like a pirate than an Ecuadorian customs service official.

At the time I didn't know that the boat trip from Muisne to Cojimíes is notorious for accidents. Mostly they occur when long canoes coming out of the estuary cross big, breaking, white-capped waves into the open sea. "Ride 'im cowboy!" Louis and I screeched as the long bow of our canoe rose up into fuming crests and smashed down with a great slap on the other side. "Man, what a roller coaster!" Louis shouted, his face wet with spray, "Let's do it again."

Once over the wave barrier, the sea rocked us gently in a smooth swell. Lines of pelicans flying in formation skimmed the tops of the waves looking for fish to snatch in

their bulbous bills. From the sea, the deserted coastline of **Ensenada** (cove) **de Mompiche**, south of Muisne looked gorgeous. Thick woods and bright green vegetation grow atop chunky cliffs overlooking secret, completely inaccessible bays and beaches. The only way to get to this wild stretch of coastline is by boat or on horseback.

Cojimíes is a barrio built on a sandbank. The foundation is an untidy assemblage of boats, shacks and shop-houses is continuously being worn away by the sea. The town has moved so many times that its cemetery is about to disappear under the water. There wasn't much to detain us here, so Louis and I grabbed something to eat and jumped into the back of an open truck heading for Pedernales.

The main **road to Pedernales** is the beach, which can only be driven at low tide. "What a ride, dude! What a ride!" shouted Louis as our truck bumped and rattled at high speed down the wide, endless stretch of sand, with pool-blue sea on one side and low cliffs and coconut groves on the other. No condos, no houses, no cottages, no tourists, there was no signs of humans on this wide, 40-km (25-mile) stretch of virgin beach. Occasionally we would pass a man on a horse or another truck belting up the beach in the opposite direction. With a rising tide, this joyride can become a white-knuckle race against the sea.

ABOVE: Trawling for shrimp larvae at Pedernales to supply the many shrimp farms along the coast.

Developers have bought up most of this stretch of coastline, and in 20 years it might well become a long strip of beach resorts and vacation complexes. There is already one hotel halfway down the beach hidden behind screen of coconut palms. In splendid isolation for seekers of solitude and deserted beaches, **Hotel Coco Solo** ✆ (02) 240404 or 461677 has cabins, a camping grounds, restaurant and horses for rent at reasonable prices. For reservations contact Safari Tours in Quito ✆ (02) 552505, or Guacamayo Tours in Bahía ✆ (05) 691412.

Pedernales is a Wild West beach resort where *vaqueros* (cowboys) ride horses down the main street (racing them during the rodeo festival in August), and all motor vehicles, most of which are pick-up trucks, sound like they have holes in their exhaust system, or none at all. It's a hot, dusty, gimcrack town with dirt roads and ugly concrete housing. The four main complaints of locals are lack of fresh water, dust, electrical blackouts and dead telephones. On the positive side, Pedernales has a magnificent beach, fine seafood, friendly inhabitants and relative safety for gringos. Another attraction of this stretch of the coast is the proximity of the **Montañas de Chindul**, the biggest coastal range of mountains in Ecuador, and the **Mache-Chindul Ecological Reserve**, home of waterfalls and to Cayapas Indians.

Until a few years ago, Pedernales was only accessible by sea, and the town had a well-deserved reputation for its independent spirit. Within living memory, a police officer assigned to the district by Quito authorities was thrown out, and not replaced for several years. Recently a road has brought the town within a four hour's drive of the capital. Developers and entrepreneurs have noted its tourist potential, and budget travelers are starting to discover its hidden charms, one of which happens to Pedernales' penchant for plaintive Mexican music.

Sadly, most of the town's charms are too well-hidden, and they certainly don't include its hotels. A new beachfront hotel was full when Louis and I met up with Frankie on a Friday night, and so was the **Hotel América** ✆ 05681174, on the road to the beach, where rooms are about US$15 per night. We had to make do with rotten rooms at one of the inexpensive hotels in the back streets of town. A note in my diary reads, "I'm fed up with showers without water, toilets that don't flush, bed bugs, torn mattresses and red smears of spanked mosquitoes on the walls."

With some speed we pushed on down the coast, **crossing the equator** just south of Pedernales and passing still more long, semi-deserted beaches, where the only inhabitants are a few fishing families. Stopping briefly at **Punta Prieta**, we visited a small lodge perched on the edge of a granite promontory. The living room balcony juts out over the cliff, with views over long, empty beaches on either side, and a sheer, 30-m (100-ft) drop to the rocks below. This isn't a place I would recommend for those who suffer from vertigo. Construction of this eccentric establishment was the fulfillment of a dream for Alonso Ordoñez, a former park ranger. You cannot phone the lodge to make reservations; just turn up and see if one or both of the guests rooms are available. One permanent guest is a Galápagos turtle whom Alonso found in the forest.

At **Punta Ballena**, near the small market town of **Jama**, the long, crescent beach is so flat and wide that the waves peter out on the sand like feathers on silk. The tide was too high for us to get around the rocky point, so we had to take the inland loop road to **Canoa**, another long, wide beach with white-topped surfing waves and huge caves in cliffs at one end. Canoa is quickly becoming a hot spot for the young beach crowd. The new-place-to-be was jumping when we arrived, with people grooving in beachside *salsatecas* in the midday sun. If you want to be near the action, stay at the Dutch-owned and -managed **Hotel Bambu** ✆ (09) 753696, a new building made of wood and bamboo that looks like a beachcomber's palace. Rooms are from US$5–10. As in most places on the coast, shower water isn't always dependable. Further down the beach you can find quieter, isolated cabañas.

We buggied on down the wide sands, passing under paragliders floating from a high cliff like brightly-colored handkerchiefs. It's hard to believe there no major tourist resorts on this long stretch of pristine coastline, though it probably won't remain so much longer. The Radisson hotel group has bought a large chunk of beachside land here, and once the runway at the nearyby airport is expanded, big jets will be able to fly in tourists from all over the world.

After 20 km (12 miles) of straight, empty sand, the beach finally folded into the **Chone estuary**, and we were confronted with an extraordinary sight. On a promontory on the other side of the water, like a mirage in the desert, was an Ecuadorian version of Miami Beach — a gleaming white forest of modern high-rise apartments, hotels and condominiums. Civilization, at last.

BAHÍA DE CARÁQUEZ

Crossing the estuary from the resort village of **San Vicente** on a small car ferry, which we shared with a truckload of cows, we landed at the upmarket playground of the Manabí coast, where politicians and a former Prime Minister have vacation residences. "There's no other Bahía, take care of it," is the town's slogan. Not surprisingly, the streets are clean, the roads well-paved and there are many smart new buildings. Expensive pleasure boats lie at anchor in the estuary, and even the road from Quito is relatively fast and well-maintained.

At the office of **Bahía Dolphin Tours** proprietor Patricio Tamariz hunched over his computer, engrossed in a live Internet feed showing current height of waves on beaches around the world, giving new meaning to surfing the net. Once out of the surf, Tamiriz introduced us to another of his passions: the history and delights of Bahía de Caráquez. "Ecuadorian nationality was founded in Bahía with the balsa sailors," he said. "They were the Phoenicians of the Americas who sailed as far as Chile in the south, and Mexico in the north." From prehistoric coastal cultures, our conversation moved on to the Incas, the Spanish conquistadors and the French astronomical expedition to Ecuador at the beginning of the eighteenth century.

More recently, Bahía was an important banana shipping center. Ecuador is still the world's leading banana republic, though most exports are now shipped through the bigger ports of Guayaquil and Machala down the coast. While still functioning as a port, tourism is increasingly important for Bahía. It is one of the country's leading and best-appointed coastal resorts, even if it might seem a tad sedate for those who prefer the party mood and beach culture of hangouts like Atacames.

What to See and Do

Not only was Bahía a focus of an ancient maritime civilization, but centuries later it became a base for Spanish ships exploring the Pacific coast of South America, and a base for their expeditions into the interior. But for a place with so much history there is surprisingly little heritage to be seen in the town itself. You can visit the Banco Central's **Casa de la Cultura**, with its collection of pre-Columbian treasures found in the sea and antique maps of the region. You can climb **La Cruz hill** for a panoramic view of the town and the coastline. Or you stroll along the pleasant and peaceful **Malecón** with its riverside views and old colonial mansions.

For close encounters with wildlife comparable to those on the Galápagos Islands, there are boat trips from Bahía to islands in the estuary. At the **Islas de Fragatas**, frigate birds can be observed and photographed at close range, along with herons, pelicans, cormorants, oyster-catchers, spoonbills and blue-footed boobies. The best time to see the magnificent frigate birds puffing up

One of the many beautiful solid gold masks on display at the Casa de la Cultura.

their red breast sacks is during mating rituals from August to January. Shrimp farms have destroyed most of the estuary's mangroves during the last 20 years, except those that are protected on the islands. For these and other excursions, including fishing and bird watching trips and visits to the coastal caves of Canoa, contact **Guacamayo Bahíatours** ☎ (05) 690597 FAX (05) 691412, Avenida Bolívar and Arenas. They also organize two-day horse trekking adventures to Río Muchacho, where you experience *montuvio* life on a organic coastal farm and sleep in a treehouse surrounded by birds and orchids.

Bahía Dolphin Tours ☎ (05) 692097 or 692086 FAX (05) 692088, on Calle Salinas, Edificio Dos Hemisferios, runs several tours, including visits to shrimp farms and villages where they make the misnamed panama hats. The company also runs a private ecolodge, archaeological site and small museum further down the coast at **Chirije** (chee-ree-hey), which can only be reached from the beach at low tide. The site is thought to have been an important seaport at the time of the Bahía culture (500 BC – AD 500) and many ceramic, gold and copper relics have been found here. Staying in bungalows overlooking the sea, guests learn about the ancient culture of this area, while enjoying a long private beach and 160 hectares (400 acres) of rare dry tropical forest, with numerous species of plants and wildlife. For more information and background on Chirije write to E-MAIL archtour@srv1.telconet.net, or visit their WEB SITE www.qni.com/~mj/bahia/bahia.html.

Where to Stay and Eat

La Piedra Hotel ☎ (05) 690780 FAX (05) 690154 on Circunvalación and Bolívar, has wonderful suites looking out over the sea, access to a beach, pool, a good restaurant and all the other ameneties of a modern hotel. Its only drawback is that it's expensive at about US$70 for a double. Also recommended in the expensive range are **Hotel La Herradura** ☎ (05) 690446 FAX (05) 690265 and **Hotel Italia** ☎ (05) 691137 FAX (05) 691092. Slightly more affordable is the upmarket oceanfront guesthouse, **Casa Grande**, which is surrounded by lush tropical gardens with a terrace and pool. The interior of this beautiful residential house is decorated with some fine contemporary Ecuadorian art. Reservations can be made through Bahía Dolphin Tours ☎ (05) 692097. Somewhere less expensive is **Hostal Querencia** ☎ (05) 690009, on Malecón 1800, or check out the hostels two blocks up from the ferry dock.

Ceviche is what you eat in Manabí and with all the prawn farms in the Chone estuary, *ceviche camarón* (raw shrimp marinated in lemon or lime with onions and various spices) is what you have in Bahía. Like a Eurasian cross between Japanese sashimi and a shrimp cocktail, *ceviche camarón* at a waterfront restaurant on the Manabí coast is one of my ideas of heaven. Try one of the restaurants by the river, such as **Restaurant Genesis**, which is popular and has a terrace on the water. As with restaurants all over the world, some of the humblest-looking places serve the most authentic cuisine. For reasonable pizzas, go to **Pizzería Donatello**, near the car ferry dock. The better hotels also have fine but rather expensive restaurants.

THE PANAMA HAT TRAIL

At low tide you can drive south along the rocky beach from **Chirije** to villages further down the coast. But many people have died in watery graves below the cliffs because their driver became stuck or mis-timed the tides.

Frankie thought he could make it. He drove like the devil along the sand and over flat, fissured rocks, keeping an eye on the advancing sea. It was touch and go. If we squeezed around the point ahead we would be home and dry. If we turned around now we would barely get back to the dirt road from the beach. We turned back. Bucking and bumping at high speed, we glimpsed some extraordinary petrified logs embedded in the cliff, part of a **petrified forest** or **fossils of pre-Columbian houses** — nobody seems to know. With the sea lapping the hubcaps,

The best panama hats are made in Montecristi, just inland from Manabí coast.

we made the road — and headed for an inland route to Manta.

Manta doesn't entice visitors with many attractions. It's a busy, working port, handling shipments of sugarcane, fiber, pepper, cacao and other agricultural products of the region. Though less crime-ridden than the other big coastal towns of Esmeraldas and Guayaquil, its less-than-pristine beaches are patrolled by naval police. We stayed on Playa Murciélago at the grandly, but inappropriately named **Manta Imperial Hotel**, a well appointed but run-down dump that is best avoided. We dined in an excellent Chinese restaurant at the **Hotel Lun Fun**. The only gringos we saw were a couple of longhaired American carrying surfboards. "Catch any good waves, dude?" asked Louis. "Sure, man," was the reply. "This place is awesome."

The next morning we hit the road to **Montecristi**, spiritual home of the misnamed "panama" hat — misnamed because the hats originated centuries ago in Ecuador, still the biggest producer. They are called panamas because they were exported to Panama in the middle of the eighteenth century and subsequently became known throughout the world. In 1855, Ecuadorian panamas caused a sensation in Paris when a Montecristi *fino* was presented to Emperor Napoleon III, after which he was rarely seen without one. Thereafter the handy, portable panama replaced the straw boater and became a sophisticated fashion accessory. The **finest panamas** in the world are made in Montecristi. Woven from long, thin fronds of the palm-like *toquilla* straw growing in the area (also known as the Jipijapa plant, after a local town), they spring back into perfect shape after being unrolled, and can hold water without leaking.

Montecristi is a dusty town that lives on the income from its **handwoven products**. Concrete and cinder block buildings are occupied by weavers and shops selling hats, hammocks, mats and tablecloths. There is a fine church and the grand former residence of **Eloy Alfaro**, liberal president and Montecristi's hero, whose father, Manuel, made a fortune trading in panamas. Thanks to Alfaro's efforst to modernize the legal code, his fight for women rights and efforts to separate church and state at the end of the nineteenth century, the panama hat is an icon of Ecuador's great liberal revolution. Sadly, in return for his vision, Eloy Alfaro was lynched in the streets by a mob incensed by his attempts to undermine the church's power.

Frankie parked the buggy by a vendor's stand and asked where we could see hats being made. A lad took us to a weaver's house on a back street. There we watched an old man sitting in the light of an open window, his long fingers flashing like knitting needles as he crossed and recrossed thin strands of white straw weaving the "wings" of a hat. Judging a hat requires experience. Tightness of weave, thickness and quality of fiber, color, smell, shape and touch all have to be considered. It used to be said that the best hats were woven by the moonlight, when there is no danger of the sun's heat damaging the straw before the hat has cured.

As for price, I bought myself a fine Al Capone-style panama for US$32 that would cost well over US$80 elsewhere. It came rolled in a neat balsa box for easy packing. A *fino* costing about US$64 in Montecristi would sell for about US$200 in London, while the *fino-finos* and *ultrafinos* are even more expensive. But the days of these greatest of panama hats are probably numbered: there are only a dozen weavers left around Montecristi capable of making them, all of whom are over 70 years old. Today, 95% of Ecuador's panama hats comes from the Cuenca area.

From Montecristi we drove south towards **Jipijapa** (pronounced delightfully as "hippie-happa"), passing **La Pila** on the way. This small village has found a unique niche in the country's economy as makers of cunning archaeological counterfeits of pre-Columbian ceramics. With growing interest in the archaeological sites in the area, village craftsmen started making so-called "antiques" but are now better-known for honest reproductions, though there are said to be workshops that still specialize in fakes. Stands selling figurines, decorated pottery and erotic sculptures, as well as weavings and wickerwork, are set up along the road to catch the eyes of passing motorists. Frankie and I bought woven hammocks.

At Jipijapa, a twisty side road branches to the right into the mountains of **Machalilla National Park**, the tallest of which (at 750 m or 2,500 ft) is marked on some maps **Cerro Perro Muerto** (Dead Dog Mountain). I don't know why it's so named but locals prefer a phrase meaning Bearded Mountain. There are large tracts of rare **dry tropical forest** in this area, also known as Sleeping Forest, because in July and August it turns into desert scrub, as brown, barren and dusty as southern Texas. In the winter the landscape is transformed by heavy rain into a green, glossy garden. Crossing the top of the range, we glimpsed the gray Pacific Ocean in the distance.

THE BEACHES OF SOUTHERN MANABÍ AND GUAYAS

The most accessible, continuous stretch of beaches and bays in Ecuador begins at Puerto de Cayo in southern Manabí and ends at Salinas in Guayas Province. The 150-km (96-mile) sweep of this popular coastline is dotted with towns and villages connected by reasonable roads and bus services.

Spread out on a long beach, **Puerto de Cayo** is a quiet, pleasant, unpretentious small fishing community with not many places to eat and stay. Yet one of its restaurants is reputed to be one of the best on the coast. There is **Restaurant Don Carlos** (no sign, on the right as you come from Jipijapa) and the restaurant across the road is a good alternative.

Aside from eating excellent seafood and drinking beer, there are few tourist activities or sights nor bars, or discos in Puerto Cayo itself. Such is the place's charm that sitting on an empty beach and looking out on the ocean is one of its main attractions. On a clear day you might see the misty outline of the mysterious **Isla de la Plata**, named after the silver (*plata*) Sir Francis Drake is reputed to have buried after a successful raid on Spanish galleons. Attempts to find the treasure have not yet been successful.

A more visible form of treasure on Isla de la Plata is its wildlife, almost as rich and varied as that of the Galápagos Islands, but with the advantage of being concentrated in one area. Frigate birds, waved albatrosses,

Young surfers make their own boards in some of the villages and towns along Ecuador's surf-fringed coastline.

occasional sea lions and iguanas and three types of boobies are just some of the stars of this insular animal kingdom. **Tours to Isla de la Plata** can be arranged in Puerto, Cayo or at **Machalilla** and **Puerto Lopez** just down the coast. Renting a five-passenger boat is about US$100, or you might join a group at about US$25 per person, not including the park entrance fee of US$20. Boats leave at about 5:30 AM and return in the afternoon, the 40-km (25-mile) journey taking about three hours each way. As well as the wildlife on the island, there are good walks, a pre-Columbian archeological site, coral reefs (the only ones on the coast of Ecuador) and great snorkeling. Dubbed the "Poor Person's Galápagos," Isla de la Plata is included by Quito travel agents in tours of this area of Manabí.

Isla de la Plata is part of the spectacular, 55,000-hectare (135,850-acre) **Machalilla National Park** that also embraces regions of dry tropical forest, a beautiful coastline, islands and a number of archaeological sites. The great curving beaches around **Los Frailes**, just south of Machalilla town but within the park itself, are said to be the finest in Ecuador; they are the most likely to appear on travel posters. A trail from the main coastal road takes you to the first, white-sand beach overlooked by green hills. A trail over the headland takes you to the other three beaches, each in its own isolated cove, one of which has black sand. Being part of the national park, there are no houses, the landscape is unspoiled, the water clear and clean for snorkeling, and often you have a beach or two to yourself.

Also within the park, the **archaeological site** and **museum** at the village of **Agua Blanca** are also worth visiting. Considered one of the most important in Ecuador, the site is about five kilometers (three miles) off the coastal road, just north of Puerto Lopez. If you don't have your own transportation, you can hike up from the dirt road, or rent a truck in one of the nearby towns. You can also walk to the site on the self-guided, eight-kilometer (five-mile) **Salaite Trail** from the village of the same name. For more strenuous hikes into the mountains, local guides are available at Agua Blanca.

The museum is full of jewelry, pottery and other objects from the **Manta culture** that flourished in the area from 500 BC to AD 1500, the time of the Spanish conquest. There is evidence that the site was occupied by the much-older **Machalilla**, **Chorrera** and **Salango** cultures. A photography exhibit shows that people in the surrounding mountains and hills have the same features as figures appearing in ancient Machalilla pottery. It is thought that the area has been inhabited for at least 3,000 years, making it perhaps the longest continuously-inhabited region of coastal South America. You can learn more about these ancient coastal cultures at another museum in the nearby village of **Salango**.

A few days before our arrival, a major storm raged over this area of the coast, causing great destruction. We would have been able to get as far as we had already without a four-wheel-drive vehicle. But even with the Land Rover we were not sure we would make it all the way down to Guayaquil. Roads were closed by mudslides, bridges washed away and houses by the side of the road were filled with mud and water. Our main concern was whether we would be able to cross the **Olón River**, just north of the surfer's paradise of **Montañita**, where reports said the bridge had been destroyed. We had no idea of when it would reopen, but not wanting to turn back, we decided to keep going and check out the situation ourselves. Our plan was to stay the night at the much-praised **Alandaluz Ecological Resort** ☎ (02) 505084 FAX (02) 543042 in Quito, or ☎ (05) 604103, a few kilometers north of Olón.

This was not to be. On arrival, we saw that Alandaluz had been utterly devastated by the hurricane. Bamboo guest houses had blown away, the palm-thatched main lodge was in tatters and the staff were far too busy clearing debris and making repairs to cope with guests, even if they had anywhere to put them. Thankfully nobody at the resort had been killed or injured. Disappointed that we would not be able to enjoy this resort, we pushed on south in the dark to Olón. To our relief, we found a temporary Bailey bridge had thrown across the river, enabling us to continue down to Montañita to meet the surfing crowd.

Nine big bonfires on the beach lit up the night sky as we drove into **Montañita**, Ecuador's most popular surfing town. In an effort to clean up, fishermen were burning driftwood washed up by the storm. We sat on logs feeling the heat from blazing fires, our faces scorching as if in midday sun. In the old days, the fishermen told us, they would have used the wood to make fires for cooking or for charcoal, now they have electricity and gas.

Tell us about the storm, we asked. "We didn't know what to think. It was *horroroso*," one man replied. "The young people had never seen anything quite like it," said another. A third man said, "The old people don't remember such a storm, either. It was like an *estampido* (explosion)." They spoke of broken riverbanks, houses destroyed, people washed away.

We had arrived the Monday night after the biggest storm this part of the coast had experienced in living memory. Not surprisingly, Ecuador's legendary party town was dead. Frankie and I dumped our bags in an inexpensive surfer's flophouse and had a drink in an empty beach bar decorated with seashells and whalebones. Janis Joplin sang *Bobby Magee*. Around the corner we munched on tasty *empanadas* made by a bubbly Colombian girl. "Where's the action?" we asked. "There's nothing going on tonight," she said. "You should come by on a weekend."

We returned to the beach to sit by the bonfires. "Sometimes this place is truly crazy," said Frankie, "jumping every weekend with surfing events, bikini contests and beach parties. The Bikini Open got so lewd they had to stop it. The girls were taking off their tops and dropping their bottoms, going nude in front of the cameras."

In the gray light of dawn the fires were still burning. I walked up to **La Punta** (the point) about a kilometer (just over a half mile) from the village of Montañita, where a handful of surfers were twisting like ballet dancers on the crests of two-meter (six-foot), white-topped waves. Sitting on the beach one said: "Ecuador is a fabulous place to surf, and Montañita is the best. From October to March the water is about 27°C (80°F). You get one to one-and-a-half meter (four- to five-foot)-waves with a hollow right-hander at low tide and a real workable wall at high. I've had a couple of big days at 10 ft (three meters). Down south at **Engabao** where you get real thick hollow beasties."

Frigate birds make their nests on the islands of Islas de Fragatas and Isla de la Plata.

Leaving the surfers to their surf, I wandered around La Punta checking out its hotels. For most visitors Montañita is a get-it-as-you-see-it place: you get what accommodation you see when you're here. Many of the less-expensive hostels and dormitory-style lodgings don't have phones anyway, making reservations difficult. Recommended hotels at La Punta include **Baja Montañita** ✆ (04) 281188, with pool, at the top end of the price range; **Rincón del Amigo**; **Casa Del Sol**; **Cabañas Cantina Tres Palmas**; **Vito's Cabanas;** and **El Pelicano** — a funky little place with a cool bar. As for dining, I found only an array of inexpensive eateries. But Montañita is growing fast, new places are opening frequently, and by the time you read this there could even be a MacDonald's in town.

Time was ebbing like the tide. We pushed down the rest of the coastline to Salinas with hardly a break. The further south we went the trees became fewer, and the landscape became drier. Crossing **Río Manglaralto**, we drove through a storm of white butterflies. We might have stopped at **Valdivia**, site of the ancient Valdivian culture that flourished between 3000 and 2000 BC. But sadly, aside from a small museum, there's not much of ancient Valdivia to see. The best of the Venuses of Valdivia sculptures, for which the culture is best known, are on display in the Museum of the Banco Central in Quito. Nor were we tempted to stop in **San Pedro**, an ugly town that once suffered from a reputation of coarseness and vulgarity.

Sticking up like a rhino horn into the Pacific, the dry scrub land of the **Santa Elena Peninsula** supports the country's second-biggest oil refinery and a fishing industry with everything from fish and shrimp packing plants to meal manufacturers and ice-making factories. Most of this industry is around the city of **La Libertad**.

Just a few kilometers west of Libertad, the glitzy resort of **Salinas** is totally dedicated to tourism with an lavish array of condos, hotels, restaurants, bars, *discotecas*, water sports facilities and the posh Salinas Yacht Club. Rich *guayaquileños* come to Salinas to show off their latest-model cars, play in their speedboats, gamble at the casino and perhaps indulge in a bit of deep-sea fishing.

A four-lane highway carried us smoothly through an urban strip into the heart of town, where modern, 15-floor apartments on one side faced an attractive, white-sand beach on the other side of the road. We got out of our car and plunged into the blue water. Wonderfully refreshed, we headed off to find some ceviche, no difficult task in a town that seems to be the ceviche center of the universe, with plazas full of clean and pleasant outdoor *cevicherías*, where fish is flapping-fresh. Working my way through a mountain of prawns, I wondered why a young kid was watching us so intently. I soon realized he was waiting for leftovers, a sign that Salinas isn't only for the rich.

As we eat, Frankie, something of an expert, gave me his take on the Salinas nightlife. "On weekends and holidays, the place goes nuts," he began. Hadn't I heard this somewhere before? "Anything goes. **Tequila-La** and **Nautica** are the most popular rockin' party bars. On weekends they are wild, packed, dancing until dawn. The fashion scene is really hip. Women wear next to nothing in the bars, maybe high heels and a bikini. The guys all act big and bad. And cars are important. People come down in Porsches and Lamborghinis, like in Miami Beach."

As for food, Frankie's view was that there were tons of restaurants in Salinas so there should be no problem in getting something to eat. And plenty of hotels, too, Frankie's recommendations being **El Carruaje** ✆ (04) 774267, **Hotel Salinas** ✆ (04) 774267, and **Calypso**. Smaller, less-expensive hotels he mentioned **Hostal Florida** ✆ (04) 772780, and **Hostal Las Rocas**.

This was the last day of our coastal odyssey and we had to be in Guayaquil that evening. But rather than driving on good roads through the peninsula, a distance of about 150 km (94 miles), we decided to take the road less-traveled around the south, passing along the most deserted and forgotten corner of the coast. On the 15-km (nine-mile)-long, empty beach of **Punta Carnero** a sign stuck into the sand read "Dangerous waters, rip tides and whirl pools present" (in English, surprisingly). Out to sea, a couple of lone surfers braved the waves.

Cutting slightly inland, the road became no more than a cattle trail through scrub, cactus and brown dust. Nothing moved in the dry landscape except for a few goats and cows. we stopped in the small, poor village of **Chanduy**, on a cliff overlooking the sea, and listened to an old man in a shack playing guitar, singing local *pasillo* (passage) music. Most of his songs were about bad loves and women who did him wrong and now were gone — Latin country music played by a Ecuadorian cowboy in a straw Stetson. Out in the bush, a man on a horse with a lasso attached to his saddle was herding goats.

Rattling and rolling along the rough trail, we passed through hamlets with the indigenous names of **Tugaduaja**, **Engunga** and **Engabao**. Each settlement has a small church and a few blockhouses positioned seemingly at random on brown earth reminiscent of an aboriginal settlement in the Australian outback. The few people we saw were Asian-looking *indígenas* with slanted, roundish faces and flat features.

The road was paved after Engabao. As the sun was setting, we hurried to the broad beach of **Playas**, a tacky, now empty resort that fills with day-trippers from Guayaquil on weekends. After driving down the coast of Ecuador, from the mangrove forests of Esmeraldas to the desert scrub of the Santa Elena peninsula, we headed for Ecuador's biggest and busiest city.

Some fishing boats on the beach near Chanduy on the southern coast of Guayas Province.

GUAYAQUIL

Guayaquil doesn't have the best reputation. People from other parts of Ecuador say their country's biggest city, with a population of some three million, is a steamy, smelly, malaria-infested seaport ridden with crime, corruption and pollution. *Guayaquileños* might agree, to a point, but will also mention that theirs is the country's richest city, contributing the lion's share to the economy, where the hotels, nightlife, shopping and business opportunities are second to none. They may add, nobody knows how to enjoy themselves better than lively *Guayaquileños*, least of all *Quiteños*.

Guayaquil is on the way up, and the city is creating a new identity. Many gleaming new high-rises have been built or are under construction, including a massive World Trade Center. Sweeping new highways and interchanges are creating a Los Angeles-style landscape. The city is cleaning itself up, literally, by collecting trash three times a week, whereas before it was only once, if ever. Though there are still crumbling tenement blocks, slums and shanty towns resembling parts of Hong Kong or Shanghai, there are also smart and affluent suburbs in the north of the city.

Guayaquil isn't perceived as a major tourist destination despite its improvements. Its crime rate is a deterrent to visitors, although residents say the streets of Quito are just as, if not more, dangerous. Most tourists come here to change buses on their way elsewhere, or to hop on plane to the Galápagos Islands.

Background

An tragic and heroic tale is the origin of Guayaquil's name. According to legend, the word is said to be the combination of the names of an Indian prince Guaya and his wife, named Quil. Guaya fought bitterly against invasions of both the Incas and the Spanish conquistadors, but came to realize he could not resist any longer. To avoid capture, the couple committed double suicide, with Guaya first killing Quil and then drowning himself. What is true about this story is that fierce fighting did occur between *indígenas* and Spanish before and after Francisco de Orellana founded the city in 1537.

The story is an appropriate foundation-myth for a city that for 450 years has seen an abundance of tragedy and heroism. Situated on flat land at the mouth of the Guayas river, the town has had its share of floods and pirates raids. With no stone in the area, the houses were built of wood and thus frequently destroyed in fires. A massive conflagration in 1896 ruined most of the city, including many of its attractive, wooden colonial houses. In addition to floods, piracy and fire, the hot and humid location of Guayaquil exposed its inhabitants to plagues and tropical diseases, especially malaria and yellow fever. Despite these challenges, *Guayaquileños* have shown heroic resilience and strength, creating the industrial and commercial capital of the country.

Guayaquil's port is its *raison d'être*, the cornerstone of its economy. Most of the vast agricultural riches of the fertile plains of the western lowlands, in particular bananas, cacao and coffee, as well as imports of cars, machinery, electrical goods, computers and other requisite consumer items passes through Guayaquil. Powered by warehouse income, Guayaquil has also developed its own industries with oil and sugar refineries, food processing, breweries and many types of manufacturing. "We create the country's wealth," say the *Guayaquileños*, "but *Quiteños* spend it."

General Information

Guayaquil is not likely, nor recommended, to be the first stop for first-time visitors to Ecuador. Those who do come here should already be comfortable with finding their way around Ecuadorian towns. Arriving by air, you'll land at **Simón Bolívar Airport**, on Avenida de las Américas, about five kilometers (three miles) north of the town center.

Alternatively, you'll come by bus and get off at the **Terminal Terrestre bus station**, about two kilometers (just over a mile) north of the airport. You can walk or take a taxi between the two. Taxis from the airport to the center of town shouldn't be more than four or five dollars, but you might have to bargain. On the opposite side of the street from the airport terminals are buses to town. There are plenty of buses and taxis between the bus station and the center.

Some travelers arrive at the **train station** in the suburb of **Durán**, on the east side of the Río Guayas. You can catch a **ferry** from here across the river, or take a taxi for a few dollars across the three-kilometer (almost two-mile)-long bridge to the city center.

Guayaquil has all the facilities and amenities one would expect for a major city, including a number of **embassies** and **consulates**. You'll find the **British Embassy** ☎ (04) 560400 at Córdova 625 and Padre Solano, the **American Embassy** ☎ (04) 323570 on 9 de Octubre 1571 and García Moreno; and the **Canadian Embassy** ☎ (04) 563580 on Córdova 812 and Rendón. Most Latin American, as well as European, countries have embassies and consulates, important for information if you are traveling onward in South America. See the telephone book or inquire at your hotel for further details.

There are a number of airline offices, both domestic and international:

Air France ☎ (04) 320313
British Airways ☎ (04) 325080 or 323834
Ecuatoriana ☎ (04) 322025
Iberia ☎ (04) 329558 or 329382 or 320664
KLM ☎ (04) 328028, (04) 200600
TAME ☎ (04) 561751
Varig ☎ (04) 560876 or 560890

The official CETUR **tourist information offices**, which in general aren't too helpful, but may have city maps, are at the airport and on the waterfront on the corner of the Malecón and Avenida Olmedo. Private **travel agents** and tour operators are likely to be of more assistance and speak better English.

WHAT TO SEE AND DO

Despite its size, Guayaquil's numerous attractions bring few tourists. A walk along the **Malecón** by the wide Río Guayas reveals the essence of the town's maritime character. Where the Malecón crosses the end of the main thoroughfare, Avenida 9 de Octubre, **La Rotunda** statue commemorates the famous but secret meeting in Guayaquil, between the two great heroes of South American liberation, Simón Bolívar and General José de San Martin, in 1822, where the two men made important decisions about South America's political future.

Continuing north beyond the Malecón, you come to the historic **Las Peñas** district, where the city was founded. Because of its elevation, Las Peñas escaped floods and fires, and is the only area that still has cobbled streets and old wooden houses, some of them now occupied by artists. These back streets are not safe alone; go with a group or join a tour with a travel agent.

For more history, Guayaquil has several good museums. In contrast to other more predictable exhibits at the **Museo Municipal**, near the Hotel Continental, you might be able to see the collection of *tsantsas*, Shuar **shrunken heads**, although they aren't always on display. The small **Museo del Banco del Pacifico**, a block up from La Rotunda on Paula de Icaza, has an excellent archaeological collection. And the **Museo Banco Central**, where José de Antepara crosses with Avenida 9 de Octubre, has good anthropological and archaeological displays. Nearby, the **Casa de Cultura** has a fine collection of gold items.

To experience the tangy side of Guayaquil's street life, go to **La Bahía black market** on both sides of Avenida Olmedo towards the river where you can buy goods that have somehow fallen off boats at rock-bottom prices. You can save a fortune here on things like clothing, shoes, electrical goods, cameras, food and drink. Be warned: the market is rife with pickpockets and snatch thieves, mostly working in pairs, who might have the watch off your wrist as quickly as flick of a snake's tongue.

To explore the modern side of Guayaquil, take a trip to the northern suburb of **Urdesa**, an almost self-contained community with many good shops, malls and restaurants and a vibrant nightlife. To get away from the crowds, visit **Jardín Botánico**, also in the north of town, which has pleasant walks, a butterfly garden, gift shop, café and a wonderful collection of orchids.

WHERE TO STAY AND EAT

Reflecting its importance a business city, Guayaquil is well appointed-with first-class hotels, some even more expensive than those in Quito. Many new hotels have been built, leading to an oversupply, so it is worth trying to negotiate a discount.

Expensive

In the US$200 per double room range, the **Oro Verde** ☎ (04) 327999 FAX (04) 329350, on 9 de Octubre and Garcia Moreno, has every facility you could expect, including pool, business center, disco and restaurants. The new **Hilton Colón** ☎ (04) 298828 FAX (04) 298827, on Avenida Francisco de Orellana-Manzana III, is also in the top of the range, but slightly less expensive than the Oro Verde. Better value is the downtown, five-star **Hotel Continental** ✆ (04) 329270 FAX (04) 325454, known for its award-winning restaurants, with singles at US$90, sometimes discounted. In the same luxury range, the **Gran Hotel Guayaquil** ✆ (04) 329690 FAX (04) 327251, has good sporting facilities, with a swimming pool open to non-guests at a reasonable charge and excellent breakfasts. Even if you're staying elsewhere this is a good place for a morning swim and hearty breakfast to set you up for the day.

Moderate

Good, mid-priced hotels are scarce in Guayaquil. Two that have been recommended are **Hotel Palace** ✆ (04) 321080 FAX (04) 322887, Chile and Luque and the nearby **Hotel Doral** ✆ (04) 327133 FAX (04) 327088, on Chile and Aguirre. Both hotels charge in the region of US$50. At about US$30 per double, the **Hotel Rizzo** ✆ (04) 325210 FAX (04) 326209, is also recommended.

Inexpensive

The best deal of all is the budget hostel **Ecuahogar** ✆ (04) 248357 FAX (04) 248341, on Avenida Isidro Ayora, near the airport and bus terminal. Rooms in this pleasant house are US$10–20, depending whether they are shared, and includes light breakfast. Laundry and storage facilities are available. If you're passing through Guayaquil but don't intend to stay, Ecuahogar is a convenient stopover.

As with hotels, good, mid-priced restaurants are also scarce in Guayaquil, though **La Canoa** at the Hotel Continental is a notable exception. This 24-hour eatery serves beautifully prepared, *típico* Ecuadorian dishes (try their *cazuela*) as well as gourmet burgers with French fries, in pleasant surroundings. Also pleasant, and good for seafood, are the floating boat-restaurants moored on the piers on the Malecón, notably **El Pirata** and **Muelle 4** and **Muelle 5**. Guayaquil, which has a large Chinese population, is well-known for its good Chinese *chifas*, **Gran Chifa** on Pedro Carbo being one of the best. For gourmet cuisine, the luxury hotels have fancy but expensive restaurants. At the other end of the scale, some of the street vendors sell excellent grilled chicken and meats. Well-known chains such as **Burger King** and **Dunkin' Donuts** are popular with *Guayaquileños*.

For Guayaquil's famous nightlife take a taxi to **VE Estrada** in **Urdesa**. Popular clubs are **Amnesia**, **Infinity Club**, and **Tequila-la** in Urdesa Norte. But if the club scene doesn't appeal, and you are more interested in a pint of English or Scottish draft beer (a change from the ubiquitous, though very good Ecuadorian *pilsna*), head for the **Rob Roy Bar** on Avenida Herradura 15 and Avenida Demetrio Agouilira, a popular gringo expat hangout.

BEYOND GUAYAQUIL

From Guayaquil. many travelers ride the fabled train up into the sierra passing through **Bucay**, up the **Devil's Nose** (the most thrilling part), and onwards to **Alausí** and **Ríobamba**. The whole journey takes 10–12 hours and costs around US$15. To save time and avoid the less interesting parts, you can take a two-hour bus ride to Bucay, transfer to the train and ride on the roof for the Devil's Nose section, and then get back onto a bus at Alausí. At the time of writing, trains leave from the Durán station, over the river from Guayaquil at 6:25 AM every morning, except Mondays and Wednesdays, arriving at Bucay at about 10:30 AM. Check the train schedules because they change often.

Tickets go on sale at 6 AM on the day of travel. The bus ride up the Andes from Guayaquil to **Cuenca**, through **Zhud**, **Cañar** and **Azogues**, is also a spectacular journey.

If you are heading for **Quito**, there are frequent, daily walk-on flights, or you can take an eight-hour bus ride. If you want to see some banana, rice, coffee and fruit growing areas in the **Western Lowlands**, you can take a bus north to **Quevedo** through **Los Ríos Province**, which as the name implies is an area of many rivers. Quevedo is known as the "Chinatown of Ecuador" because of its descendants of Chinese who helped construct the railway at the end of the nineteenth century.

Santo Domingo de los Colorados, further north, is the home of the **Colorados Indians**, but visitors are no longer likely to see them in their bowl-shaped, bright red hair styles, dyed with achiote plant, and faces painted with black stripes. A few kilometers southeast of the fast-growing town of Santo Domingo is the well-known **Tinalandia Hotel** ☎(02) 247461 FAX (02) 442638 in Quito. Established by a Russian émigré many years ago, the hotel is surrounded by subtropical forests with many species of plants and birds. They also have a nine-hole golf course, one of the few in Ecuador.

The road south from Guayaquil passes through the **Manglares Churute Ecological Reserve**, one of the few areas of mangroves left on the coast. Beyond the reserve, bananas, pineapples, citrus fruit and coffee take over. **Machala**, the capital of El Oro Province, 200 km (125 miles) south of Guayaquil, is known as the Banana Capital of the World, and indeed a banana festival takes place in the town each September. The town isn't big on tourism, though the beach of **Jambelí**, on a nearby island, is said to be beautiful but primitive, and treasured by birders in search of the rare rufous-necked wood-rail.

From Machala, a road branches southeast towards **Piñas** and the old mining town of **Zaruma**. Though way off most travelers' paths, this is a picturesque area, and Zaruma, perched on a hill, has some charming old wooden buildings. White-skinned, blue-eyed descendants of Spanish colonialists still work old and exhausted gold mines, some dating back to pre-Columbian days. Recently-discovered pre-Columbian ruins indicate the area was well-populated before the Inca invasion.

Most travelers head directly south from Machala to the **Peruvian** border. The last Ecuadorian town is **Huaquillas**, an untidy, dismal place with a reputation for smuggling and pickpocketers. But inexpensive Ecuadorian goods have made it a shopping center for Peruvians who nip across the border for cut-price shopping. Travelers leaving Ecuador must complete immigration formalities in the town before crossing the **International Bridge** at the border.

LEFT: The fruit of the land in the Western Lowlands. ABOVE: Riding the rails from the coast to the sierra up the flanks of the Andes, passing along Devil's Nose en route.

The Galápagos Islands

STEPPING ONTO A BEACH ON ONE OF THE GALÁPAGOS ISLANDS you could well find yourself surrounded by dozens of sunbathing sea lions lying about on the sand like so many sacks of potatoes. As you approach, they don't blunder off into the sea or shuffle behind a rock, as you might expect; they keep on sleeping in the sun or stare at you with studied indifference. If you stand within a meter or two they might snarl or bark with a sound that's a cross between a pig's oink and the klaxon of antique car, as if to say, "This is my space." But they are unlikely to be aggressive towards you, nor frightened.

Walking along rocky shorelines, you encounter blue-footed boobies laying eggs on the pathways who show not the slightest concern at your presence. They don't bat an eye if you approach within a meter. Prehistoric marine iguanas, which look like miniature dragons or extras from a science fiction movie, eye you languorously from jagged lava rocks and hardly deign to move if you poke a camera lens within a few inches of their glistening heads.

For hundreds of years human visitors have commented on the abundance and tameness of the wildlife in these remote and isolated islands that straddle the equator in the Pacific Ocean, about 1,000 km (625 miles) off the coast of Ecuador. In fact, the word tame isn't quite accurate since it implies domesticated wildlife. For the most part animals of the Galápagos have evolved and lived without fear of predators common in other parts of the world, neither human nor four-legged. This absence of fear on the part of the birds and animals, make human visitors feel an extraordinary, uplifting harmony with nature that cannot be experienced anywhere else on earth. It's for good reasons the Galápagos Islands have often been called the Garden of Eden.

For equally good reasons, the archipelago is also known as the world's greatest natural laboratory of evolution. Ever since Charles Darwin's visit in 1835, scientists have been drawn to the islands to study creatures that evolved in isolation from their cousins on the mainland. Darwin was interested in the various species of finches, all of which had adapted to local conditions and evolved in different ways. The islands continue to attract scientists from all over the world, and the Charles Darwin Research Station on Santa Cruz is an important center for their activities.

In 1959, responding to a growing awareness of the environmental and scientific importance of the archipelago, Ecuador designated 97% of the 8,000-sq-km (3,088-square-miles) land area of Galápagos as a national park. In 1986, the Galápagos Marine Resources Reserve was established, protecting the water around the archi-pelago. UNESCO has also recognized the islands as a Man and Biosphere Reserve, and as a World Heritage Site.

Ecuador manages the islands through the Galápagos National Park Service, which has offices in Puerto Ayora on Santa Cruz. Nearby is the Charles Darwin Research Station, run by the Charles Darwin Foundation. The Research Station carries out scientific research and assists the Park Service.

The Galápagos National Parks Service has designated more than 60 visitors' sites on the islands, enabling visitors to see all the interesting wildlife; the rest of the park is off limits to tourists. At each visitors' site a discreetly marked trail provides excellent views of wildlife, vegetation and landscape of the island. Most of the trails are less than a mile long but can be difficult underfoot, leading over rough lava or uneven boulders. There are also one or two longer hikes in the highlands.

The different sites are varied in their scenery and vegetation but some animals are common at nearly all of them. These include Galápagos sea lions, marine iguanas, lava lizards and a variety of coastal birds. In addition to the visitors' sites on land, the Galápagos offer excellent scuba diving, though these aren't recommended for beginners. However, many snorkeling spots offer anyone the chance to see the colorful underwater life of the Galápagos Islands.

Almost without exception, visitors are extremely impressed with what they see and do on the Galápagos Islands. "The trip of a lifetime," they say, "Like nowhere else on earth" or "Paradise on this planet." The

PREVIOUS PAGES Sunset/sunrise LEFT over Santa Cruz/Santa Fé Island. Sea lions RIGHT inhabit most islands of the Galápagos and are generally not frightened of nor aggressive towards human visitors. OPPOSITE: Marine iguanas on Hood Island.

only negative things you'll hear anyone say will be about increasing threats to the environment and wildlife, and fears that the fragile ecosystem will be further damaged.

BACKGROUND

Although they had no aboriginal human population, the Galápagos Islands have been a magnet for naturalists as well as a refuge for pirates, prisoners, castaways, rogues and eccentrics over the centuries. Potsherds examined by the Norwegian anthropologist and explorer, Thor Heyerdahl, suggest that the first sailors to the islands came from the coast of northern Peru. It is also thought that one of the great Incas, Tupac Yupanqui, sent an expedition to the islands at the end of the fifteenth century.

The Bishop of Panama, Fray Tomás de Berlanga, who was blown off course onto the islands while on a mission to Peru in March 1535, made the first written record of the archipelago. In a letter to King Charles V of Spain, he wrote of finding seals and turtles and tortoises so big that each could carry a man, and many serpents-like iguanas, and "birds so silly that they did not know how to flee." On one island there was "not even space to grow a bushel of corn because it was as if God had showered the land with very big stones." The bishop is credited for naming the islands Las Encantadas, the Bewitched or Enchanted Ones, because they seemed to move in the swirling mists. From his and the pilot's report of the voyage, the Flemish cartographer, Abraham Ortelius, learned of the islands and marked them as *Isolas de Galápagos* on his *Orbis Terrarum* of 1574, the word *galápagos* being Spanish for turtles.

BRITISH BUCCANEERS

During the sixteenth and seventeenth centuries the Galápagos Islands were a refuge for British buccaneers pillaging the Spanish colonies on the western coast of South America and attacking Spanish galleons laden with Inca gold on their way back to Spain. One such ship, the Bachelor's Delight, made several visits to the islands in the 1680s. A member of the crew, William Ambrose Cowley, drew maps and named each island after leading personages of the day.

Thus these remote, uninhabited islands of the eastern Pacific acquired bizarre names like King James Island, the Duke of Albemarle's Island, the Earl of Abingdon's Island, the Duke of York's Island, Lord Cullpeper's Island, the Duke of Norfolk's Island, and Sir John Narborough's Island. Subsequently the islands were re-named by the British, United States and the Spanish, as well as the government of Ecuador when it claimed sovereignty of the islands in 1832. The result has been a quaint confusion about names, so even modern maps show as many as three names for one island.

The Duke of Norfolk's Island, for instance, has been known variously as Indefatigable, Porter Island, Valdez, Chavez, San Clemente and finally Santa Cruz, by which it is now known. It is shown on maps as Santa Cruz, with Indefatigable and sometimes Chavez. Isla Santa María is usually known by its fomer name of Floreana and its even older name, Charles, is still shown on contemporary maps. One island is simply called Sin Nombre, or Nameless.

To add to the confusion, the islands themselves were officially named Archipelago de Colón by the National Assembly of Ecuador

in 1892 to commemorate the 400th anniversary of Columbus's first voyage, Colón being the Spanish spelling of his name. But they are still called the Galápagos Islands in everyday usage.

The First Resident

The first human resident of the Galápagos Islands on record was Patrick Watkins, an Irish castaway. According to Captain David Porter's journal, a United States Navy officer who served in the archipelago during the Anglo-American war of 1812, the man's appearance was the most dreadful that can be imagined. His ragged clothes were infested with vermin and scarcely sufficient to cover his nakedness; his red hair and beard matted, his skin much burned from constant exposure to the sun; and so wild and savage was his manner and appearance that he struck everyone with horror. He had no apparent desires aside from getting enough rum to keep himself intoxicated. Mostly he was found in a state of perfect insensibility, rolling around the rocks of the mountains.

After several years on Charles Island (now known as Floreana), where he supported his thirst by growing and selling vegetables to visiting ships, Watkins got some sailors extremely drunk and kidnapped them. He then stole a boat and embarked with these men. The boat arrived in Guayaquil on the coast of Ecuador with only Patrick Watkins on board; nobody knows what happened to his slaves. Watkins was thrown in jail in Peru and nothing more was heard of him.

During the nineteenth century there were various attempts to colonize the Galápagos Islands, none of them very successful. A General José Villamil tried to develop an enterprise to cultivate and export orchilla for the manufacture of dyes, for which he

OPPOSITE: Fishing boat off Rábida Island, one of the best spots for snorkeling in the Galápagos Islands.

brought the first colonists to Charles Island. These were a group of eighty Ecuadorian soldiers who had been condemned to death for mutiny, but reprieved on condition they worked for the general. The islands were also used as a dumping ground for political exiles, common criminals and prostitutes deported from Guayaquil.

At the same time, the islands were regularly visited by whaling boats, naval ships and scientific expeditions. In 1825, Captain Lord Byron of the British Royal Navy, son of the poet, anchored off Albemarle Island. He

wrote in his diary, "The place is like a new creation; the birds and beasts do not get out of our way; the pelicans and sea-lions look in our faces as if we had no right to intrude on their solitude; the small birds are so tame that they hop upon our feet; and all this amidst volcanoes which are burning round us on either hand. Altogether it is as wild and desolate scene as imagination can picture."

CHARLES DARWIN

Ten years later, another Englishman, the naturalist Charles Darwin, spent five weeks in the archipelago as part of his five-year journey of exploration and scientific discovery aboard HMS *Beagle*. "Nothing could be less inviting than the first appearance," he wrote. "A broken field of black, basaltic lava... crossed by great fissures, is everywhere covered by stunted, sunburned brushwood... the many craters vividly remind me of parts of Staffordshire, where the great iron foundries are most numerous."

Notwithstanding those bleak first impressions Darwin found the islands "infinitely strange, unlike any other islands in the world." And he recorded that the natural history of the archipelago was "very remarkable: it seems to be a little word within itself; the greater number of its inhabitants, both vegetable and animal being found nowhere else."

Despite intense heat and a shortage of drinking water, Darwin worked hard at collecting his specimens. Only later, during the years he spent examining his collection on his return to England, did he recognize the full significance of his work. He noted important differences between similar species collected on different islands, particularly in the shapes of the beaks of finches. He concluded that over the millenia, the finches had adapted to the varying conditions of the islands. One type of finch would have thick beaks for cracking nuts, for example, while another would be adapted for pecking at fruit or flowers, and yet another finch used twigs to dig insects from the bark of trees.

These and other observations eventually led Darwin to his theory that man had evolved from apes, in direct contradiction to the accepted ideas of divine creation. Darwin set forth his views in his controversial book, *On the Origin of the Species by Natural Selection*, which he published in 1859, nearly 25 years after his visit to the Galápagos Islands. The first edition of 1,250 copies sold out on the day of issue. Darwin's theory that our human ancestors had emerged from primordial slime stimulated the most vigorous intellectual debate of the nineteenth century.

CURIOUS COLONISTS

Darwin's writings stimulated worldwide interest and further scientific expeditions to the Galápagos Islands. Wealthy Americans cruised down on their yachts and in the 1920s American journalist, William Beebe wrote a best-selling book about the islands: *Galápagos: World's End*. The book sold particularly well in Norway, and inspired several Norwegians to come and live on the archipelago. In the 1930s, a German couple settled on Floreana and attracted international interest because of their curious lifestyles. Before leaving Germany, Dr. Friedrich Ritter and his companion took the precaution of having all their teeth removed and replaced with steel dentures, because they would be unable to obtain dental treatment on the island.

Three years later another German couple, Heinz and Margaret Wittmer and their 12-year-old son, joined these two lone inhabitants of the 250-sq-km (96-sq-mile) island. The two families did not care for each other. The atmosphere on the island became more poisonous when a self-styled Austrian baroness arrived on the island with her three male lovers. The scene was set for one of the world's most intriguing true-life, unsolved mystery stories. First one lover, then the baroness with another lover disappeared. Dr. Ritter died in mysterious circumstances. At the time of writing, the aged Margaret Wittmer, the only survivor, still lives on Floreana.

THREATS TO THE ENVIRONMENT

In the past two decades colonization and tourism to the Galápagos Islands have increased rapidly. Although the National Park accounts for 95% of the islands' land area, there are serious problems with settler encroachment. Ten years ago the population of the islands was around 6,000, of which some 2,500 lived on Santa Cruz, the center of the tourist industry. The present population of the islands is thought to be approaching 20,000, with an annual growth rate of eight percent.

An even greater threat to the environment is the animals and plants human visitors and colonists have brought with them. Feral cats, dogs, rats, pigs, goats, donkeys, deer and cattle have contributed to the destruction of eggs, hatchlings and the vegetation, on which all the native species depend. On Española the tortoise population was almost extinct by the 1960s. A captive-breeding program for tortoises was started at Darwin

The endemic giant Galápagos tortoise LEFT, after which the islands are named, are the biggest tortoises in the world and weighs up to 250 kg (550 lb). ABOVE: Sea lions are one of the main attractions in the Galápagos Islands.

Station, and the goats were eliminated. Young tortoises have now been returned to their ancestral island and the unique subspecies has been saved from extinction.

Served by some 100 cruise ships, the fast-growing tourist market also threatens the ecological balance. The National Parks Authority imposes strict control on where visitors are allowed to land, and all visitors are strongly requested to obey common-sense rules, such as not to stray from the paths, nor feed or touch the birds and animals.

CENTRAL ISLANDS

In rough terms, there are about a dozen major, a dozen minor and about 50 small islands and islets in the Galápagos chain. Of these only five are inhabited: Santa Cruz, Baltra, San Cristóbal, Santa María (usually known as Floreana) and Isabela. The capital of Ecuador's Galápagos Province is Puerto Baquerizo Moreno on San Cristóbal Island, although the largest town is Puerto Ayora on Santa Cruz.

BALTRA

Most visitors land at the airport on the small, flat island of Baltra, just north of the main tourist island of Santa Cruz, where they are confronted by a dry, desert-like moonscape of brown lava rock and tall cactus plants and wind-blown trees. American forces built the runway to defend the Panama Canal in World War II. The airport was given to Ecuador after the war, and is now the main entry point for tourists to the islands. There is an Ecuadorian naval base to the west of the island and a small port for cruise ships and cargo boats. The Ecuadorian army supervises the island. On landing, visitors have to pay a National Parks Entry fee of US$80 and port fee of US$12. There are no visitors' sites on the island.

NORTH SEYMOUR

This small island, close to the airport on Baltra, is a popular stopping point for cruise boats because it has one of the most active nesting colonies of frigate birds. Here visitors can see the splendid sight of the male frigate bird puffing up its big red chest pouch in a flamboyant courtship display to attract females. Blue-footed boobies, marine iguanas and sea lions are also plentiful on the island. North Seymour is often the last stop on a cruise before passengers fly out from Baltra, formerly known as South Seymour. The nearby islet of **Mosquera**, only 600 m (2,000 ft) long, has a sandy beach with a sea lion colony, and is sometimes the first stop on a boat tour of the islands.

DAPHNE MAJOR AND MINOR

These two small, barren tips of submerged volcanoes are surrounded by steep cliffs, undercut by waves, making it very difficult to land. The main claim to fame of Daphne Major is that for nearly two decades it has been the site of a major scientific research program. Peter and Rosemary Grant and their assistants, have been investigating and measuring the characteristics of the island's varying population of Darwin's finches over some 20 generations. The results of their work, shows an intimate and fascinating portrait of evolution as it happens in real time. Jonathan Weiner, author of a book about this research, *The Beak of the Finch*, which won the 1995 Pulitzer Prize, described the Grants' project as "one of the most remarkable works in progress on this planet."

SANTA CRUZ

Most visitors get to know Santa Cruz better than the other islands. Unless they are met by a cruise boat, passengers arriving at Baltra take a bus from the airport (no taxis are available) before transferring to a small ferry to cross the Itabaca Channel to Santa Cruz. Another bus then takes them on a 40-km (25-mile), one-hour ride over the top of the island and down to the small town of Puerto Ayora. This empty, straight, narrow road cuts through vegetation zones of the island, from arid north shore to wet, green highlands. Some tour buses stop in the highlands so passengers can stretch their legs

OPPOSITE: Ninety-five percent of the land area of the remote and isolated Galápagos Islands are designated parklands.

and look at the twin craters, known as **Los Gemelos**, one each side of the road, outside the village of **Santa Rosa**. These 30-m (100-ft)-deep holes in the earth look as if they were caused by volcanic explosion or blasted by meteorites, but in fact are thought to be caved-in magma chambers. Dense scalesia forest surrounding the craters abounds with wildlife. Birders should watch out for vermilion flycatchers and the diurnal short-eared owl.

For people used to living in big cities, **Puerto Ayora**, with a population of some 10,000, is a pleasant, peaceful, fishing port. Big-billed pelicans dive for fish in Pelican Bay, while sea lions and marine iguanas sunbathe on the rocks by the shore and on the terraces of seaside cafés. Bicycles, pick-up trucks and motor scooters make up most of the traffic around the waterfront, and there are only two sets of traffic lights in town. Most visitors board boats here for island cruises, while others simply enjoy a few day's break onshore, availing themselves of a choice of bars, restaurants, hotels, dive shops, souvenir shops, travel agents and banks.

Many residents and others who have known the island for decades are shocked by the development of Puerto Ayora in recent years. In 1980 the population was a quarter of what it was in 1998. A former Galápagos tour guide told me there was only one car on the island when he first came to Santa Cruz in the 1970s. Jimmy Perez, owner of Hotel Sol y Mar, arrived in the early 1960s as a beachcomber, when there were only 120 inhabitants on the whole island, most of them farmers.

The main concern of Señor Perez and others is that rising population, mostly from mainland Ecuador, is harming the archipelago's ecosystem through illegal fishing and encroachment on national parks. Insufficient electricity, fresh water, garbage disposal services, education and medical facilities are also problems caused by population pressure and the increasing number of tourists. Proposals are now being considered on limiting the number of tourists and immigrants from the mainland who come to the archipelago hoping to make a living from tourists.

What to See and Do

Aside from the warm climate and the vacation atmosphere, the main attractions at Puerto Ayora are the **Charles Darwin Research Station** and the Headquarters of the **Galápagos National Park**, a 15-minute walk northeast from town. At the Darwin Station giant tortoises are born and bred in captivity.

Visitors see how hatchling giant tortoises are incubated in dark boxes for the first two weeks of their lives, then transferred to outdoor corrals for two or three years. Then they are released into bigger, adoption corrals, which simulate natural conditions of the islands, where they learn to walk on lava rocks and how to find water. At four or five years old their shells are hard enough to protect them from predators, and they are released into the wild.

The last dozen or so remaining tortoises on Española island were taken in to the center, where some 200 offspring were brought up in captivity before being taken back to their island. A similar scheme for the Pinzón tortoise has been equally successful. The center has returned some 2,000 tortoises to their native islands throughout the archipelago. By the year 2000 that number should reach 3,000.

One tortoise who will probably never leave Darwin Station is Lonesome George, the sole survivor of the Pinta breed. Found unexpectedly on Pinta in 1971, he is now a resident of Santa Cruz. In spite of thorough searches of his birthplace, no mate has been found for George. There is a US$10,000 reward for anyone who does — a tricky proposition for a bounty hunter because only qualified scientists are allowed on the island.

George, who is from the biggest of the saddleback subspecies, shares his corral at the Darwin Station with two females from Volcán Wolf on Isabela. Although from a subspecies that is very similar to George's, the old man doesn't show interest in mating. Scientists have taken the precaution of extracting and deep-freezing George's sperm for possible use in the future.

The chance to say good-bye to a dying breed is one of the high points of a visit to the Darwin Center, but also interesting is the walk-in tortoise enclosure for almost face-to-face meetings with other incredible, armor-plated hulks, though visitors should refrain from touching them. In addition there's a museum, an exhibition center, a souvenir shop selling T-shirts to support the research station, and trails through salt bush, mangrove and cacti plantations populated by Darwin's finches and other birds.

A visit to the Darwin Station can be a hot and exhausting experience, after which a swim might be very welcome. The best place for this is **Tortuga (Turtle) Bay**, three kilometers (just under two miles) southwest of Puerto Ayora. The bay has a fine white beach, one of the best on the archipelago, beautiful blue sea and a lagoon protected by a spit of land. Sea turtles come to lay their eggs here, but you're more likely to spot pelicans, marine iguanas and flamingos. Although the wildlife is protected you don't need to be accompanied by a guide and you could well have the beach to yourself.

Most visitors don't spend much time, if any, in Puerto Ayora because they are on cruises from the beginning to the end of their island stay. And it's true that the best way to see the wildlife is by boat. However some people make their reservations when they get to Puerto Ayora, which means they usually get it for less, last minute price for a cruise (in the low season), though they might have to spend a few days on Santa Cruz. This is no hardship. Aside from relaxing in the warm sunshine, there are plenty of places to explore and things to do on Santa Cruz.

OPPOSITE: The small, dark Lava Heron, seen here at St. James Bay on Santiago Island, is endemic to the Galápagos. ABOVE: A giant Galápagos tortoise on Isabela Island.

The fit and adventurous go hiking or horse riding in the highlands. A bus from Puerto Ayora takes you to the inland villages of **Bellavista** and **Santa Rosa**. Check departure times with a local travel agent or the CETUR office because service isn't frequent. From Bellavista you can climb the cinder cone of **Media Luna**. The base of the tallest peak of Santa Cruz, **Mt. Crocker** (864 m or 2,880 ft), is three kilometers (nearly two miles) further on. The view from the peak of Mt. Crocker is spectacular, taking in the scalesia forest pushing up the lava slopes of the barren volcano and some surrounding islands studded in the emerald sea.

From Santa Rosa, you can visit the wild **Tortoise Reserve** — wild because of the dense, unruly vegetation, and because the tortoises aren't tame like those at Darwin Station. The best way to see the reserve is with a guide and atop a horse. Guides can be hired and horses arranged through travel agents in Puerto Ayora. There are also a couple of private farms in the area, which supply refreshments and allow you to watch tortoises drinking at a watering hole for a small fee. Another place to watch the lumbering giants in the wild is on Volcán Alcedo on Isabela.

From Bellavista, it's a short walk to the nearby **Lava Tunnels**, long tubes of rock formed by the solidification of a lava flow during a volcanic eruption. There are several such tubes on the island but these are the most impressive, one of which is about a kilometer (just over a half mile) long and as high and wide as a subway tunnel. It is known as "The Tunnel of Endless Love," because of a heart-shaped hole in its roof. Guides with torches can be hired at Bellavista to explore these dark labyrinths.

Several coves and beaches cut into the isolated and rarely visited northwestern shore of Santa Cruz. The most interesting of these is **Caleta Tortuga Negra** (Black Turtle Cove) where green turtles can sometimes be seen during the breeding season from September to February.

Where to Stay

Santa Cruz is the only one of the five inhabited islands that has a decent choice of land-based accommodation ranging from budget to almost first class. During the popular vacation times of June, July, August, December, early January and Easter it's advisable to make reservations.

EXPENSIVE

At the top end of the scale is the well-established though not quite deluxe, **Hotel Galápagos** ☎ (05) 526330 with a hectare (five acres) of gardens and bungalow-style rooms from US$72, tax and service included. All 14 rooms have baths, hot showers and wide ocean views over Academy Bay. A scuba school attached to the hotel makes it popular with divers. Similarly-priced and also with a fine view across Academy Bay from its wide, wooden terrace is the very upmarket but informal **Red Mangrove Inn** ☎ (05) 526564. With only four guestrooms, this boutique hotel has an especially personal touch. If he's home, owner Polo Navaro will help with any arrangements you make, from islands tours to horse riding, kayaking and diving. Also in the top league for both price and quality is **Hotel Delfín** ☎ (05) 526297, which has its own private beach on the opposite side of Academy Bay and can be reached only by boat. The newly-renovated **Hotel Angermeyer** ☎ (05) 526186, with nearly 30 clean and comfortable rooms has a swimming pool and room service, but lacks character.

MODERATE

Mid-range hotels are in short supply at Puerto Ayora. For individuality and a splendid location on the waterfront in sight of fishing boats and diving pelicans, **Hotel Sol y Mar** ☎ (05) 526281, owned by Sr. Jimmy Perez, is recommended. Marine iguanas eye you calmly as you have breakfast on the terrace. Prices range from US$10 to $30 depending on the season and whether the room overlooks the sea. Accommodation is clean and functional, if not wildly comfortable.

INEXPENSIVE

Further down the scale, **Hotel Darwin** ☎ (05) 526193 has a pleasant courtyard and relaxed atmosphere, but at about US$5 per night you can't expect Hilton-standard beds and plumbing. Other hotels and hostels worth checking out are **Hotel Fernandina** ☎ (05) 526122 or 526499, which does full board and is suitable for families, and **Bed and Breakfast Peregrina** ((05) 526323. Hotels open, close and change hands frequently on Santa Cruz so it's worth asking fellow travelers and agents for the latest recommendations.

Where to Eat

For excellent, but quite expensive, Italian food in candle-lit atmosphere try **Las Cuatro Linternas** (The Four Lanterns), on Avenida Charles Darwin on Pelican Bay. Nearby but on the other end of the price scale is the **Iguana Café**, owned by a former Lufthansa stewardess, a good place for a beer or a late night snack. **La Dolce Vita** in the same area has a pleasant garden in which to sit and chat, or study Spanish while nursing a coffee or a cool drink. Further up Avenida Charles Darwin towards the harbor is the popular **La Panga** restaurant with adjoining *discoteca*. The food is reasonable and the disco usually very active. Almost next door is the well recommended **La Garrapata**, a popular watering hole for travelers. The road leading up from the harbor, Avenida Padre Julio Herrera, has a number of good-value bars and restaurants including **Restaurante El Sabrosán**, which serves excellent grilled meats and seafood. **Rincón del Alma** facing the waterfront park is also reasonably priced and popular.

NORTH AND SOUTH PLAZA

The twin islands of North and South Plaza lie just off the east coast of Santa Cruz. North Plaza is reserved for scientific research and is closed to visitors, while South Plaza has plentiful wildlife and makes an excellent day trip from Puerto Ayora. But if you are on a cruise boat it's better to visit South Plaza in the early morning or late afternoon to avoid other day-trippers. South Plaza's best-known resident is a huge, bad-tempered gentleman by the name of Charlie who jealously guards his harem. Charlie sometimes sits on the landing dock in an attempt to keep visitors away, but a few loud hand claps should be enough to make him let you pass. Charlie's entourage of females and pups are a playful, frolicsome bunch who play chicken with snorkelers by swimming up close to them underwater and veering off at the last moment. Such an encounter makes for one of the most breathtaking Galápagos experiences, but isn't dangerous

Puerto Ayora on Santa Cruz Island, the largest town on the Galápagos with a population of 10,000.

unless Charlie himself mistakes you for a competing male. Sea lions from a bachelor colony live above the cliffs on the other side of the island, sharing their rocky home with a host of seabirds from blue-footed and masked boobies to frigate birds, tropical birds, pelicans and swallowtail gulls. Large, brown-yellow land iguanas scuttle over the lava rocks in search of fruit from colossal prickly pear cacti.

Santa Fé

This small island, just 24 sq km (9.2 square miles) and only 20 km (12 miles) southeast of Santa Cruz, home to a unique subspecies of land iguana which is bigger than its cousins on other islands of the archipelago, sometimes growing up to 120 cm (four feet) in length. These unfriendly-looking, cactus-guzzling reptiles with long tails, clawed feet, spiny dorsal crests and blood-shot eyes look like mythical creatures from the medieval traditions. There are two marked paths on the island. One is a steep trail of about one and a half kilometers (nearly a mile), which heads for the iguana colony in the highlands. The other is a short walk from the landing point to a stand of giant cactus. Popular with day visitors from Santa Cruz, the island has a sea lion colony and a pleasant blue lagoon, though swimmers should keep an eye out for stingrays. Santa Fé's unique subspecies of giant tortoise was exterminated about a hundred years ago by American and European whalers and sealers who hunted them for meat.

Pinzón

At the end of the nineteenth century the Pinzón tortoise was dangerously near extinction because of depredations by whalers, sealers and scientific collectors. However, a captive breeding and re-introduction program at the Darwin Center, and the eradication of black rats that eat tortoise eggs and young hatchlings has rescued this saddleback breed. Visits to this cliff-ringed, 12-sq-km (four-and-a-half-square-mile) island, also known as Duncan, are usually restricted to scientists.

Rábida

Formerly known as Jervis, this five-square-kilometer (two-square-mile) island is one of the best snorkeling spots of the Galápagos, as well as the best place to see nesting pelicans. The ubiquitous sea lions lounge on a red sand beach and pink flamingos can occasionally be seen wading in a brackish lagoon.

San Salvador

The fourth-largest island of the archipelago, San Salvador (often referred to by one of its former names, Santiago and James) is also the largest uninhabited island. In the 1920s, and again in the 1960s, salt was mined from the inside of a volcanic crater on the western

end of the island. When Galápagos National Park was created in 1968, all property and mining rights were annulled and the island lost its small human population. San Salvador is overpopulated by feral goats, and other animals left behind, despite the National Park authorities' attempts to control them. Some abandoned buildings are all that can be seen of the old salt mine.

What to See and Do

San Salvador is a popular destination for cruise boats and there are four sites where visitors are allowed to land. The most impressive is the black sand and lava shoreline of **Puerto Egas** in **James Bay** on the west coast, with its eroded rock formations, caves and inlets which are home to a variety of wildlife including fur seals and a large colony of marine iguanas. Rock pools in the area known as **Grottoes** abound with hermit crabs, anemones and tiny fish that are a feast for herons, oystercatchers and other seabirds.

Energetic hikers can take a rocky, two-kilometer (just over a mile) trail from Puerto Egas to the peak of Sugarloaf Volcano for a magnificent view of the island. A less demanding hike goes to the crater with the old salt mine. The Puerto Egas site was temporarily closed in 1995 because of damage caused by too much foot traffic. At the north end of James Bay, best reached by

A stand of giant opuntia cactus lines the shore on Santa Fé. The island is also home to a unique subspecies of giant land iguana.

boat, is **Playa Espumilla (Foam Beach)** where the swimming is good and the sand is golden.

Beautiful **Buccaneer Cove**, further northwards along the coast from James Bay, was a popular haven for pirates in the seventeenth and eighteenth centuries. On the red beach below the dramatic palisade of cliffs the mariners tilted the hulls of their boats. In search of food supplies, they hunted for giant tortoises and the island's now-extinct land iguanas. Today, Buccaneer Cove is better known for its sea lions, seabirds and snorkeling.

Instead of a sandy beach, **Sullivan Bay**, on the eastern tip of San Salvador, boasts a wide moonscape of solid black lava, which might be the most extraordinary coastline you will ever see. In the middle of this enormous field of ropy lava formations are two imposing tuff cones, rocks which were surrounded by the flow of molten lava about a hundred years ago.

Bartolomé

Bartolomé's popularity is way out of proportion to its size. Just over a square kilometer (less than half a square mile) in area, the island is not much more than a stone's throw from San Salvador. A short walk to the 114-meter (380-ft) peak of the island is rewarded by magnificent views of the archipelago. Looking westwards towards Santiago, you see one of the most photographed views in the Galápagos with **Pinnacle Rock** on the northern shore of Bartolomé standing like a finger pointing defiantly to the sky. Galápagos penguins swim the waters below this rock. This is the best place to see these comical creatures, unless you have the time to visit colonies on Fernandina and the western side of Isabela. Bartolomé is truly a lunar landscape with twisted lava formations, sparse plant life, but plenty of sea creatures, including nesting turtles (late December until early March) and great blue herons.

Sombre Chino

Also just off the coast of Bartolomé lies the tiny, conical island, whose name translates as "Chinese Hat." A beautiful blue lagoon separates it from the larger island, where there are some good swimming and snorkeling spots. A small colony of sea lions inhabits a beach on the north shore, where there is a visitor site.

Isabela

Isabela, at 4,588 sq km (1,766 square miles), is by far the largest island and boasts the tallest point of the archipelago, the 1,646-m (5,487 ft) Volcán Wolf. Stretching 132 km

(83 miles) from north to south and 84 km (53 miles) at its widest, the island includes more than half of the land area of the Galápagos. A wild and inaccessible place of rumbling volcanoes, the island supports a population of about 1,000.

The main settlement, **Puerto Villamil** on the southeast coast, has a grim history and some visitors feel a dismal, end-of-the-world feeling hanging in the air. Not many cruise boats visit Puerto Villamil because of its distance from the main tourist areas and because of the difficulty entering the bay in rough weather. A few kilometers west of the village is the site of a penal colony, now destroyed, which had a reputation for cruelty. Little remains except an enormous basalt wall, known as the **Wall of Tears**, which was built from lava blocks by prisoners. Further on from here there's an airport which had to be abandoned because the runway was badly positioned.

Despite its size, Puerto Villamil has a few shops, one or two excellent budget hotels, and the odd bar and disco. A short walk from the village is the white sand **Lover's Beach** and a lagoon, said to be the best place to see water birds in the Galápagos. Puerto Villamil might well turn into a major tourist area like Puerto Ayora.

What to See and Do

From Puerto Villamil, visitors can take a bus or a rental truck to the little hamlet of **Santo Tomás** on the slopes of the volcano of the same name (but also called **Sierra Negra**). From there it's a nine-kilometer (just over five-mile)-hike or horse ride (horses can be rented in the hamlet) to the rim of the volcano. The views here are magnificent — weather permitting. It's a further eight-kilometer (five-mile)-hike around the rim to see the belching fumaroles.

Isabela is well known for its population of several thousand giant Galápagos tortoises. Tortoise subspecies on the island have developed over hundreds of years around each volcano. Intervening fields of jagged lava rocks has prevented tortoises lumbering from one volcanic area to another, intermingling the species. Feral goats, descendants of domestic animals brought by humans, are more agile and able to cope with the rugged terrain. Goats eat cactus, the staple diet of the tortoises, and thus threaten the older inhabitants with extinction. In an attempt to prevent such an ecological tragedy, shooting parties regularly venture to Isabela to control the goat population.

The best place to see giant tortoises is on **Volcán Alcedo**, home to the biggest population on the island. It isn't a quick and easy journey. The usual procedure is to join a boat in Puerto Ayora that takes you to **Shipton Cove**, halfway down the eastern coast of Isabela. From the beach, a three-to five-hour hike takes you to the rim of the volcano, the last steep haul being particularly difficult because of loose volcanic scree. The slopes of Alcedo become very hot in the middle of the day so it's advisable to start your climb before dawn. With little shade en route, you must bring water and other supplies with you. If possible, arrange to camp for one or

The sun setting over the small island of Bartolomé, one of the most beautiful in the archipelago, with Pinnacle Rock jutting into the sea.

two nights on the rim of the volcano from where there are wonderful views across the island and down 200m (670 ft) into the immense lava field of the seven-kilometer (four-and-a-half-mile)-wide caldera itself.

Walking around the rim for another three or four hours, you will come to fumaroles of spewing vaporous gases. Tortoises tend to hide under bushes or in burrows in hot season to avoid the sun, but during rainy season, from June to December, hundreds of giant tortoises can be seen in or around the caldera wallowing in muddy pools.

Isabela is also a breeding ground for the world's only flightless cormorant. Occasionally these rare birds can be seen around **Punta Garcia**, further northwards up the coast from Shipton Cove, but the birds may have deserted this area for the more populous and inaccessible colonies in the west of the island. Moving up to the northern tip of Isabela, **Punta Albemarle** is a remote and seldom-visited promontory, which was an American radar base during World War II. It was one of the few places on the planet from which to see the total eclipse of the sun on February 26, 1998.

Unless you spend a few weeks in the Galápagos Islands, you are unlikely to have time to discover the desolate charm and teeming bird life of western Isabela. But if your heart is set on seeing the unique flightless cormorant, you can find several colonies along the coast. The other flightless bird, the Galápagos penguin, also resides here. One of the best places to see them is from a boat off the cliffs of **Tagus Cove**. Some of the cliffs and the rocks of the cove are covered with names of boats and people inscribed by sailors who used the bay for refuge. If you land here you can take a wooden stairway to a viewpoint overlooking **Darwin Lake**, a circular, lagoon which was raised above sea level by tectonic movements. Walking on further, you come to another panoramic viewpoint. So jagged are the lava rocks here you could lose the soles of solid boots if you walked over them for more than four kilometers (two and half miles). Wild dogs in the area have adapted to their environment by growing extra-thick pads on their feet and acquiring the capacity to drink sea water.

There are some 28 endemic and 60 resident bird species and in the Galápagos. LEFT TO RIGHT: A hawk, a brown pelican, a red-footed booby, and a blue-footed booby.

Other visitors' sites on the west coast of Isabela include **Urvina Bay**, **Elizabeth Bay**, and **Punta Moreno**. Giant tortoises can sometimes be seen at Urvina Bay along with iguanas, flightless cormorants and pelicans. A short walk after landing on a white sand beach is the bizarre sight of coral reef stranded on land, tectonically uplifted from the ocean floor in 1954. Further down the coast, an inlet on **Elizabeth Bay** penetrates deep into an aquatic mangrove forest before opening up into a maze of convoluted channels and lagoons inhabited by green turtles, rays and an array of seabirds. There is no landing site at Elizabeth Bay. At Punta Moreno visitors can land on a lava flow where there are pools and small lagoons, the feeding grounds for a variety of birds, including flamingos, pintails and great blue herons. Feral dogs prowl the area on the lookout for a tasty morsel of marine iguana or baby sea lion.

Where to Stay

Though limited to the budget end of the market, accommodation in Puerto Villamil is surprisingly good for such a small town. Well-known and highly recommended is **Hotel Ballena Azul** and **Cabañas Isabela del Mar** ((05) 529125 (same phone number for both). Large airy rooms, mosquito nets, ocean views are an excellent value at less than US$10. Hostess Dora Gruber enjoys chatting with her guests in several languages. On the road to the highlands, **Hotel Terro Real** ((05) 529106, with its triangular, red-roofed bungalows, has friendly management and is an excellent value at less than US$5 per person. Also recommended and slightly less expensive is **Posada San Vicente**, where the owner can arrange horses rides up the volcano.

Where to Eat

Ballena Azul also has a good reputation for fine food at reasonable prices. Breakfast is particularly scrumptious, but it's advisable to let Dora know in advance if you would like lunch or dinner. On the beach, the restaurant at **Hotel Loja** is recommended. Other restaurants in town worth checking out are **Costa Azul**, **Ruta**, and **Restaurant Iguana**. Don't expect a wide choice of fare at any of these establishments.

How to Get There

Most people come to Isabela on cruise ships, but the adventurous who want to spend more time on this beautiful island should travel independently. There are occasional flights on a five-seat planes from Baltra. Check with your travel agent or call Dora at the Ballena Azul for more information. Alternatively, the government-run transporta-

tion service INGALA (Instituto Nacional Galápagos) operates weekly ferries that leave Santa Cruz for Isabela on Thursdays at 8 AM and return on Fridays at 10 AM. There's also a private ferry, the *Estrella Mar,* which leaves Isabela to Santa Cruz on Tuesdays at 10:30 AM and returns the next day at the same time. Be sure to double check these schedules and buy your ticket at least a day in advance. Fares are around US$30 each way. Ask around for passages on private boats and yachts.

FERNANDINA

Fernandina is the third-largest, the geologically youngest and most volcanically active of the Galápagos. This uninhabited island is also the most remote and least visited of the main islands. **Volcán La Cumbre** (1,463 m or 4,877 ft) erupts regularly, most recently in 1995 when lava flowed into the ocean for over a month, and the cone of the volcano shifted and changed in shape. Columns of sulfurous smoke and steam rose 4,000 m (13,332 ft) into the air, with extremely loud echoing explosions and a cacophony of hissing and popping and low-level thumps. Dead mesopelagic fish from the depths floated on the steaming and bubbling surface of the water, which reached a temperature of 60°C (140°F). Biology was in confusion.

Exactly 170 years earlier the captain of the American schooner *Tartar,* which was off the coast one night in February 1825, wrote this account of an eruption on Narborough, as the island was then called. "The heavens appeared to be one blaze of fire, intermingled with millions of falling stars and meteors; while flames shot upwards from the peak of Narborough to the height of at least two thousand feet in the air… the boiling contents of the tremendous caldron had swollen to the brim, and poured over the edge of the crater in a cataract of liquid fire. A river of melted lava was now seen rushing down the side of the mountain, pursuing a serpentine course to the sea… the demon of fire seemed rushing to the embraces of Neptune; and dreadful indeed was the uproar occasioned by their meeting. The ocean boiled and roared and bellowed…." The captain also recorded that when the temperature of the sea rose to 150°F (65°C), melted pitch ran from the vessel's seams and tar dropped from the riggings. Had not a lucky breeze helped its escape, the *Tartar* would certainly have fell apart and sank.

As well as one of the world's most volcanically-active islands, Fernandina is also considered one of the most pristine for lack of non-native plants and animals. There are no feral dogs or donkeys on Fernandina, nor goats, rats, pigs or cats. With such an environment to protect it is easy to understand why the National Park Service insists on precautions to avoid transportation of seeds or any animal forms to the island — visitors are required to wash their shoes before landing. Because of these measures, neither marine iguanas nor flightless cormorants have predators on the island and are left to multiply in safety. In this sense Fernandina is the only place in the Galápagos where you can travel back in time and see the island before the arrival of humanity.

Fernandina has been associated with illegal harvesting and smuggling of protected sea cucumbers. Encouraged by Japanese fishermen, Ecuadorians have harvested huge quantities of these creatures off the coast of Fernandina for shipment to Asia.

What to See and Do

Fernandina has only one visitors' site, at **Punta Espinosa** on the northwest coast, opposite Isabela. Here thousands of marine iguanas lie about in the sun, digesting their dinners and shooting sprays of salt water into the air in fits of iguanic sneezing. There are also sea lions, flightless cormorants and a few Galápagos penguins. Snorkelers swimming in the clear waters of the lagoon will see rays, white-tip sharks, turtles and plenty of brilliantly colored tropical fish.

THE SOUTHERN ISLANDS

SANTA MARÍA

Usually known as **Floreana**, sometimes called Charles, Santa María was colonized by convicts in the nineteenth century, the first of the Galápagos islands to sustain a human population. The island has since acquired a reputation for murder, mystery and curious goings-on. The best known murder mystery is that of the Germans who came to the islands in the 1930s and then disappeared one by one, as in Agatha Christie's story, *The Ten Little Niggers* (see page 215). The last survivor is Margret Wittmer, who was over 90 years old at the time of writing and still in charge of the island's only guest house and restaurant. Several books have been written about this unsolved mystery, including Margaret Wittmer's own fascinating account of life on the island, *Floreana,* though she leaves many questions unanswered. It is said that Señora Wittmer is the only one who knows the full story of what happened.

Floreana boasts one of the most charming curiosities of the Galápagos Islands: the mail box of **Post Office Bay**, perhaps the most unusual in the world. In the days before radio and air travel, when whaling ships cruised the Pacific for years on end, a thoughtful English captain established a "post office" barrel on Floreana. The idea was that mail could be deposited in the barrel, which ships heading home would pick up. The system worked so well that during Anglo-American hostilities at the beginning in 1812, information obtained from letters stolen from the mail barrel helped an American captain destroy more than half the British whaling fleet. The original barrel is long gone, but a replacement box is still used in the same way. A Canadian visitor recently sent a letter from the Floreana mail box that arrived before a letter to the same address in Canada, which had been sent a few days earlier through the regular Ecuadorian mail.

Margaret Wittmer on Floreana, the last survivor of a remarkable band of expatriate islanders.

What to See and Do

Though there are more imported plants and animals than on other islands, descended from those brought by early inhabitants, Floreana has some fine visitors' sites with a wealth of fascinating Galápagean wildlife. The best site is **Punta Cormorant**, on the north shore, where the beach has a green tinge because of olivine crystals in the sand. There are plenty of sea lions on the beach, and the swimming is good. Walking eastwards over a small isthmus, you pass a lagoon, where there are often flamingos and other water birds, before coming to another pleasant beach. There are a number of stingrays here so it's important to shuffle your feet in the sand as you wade out to sea. Just off the coast is one of the best snorkeling spots in the Galápagos Islands, the tip of a submerged volcano known as the **Devil's Crown**, where you will see big cast of glittering tropical fish of all colors and shapes and perhaps sea lions and sharks. Take heart, that it is said that nobody has been killed by a shark in the Galápagos Islands — yet!

Where to Stay and Eat

If you do find your way to the island's small port of **Puerto Velasco Ibarra** (population 100) you're not spoiled for choice; in fact, you have none at all. The only place to stay and eat is the small, inexpensive guesthouse and restaurant ☎ (05) 520150 run by Margaret Wittmer and her family. Margaret's son Rolf was born on Floreana in January 1933, and his was the first historically documented birth on the Galápagos islands. Rolf now runs a travel company and his charter boat, *Tip-Top III*, regularly anchors off his birthplace.

How to Get There

Few independent travelers stay overnight on Floreana. Visitors usually come by cruise boat for a short visit. However INGALA ferries stop in Floreana on their way from Puerto Ayora to Isabela on Thursdays, or from Isabela to Puerto Ayora on Fridays. Check with INGALA ☎ (05) 526151 in Puerto Ayora to confirm.

ESPAÑOLA

Despite its small size, the southernmost island of Española, formerly known as Hood, has a rich variety of wildlife, making it popular with cruise boats. Ninety kilometers (55 miles) from the main tourist center of Puerto Ayora, this uninhabited island is often the first stop of a one-week itinerary after an overnight crossing. In a typical routine, visitors are woken early with a morning music call piped into their cabins. After a breakfast with a variety of delicious and unfamiliar fruits and juices, the dozen or so passengers descend from the cruise ship into a *panga*. This small dingy ferries them a hundred meters or so to the visitor site of **Punta Suárez**, a long, low headland of twisted volcanic rock. Laden with cameras, binoculars, large sun hats and suntan lotion, the pink-skinned, bare-footed bipeds are helped off the panga for a "wet landing" onto the black lava rock by a strong-armed boat boy.

Immediately visitors feel like they have arrived somewhere between the Garden of Eden and Dante's inferno. Prehistoric marine iguanas, which Darwin called "Imps of Darkness," lounge on black rocks while sleek and slithery sea lions bask in the sun on the beach. If this is your first major encounter with the wildlife of the Galápagos, you will be astounded that the animals don't scurry away when you approach.

Even the birds appear quite tame, pecking about at your feet and perhaps even landing on your shoulders. We spotted a rare Galápagos hawk and several endemic Española mockingbirds at close range.

About a kilometer's walk (just over a half mile) from landing at Punta Suárez, along the path marked by black and white stakes in the ground, the visitor comes to the edge of a high cliff overlooking a vibrant blue sea flecked with white-tipped waves. Fork-tailed frigate birds soar and glide in the thermals, while the breakers crash on the rocks below. At one point the surf thrusts itself into the entrance of a lava tube blowhole and bursts out the other end in a 30-m (100-ft) fountain of white spray.

What to See and Do

The usual cast of Galápagos wildlife takes the stage on Española. Blue-footed and masked boobies are always in the spotlight, while marine iguanas and the ubiquitous sea lions aren't shy of appearances. Galápagos doves, mockingbirds, hawks, lava herons, night herons, oystercatchers, swallowtail gulls, various finches, lava lizards and the occasional snake are among the supporting cast. Always hiding in the wings, however, is the reclusive Española subspecies of the giant saddleback tortoise, some 700 of which have been reintroduced to the island during the last 20 years after captive breeding at the Darwin Station on Santa Cruz.

The bird most closely associated with the island is the waved albatross, a creature famous for its elegant flight, elaborate courtship display and its size — it's the biggest bird of the archipelago. It's also the most monogamous. Birds mate for life, though they repeat their courtship ritual each year. Only a few thousand of these white-necked, yellow-billed beauties exist on the planet, all from Española, except for a few which breed on Isla La Plata, off the mainland. Breeding season, from about April to mid-December is the time to see them. The rest of the year they spend at sea.

After a thrilling but hot walk among the creatures on Española, visitors return to the cool and comfort of the cruise ship for lunch. In the afternoon there is often a snorkeling expedition around **Gardner Rock**, off the northeast shore where the waters glint and flicker with millions of tropical fish. If you're lucky you might see a few turtles in these waters. Or a white-tipped shark may cruise silently past you underwater, like a police officer of the deep.

Then it's time to relax with sea lions on the long, golden beach of Gardner Bay. Life isn't all sun, sea and sleep for the sea lions. Many big scars on the sleek fur of the males are evidence of fights with other males to dominate the female herd. We saw one pathetic youngster who was rejected by the group. Perhaps a shark had eaten its mother, but there was evidently no hope for this little one. Our guide, Carmen Guzman, said it would die of starvation a couple weeks.

As the sun sinks towards the horizon, sunburned bipeds climb aboard the panga and head back to their natural habitat on the cruise ship. Delicious fruit cocktails are

OPPOSITE: A giant opuntia cactus on South Plaza Island. ABOVE: Marine iguana on Hood Island. Charles Darwin called them "Imps of Darkness."

served on deck, marking the end of a typical day on a Galápagos cruise.

SAN CRISTÓBAL

Small and somnolent, the main town of the island of San Cristóbal has a big name: **Puerto Baquerizo Moreno**. Such an elegant appellation is appropriate for a place that boasts a naval base, a radio station and is the provincial capital of Ecuador's Galápagos Province. Most of the basic utilities are available in Puerto Baquerizo Moreno, including an EMETEL telephone office, a hospital, an airline office, a police station and a bank. But the town (population 3,000) has a run-down, backwater atmosphere, and from a tourist's point of view isn't as pleasant as its sister, Puerto Ayora, over on Santa Cruz. This might change, however, because Puerto Baquerizo Moreno has a new airport, which makes it a second gateway to the archipelago.

What to See and Do

One of the town's few tourist attractions is the small **natural history museum** full of dusty stuffed birds, iguanas, sea lions and dolphins as well as whalebones, tortoise shells, corals and crabs. The sole living exhibit in the museum is a tortoise called Pepe, who lives in an enclosure behind the main building. Included in the admission to the museums (2,000 sucres) is a fistful of green leaves to feed the gentle giant. Nobody knows how old Pepe is because scientists haven't found a way of determining the age of tortoises though it's known that they often live well over 150 years. It's possible that Pepe was around when Charles Darwin visited these islands.

A notice on the wall of the museum gives a short version of the horrendous story of one Manuel J. Cobos, who operated a sugar plantation and refinery up in the hills of Chatham, as San Cristóbal was then called, at the end of the nineteenth century. Cobos was a dreadful tyrant with a taste for flogging his convict laborers to death and taking advantage of their women. Rebellious workers murdered him in 1904. In recording the story of Cobos, author of *The Enchanted Islands*, John Hickman writes: "These stories — and there must be many similar unrecorded incidents — show the Galápagos archipelago as a sinister backdrop against which all human dramas are doomed to tragedy. There seems to be something inimical to human life or at least to human happiness in the very atmosphere."

In spite of a dire history, the island of San Cristóbal a has plenty to offer visitors. **El Progreso**, as Cobos' small plantation village was ironically called, still exists and can be reached by truck or bus from Puerto Baquerizo Moreno, or by walking eight kilometers (five miles). Ten kilometers (six miles) further up the road is the beautiful crater lake of **Laguna El Junco**, where you can walk around the rim, which is rich in plant and bird life. From the crater you can look out over most of the island, including the 900-m (3,000-ft) peak of **Cerro San Joaquín**. To the northeast you can also see the cliffs of **Punta Pitt**, the most spectacular visitors' site on San Cristóbal.

As with most visitors' sites on the Galápagos, the only way to reach Punta Pitt is by boat. Disembarking onto the small beach, visitors are confronted by the strong stench and cacophony of barking sea lions. At certain times of the year there are as many of these beautiful beasts are as bodies on West Palm Beach on spring break. This is a bachelor colony, and most are exhausted from fighting and mating. They won't budge an inch as you approach so you have to step around their basking bodies while being careful to avoid the source of the strong stench. A steep gully leads up the cliff to a breeding ground for boobies of all three varieties: red-footed, blue-footed and masked. It's the only place in the Galápagos where you can see all three species nesting together.

The view from the top of the cliff over the beach of sea lions is magnificent, as are the contours of the barren, wind-eroded peaks of the island. The trail across the Punta Pitt site offers a closer look at the hardy vegetation that manages to thrive in this volcanic wasteland. From saltbush and spiny shrubs by the beach the trail leads up to an area of palo santos trees, big yellow-green shrubs, tiny cacti and, in the dry season, carpets of red sesuvium. A short distance westward along the coast from Punta Pitt is the new visitors' site of **Galapaguera**, where giant turtles can sometimes be seen. Getting there involves a long hike so it's advisable to go with a guide.

Off the coast of San Cristóbal are a number of steep, rocky islets that rise almost vertically from the sea. There's good snorkeling around the islet opposite Punta Pitt, but the most impressive of these solitary, sea-girt towers is **Leon Dormido** (Sleeping Lion). Also known as **Kicker Rock**, this twin-peaked cathedral of stone looks as if it had been split by a divine karate chop. Huge, cackling colonies of sea birds nest in its vertiginous walls.

Where to Stay

The top of the range accommodation at Puerto Baquerizo Moreno is the **Grand Hotel San Cristóbal** ((05) 520179, which faces Playa Mann beach, just to the east of town. It has large rooms, ceiling fans, private bathrooms and a good restaurant that is popular with locals. Double rooms are from US$30. Nearby is **Cabañas Don Jorge** ((05) 520208. Double cabins start at US$10. One of the most popular hotels in town is the **Mar Azul** ((05) 520139, which has pleasant, shady courtyards and equally pleasant prices with single rooms starting at US$4 and doubles from US$9. Also well-recommended is **Hotel San Francisco** ((05) 520304 on the waterfront where a single room with fan, television and bathroom is less than US$4.

Where to Eat

Restaurante Rosita behind Hotel San Francisco has legendary status because of Rosita's skill at cooking fish. Prices are reasonable and you can dine inside or out. The restaurant at the **Grand Hotel San Cristóbal** is more expensive but has a good reputation and is popular with locals. Otherwise follow your nose and trust your judgment. *Ceviche* lovers can choose from a number of *cevicherías* well-supplied by local fisherman. Also recommended are restaurants **Casa Blanca** and **La Zayapa** and **Galapan** bakery.

Nightlife

Though not the most swinging of provincial capitals, Puerto Baquerizo Moreno does have a couple *discotecas* near the center of town, **Blue Bay** and **Neptunus**, which are most lively Friday and Saturday nights.

How to Get There

After Baltra, San Cristóbal, is the second entry point to the Galápagos Islands from Quito and Guayaquil. SAN-SAETA flights land at San Cristóbal while TAME flies into Baltra. There is also passenger boat service between San Cristóbal and Puerto Ayora on Santa Cruz run regularly by INGALA. Boats leave San Cristóbal every Monday and Wednesday at 10 AM and return Tuesdays and Saturdays, departing at the same time. Most tourists visit Puerto Baquerizo Moreno for just a few hours from their cruise boats.

THE NORTHERN ISLANDS

GENOVESA

Seldom visited by tourists, the remote northern island of Genovesa, also known as Tower Island, is a paradise for bird lovers. The avian abundance is a strong incentive to endure a sometimes rough 10- to 12-hour boat ride from Puerto Ayora. The island has a thriving red-footed booby colony, as well as plentiful masked boobies, swallow-tailed gulls, red-billed tropical birds, storm petrels and great frigate birds. There are two visitors' sites. A path through woods and nesting colonies to the top of a cliff is known as Prince Philip's Steps after the prince's 1964 visit to the islands, which helped stimulate international interest in the Galápagos' survival. The second site is Darwin Bay, a collapsed caldera filled with sea water, surrounded by a ring of cliffs, where there's a coral beach and several seabird colonies.

MARCHENA

This desolate island is the seventh-largest in the archipelago and the biggest island lacking an official visitors' site. Though landings are possible on the black sand beach on the southwest of the island, Marchena is best known for scuba diving. The 343-m (1,144-ft) volcano in the center of the island erupted in 1991.

PINTA

Though tourists rarely visit the ninth-largest of the Galápagos islands, it has had one celebrated resident. He is the solitary survivor of the Pinta breed of tortoises, Lonesome George, who now lives at the Darwin Research Station on Santa Cruz, as mentioned above. There are no visitor sites on Pinta and anyone wishing to go there for research has to obtain special permission.

DARWIN AND WOLF

These two small, remote islands, about 100 km (63 miles) northwest of the central islands, are seldom visited except by scuba divers. Though plenty of seabirds make their homes here, steep cliffs encircling the islands make landing difficult from a boat. A rare expedition to Darwin in 1964 landed by helicopter.

THE WILDLIFE

The Galápagos Islands, the world's greatest natural history museum, are one of the most exciting places on earth for wildlife watching and photography. Large number of species are endemic to (found only on) the islands, most of which are easy to see because they have not learned to fear humans. One piece of advice that every visitor should heed is to bring twice as much film as you originally intend — and then to double that amount. The following are some of the more interesting species to watch for.

REPTILES

The Galápagos Islands are well-known for their variety and abundance of various forms of primeval reptiles, most of which aren't founed anywhere else on earth. Out of 22 species of tortoises, iguanas, snakes, lizards and geckos, 90% are endemic to the archipelago.

Giant Tortoises

Giant tortoises are the big stars in the pantheon of the Galápagos Islands. Numbering some 15,000 and weighing up to 250 kg (550 lb), these are the biggest tortoises in the world. It is estimated that between two and three hundred thousand were killed or captured as sources of fresh meat by whalers and sealers or taken away by collectors in the eighteenth and nineteenth centuries.

Fourteen subspecies of giant tortoise inhabited the archipelago when it was discovered in 1535. Today, only five subspecies are numerous enough to be considered safe, five are threatened and three are extinct. One subspecies has just one surviving individual, Lonesome George, who lives at the Charles Darwin Research Station on Santa Cruz (see SANTA CRUZ, page 218). Though it is known that tortoises once inhabited Santa Fé, no evidence remains to tell us what that particular breed was like.

There are two basic types of Galápagos tortoise: those with shortish necks and high-domed carapaces, which come down low over both head and tail. These big beasts inhabit the lusher, thicker vegetation on the uplands of Santa Cruz and some of the Isabela volcanoes. The second, smaller type have longer necks and legs with carapaces shaped more like Spanish-style saddles, flatter on top and rising up at the front. They are able to reach up to cactus and high foliage and come from the arid zones. A continuum exists between the the very pronounced saddleback shells, which come from the low, flat islands of Pinzón and Española, to the roundest dome-shaped shells from the lusher parts of Isabela.

Saving tortoises threatened with extinction through captive breeding and reintroduction to the wild is a major part of the work of the Charles Darwin Station on Santa Cruz.

Marine Turtles

Though not an endemic to the islands, Pacific green sea turtles lay eggs and breed in the islands. At night, during the breeding season from January to June, females waddle up island beaches above the high water mark, dig holes and bury dozens of eggs. When hatched, baby turtles try to make their way to the sea, though they are vulnerable to predators such as rats, dogs, pigs and humans. If they make it safely, they disappear for years and travel huge distances. Incredibly, females are able to find their way back to the beach where they were born to lay eggs for the next generation. One of the big excitements of the Galápagos islands for snorkelers and divers is the sight of a turtle swimming nearby.

Marine Iguanas

Darwin called them Imps of Darkness… hideous looking creatures, stupid and sluggish in their movements. But he was fascinated by these endemic reptiles, the only sea-going lizards in the world, which probably evolved from land iguanas who found their way to the Galápagos on rafts of vegetation. With spines like teeth running down their backs, long tails and growing to a meter (three feet) in length, these fearsome-looking creatures seem to predate man by millions of years. Most are dirty black when wet and gray when dry, easily blending into their rocky environment.

Marine iguanas live on lava rocks on the water's edge, dine on seaweed and can swim underwater for as long as an hour. Darwin discovered this by throwing them into the water with weights attached to their legs, and then pulling them back up at various intervals to see which ones survived. They are common on most Galápagos islands and can often be seen in groups of similar age basking in the sun, all facing the same way, or even piled on top of each other.

In spite of their aggressive appearance, vegetarian marine iguanas won't bite humans unless provoked. After feeding on algae, these cold-blooded creatures sun bathe on the rocks to warm their bodies and digest their food. They even bask on hotel terraces in Puerto Ayora on Santa Cruz. With desalination glands in their heads to filter out salt from sea water, they snort out sprays of salt through their noses like Puff the Magic Dragon.

During their mating season, which varies from island to island, males become aggressive and territorial, fighting head to head and mating with several females. Their scaly skin becomes blotchy red and green at these times, though marine iguanas on Española are colorful all the year round. Females lay two to four eggs in sandy nests and defend them until they hatch but don't pay much attention to their young after that.

Charles Darwin was fascinated by the only sea-going lizard in the world, the marine iguana, which can swim underwater for up to an hour.

Land Iguanas

Thought to have the same ancestors as marine iguanas, land iguanas are now totally different in habit and habitat. At one time the Galápagos land iguana lived on almost all the islands of the archipelago, but hunting and competition with introduced animals, such as pigs, goats, dogs and rats, have confined them to Isabela, Santa Cruz, Fernandina, Seymour and South Plaza islands. This yellowish lizard, slightly bigger than its aquatic cousin, has a tough, leathery mouth, enabling it to feed on the spiky prickly pear cactus. A second species of land iguana, the Santa Fé land iguana, is bigger and more yellow than the Galápagos land iguana and is confined to Santa Fé island.

Snakes, Lizards and Geckos

Though rarely seen by visitors, two kinds of snakes inhabit the archipelago: the Galápagos land snake and the yellow-bellied sea snake. The constricting, but inconspicuous brown or gray land snake, with yellow spots or stripes, grows to about a meter (three feet) in length. It asphyxiates insects, lizards and hatchling but isn't dangerous to humans. The black and yellow sea snake is rare, though its venom can be stronger than a cobra's. Harmless lava lizards can be seen scurrying around most of the islands, as can the equally-harmless nocturnal geckos who climb vertical walls and walk upside down on ceilings hunting for insects.

Mammals

There are few native species of mammals on the Galápagos because the islands' separation from the mainland and because of the difficulty for land mammals to survive an ocean crossing. Aside from two species of seals, the only mammals not introduced by man are some species of rats and bats. Animals brought to the islands by man include goats, dogs, cats, donkeys, horses and the black rat (*Rattus rattus*).

Sea Lions

These sleek, blubbery, playful creatures are one of the main attractions of the Galápagos. Close relatives of this endemic subspecies exist in the Sea of Japan, on the

California coast, and in sea-life aquariums all over the world, but on the beaches of the archipelago the Galápagos sea lions are abundant, easily approachable and not intimidated by humans.

Landing on some beaches you might find yourself in colony of scarred and tired males, exhausted after fighting off male rivals and looking after their harems of cows. On another beach there may be families of cows with their pups and a sea lion bull patrolling the nearby waters, trying to keep his females to himself. In practice, a jealous male may guard his females for up to a month, until hunger and lack of sleep exhausts him. At this point a rival male takes over the harem and the old bull skulks off back to the bachelor colony.

Male sea lions are easily distinguished from females because they are generally much bigger, growing up to 250 kg (550 lb), and because they have a high, bulging foreheads in contrast to the flatter female skulls. Mothers give birth to one cub at a time and nurse them for up to two years. Females are tamer than the males and can be approached to within a meter or so. Be careful of bull sea lions, especially when they are guarding their cows.

Fur Seals

Although about as numerous as sea lions, endemic fur seals aren't as easy to see because they don't lie around sunning themselves on the sand and rocks, preferring instead the cool of caves and grottoes. They are more timid towards humans than other animals, probably because they were almost hunted to extinction for their luxuriant, cinnamon-brown fur, made of two layers of hair. They are smaller than sea lions, broader headed, and they emit a bovine lowing sound rather than a canine bark. Thanks to conservation efforts their numbers have increased and the fur seals are no longer in danger of extinction.

Whales and Dolphins

One of the great thrills of cruising the islands is when somebody shouts: "Dolphins on the bow!" Everybody rushes to lean over

The beaches of the Galápagos Islands are alive with colonies of sprawling sea lions, like these on North Seymour Island.

the rails and watch these streamlined torpedoes racing along at the sharp end of the boat, breaking surface for a split second in a shower of spray. There are so many dolphins in the Galápagos waters that if you take a boat cruise you're almost certain to have this exhilarating experience. If you're lucky you'll see a mother swimming at high speed with cubs who keep so close that they seem to be joined by an invisible cord. Suddenly, as quickly as they've come, the playful dolphins disappear, leaving you wondering where they've gone and what they're doing next.

Several species of dolphins have been sighted here, but the ones that play with the ships are the bottle-nosed variety. Several whale species are also sighted regularly, including the common rorqual, sei, sperm, killer, humpback and blue. Whale sightings are usually so brief and distant that it's difficult to identify the species.

BIRDS

The attraction of bird life in the Galápagos isn't only the abundance of rare and interesting species (nearly 60 resident species on the islands of which some 28 are endemic). It is also the fact that many birds are unafraid of humans and therefore easy to see close up. There are also dozens of migrant birds which almost always can be spotted.

The comical **boobies** are likely to be among the first birds you'll meet on the islands. As you wander along pathways through their nesting colonies, they continue on with their rituals and activities, such as courtship dancing or incubating eggs under their webbed feet. Even within a few feet of hundreds of birds they appear as indifferent to you as you might be to a passing stranger on a street. **Blue-footed boobies** frequently lay eggs right in the middle of a path, their nest being nothing more than a circle of guano defining a boundary for their young chicks. **Masked boobies** also lay their eggs on the ground, while **red-footed boobies** make primitive nests in bushes or low trees. Each of the booby species has carved out its ecological niche, with the blue-footed birds feeding from the shore, and the red-footed variety diving for fish away from the breeding colonies.

The friendly **Galápagos penguin** is one the world's smallest, rarest and least-studied penguins, and lives further north than any other species. These flightless birds charm all as they hop about the rocks and plop feet-first into the sea. The world's only other flightless seabird is the **flightless cormorant**, another rare and endemic species. Its small, atrophied wings are thought to be the result of evolution, where swimming and hunting became more important than flight. The tallest of the world's 29 species of cormorant, it is curiously ungainly on land but is a powerful swimmer. It's also one of the few seabirds that doesn't keep the same mate from one nesting to the next.

Of special interest among seabirds, the **waved albatross**, one of the rarest and by far the largest bird in the archipelago, is endemic to Española, aside from some pairs on Isla de la Plata, off the mainland coast. Albatrosses spend their first few years at sea before returning to breed, and all are at sea from mid-January to mid-March. One of the most spectacular sights on the Galápagos is their courtship dance, when they bow and sway, honk and whistle, point to the sky and fence with their long, yellow bills.

Various species of **petrel** are common on many of the islands, of the archipelago but the **dark-rumped petrel** has been in danger of extinction. Also known as the Hawaiian petrel, this shy, nocturnal seabird, which mates for life, is nearly extinct on those islands. Early settlers on the Galápagos found these petrels in immense numbers. Reports say that during nesting season, the night air was filled with their howls and weird cackling calls. By the 1960s very few young were surviving because rats and pigs were eating their eggs, and dogs and cats were killing chicks and adult birds. An intensive predator control program by the Darwin Station and the Park Service has had promising results.

One of the most spectacular seabirds of the Galápagos is the **frigate bird** of which there are two difficult-to-distinguish species: the augustly named **great** and **magnificent frigate birds**. With deep, forked tails and long pointed wings spanning over two meters, they have the highest wingspan-to-body ratio of any other bird. Elegant and streamlined, they can be seen cruising thermals above many parts of the islands on the lookout for prey. Frigate birds aren't hawks; they are air pirates, or cleptoparasites. Their technique is to harass other birds such as boobies to drop or regurgitate their food. With atrophied preening glands, they are unable to secrete enough oil to waterproof their wings. This is why frigate birds cannot dive or land in the water, though they can fish on the surface with their hooked beaks.

The male frigate bird has an enormous red pouch of skin under his beak, which he inflates almost to the size of a football to attract females. One of the most extraordinary sights of the Galápagos is that of a courting male frigate bird sitting in a tree, or even flying overhead, with a big, bright red balloon puffed up on his chest. Frigate birds are opportunistic breeders and mate all year-round. The females lay one egg annually because feeding the chick until it can fly and get food for itself means another year of hard-line aerial piracy.

Other special, mostly endemic seabirds to watch for on the Galápagos Islands include: the beautiful **swallow-tailed gull** with its crimson eye-ring, which travels great distances out to sea and is the only gull to feed only at night; the **lava gull**, considered to be the rarest gull in the world; the splendid **red-billed tropical bird**, with its two elongated tail streamers; and the **brown pelican**, with its huge "scoop-fishing" bill and prehistoric appearance.

Among shorebirds, the stately but shy **greater flamingo** is literally head and shoulders above other birds in its habitat of salty lagoons, though it's slightly shorter than the more ubiquitous **common egret**, also known as the great egret or the American egret, which favors the rocky coastline. Though flamingos breed in other parts of the world, the Galápagos subspecies is rare. It doesn't like to be disturbed, and is likely to desert its mud nest if disturbed. Bird-watchers are advised to be especially sensitive. On the shorebird watch you may also spot **oystercatchers**, **plovers**, **sandpipers**, **turnstones**, **whimbrels** and **stilts**.

Of the land birds, the most scientifically important are the 13 species known as **Darwin's finches**, so-called because these birds were a key in the development of the scientist's theory of evolution by natural selec-

Masked boobies on Hood Island. These comical creatures became known as boobies because human visitors mistook their tameness for stupidity.

tion. By studying the sizes and shapes of their beaks Charles Darwin observed how the finches had adapted themselves and survived in the harsh habitats of the volcanic Galápagos islands. His belief that all the finches shared a common ancestry was a major factor in the formulation of his theories about the origins of species and the beginning of life itself.

Since Darwin's visit in 1835, many scientists have studied his famous finches in great detail researching the mechanisms of evolution. As an indication of the number of such studies, *The Beak of the Finch,* by Jonathan Weiner, lists some 300 bibliographical references.

On the Galápagos islands, 13 species of finches can be classified into four subspecies. There are those that live in trees and eat fruits and bugs; those that also live in trees but are vegetarians; birds that live in trees, but look and act like warblers; and birds who spend much of their time hopping on the ground. Among these species there are great differences in behavior. The **woodpecker finch**, for example, has the extraordinary ability to break a cactus spine or a twig to make a tool, which it uses to dig for insects in a tree, while the sharp-beaked **ground finch** picks at the tail feathers of molting boobies and drinks their blood.

On most of the Galápagos islands you see finches flying about, picking up crumbs, bathing in puddles. They are all small, black or gray-brown birds, no bigger than sparrows, with short wings and tails. Their differentiating characteristics are the shapes and sizes of their beaks. Unless you are an expert bird watcher it's unlikely you'll be able to distinguish one species from another. As one field guide states: "It is only a very wise man or a fool who thinks he is able to identify all the finches which he sees."

Like the finches, **Galápagos mockingbird**, of which there are four endemic species and six subspecies, has been the subject of painstaking scientific research. These noisy, curious, sociable birds are on all the islands except Pinzón.

There is thought to be just a hundred pairs left of the endemic **Galápagos hawk**, the only raptor that breeds on the islands. The birds practice cooperative polyandry, in which a female mates with two or more males and all the adults help raise the young. There are also two endemic subspecies of owl on the islands: the **short-eared owl** and the **barn owl**.

FISH

The wealth of marine life makes the Galápagos waters a paradise for divers and snorkelers. Within the 70,000-sq-km (27,000-sq-mile) Galápagos Marine Reserve more than 300 species of fish have been identified and, with further research, the number is expected to go beyond 400. About 50 of those identified are endemic. With water often as clear as glass, you can see many sorts of colorful tropical fish when you dive. There's a good chance these will include one or more of about 12 species of sharks which swim in these waters, the most common being the **white-tipped reef shark**, the **black-tipped reef shark**, the **gray reef shark** and the **Galápagos shark**. In some areas **hammerheads** and **tiger sharks** are also common. Fortunately there have been no serious sharks attacks in the Galápagos waters, and the dangerous great white shark is not an inhabitant of the archipelago. Several marine life guidebooks, available in Quito or Puerto Ayora on Santa Cruz, list most of the fish to be seen in the Galápagos.

Commercial fishing is permitted within the archipelago, though illegal fishing threatens the environment. Local and Japanese fishing pirates have seriously depleted shark, lobster and sea cucumber stocks, upsetting established ecosystems. Some islanders see fishing regulations as a threat to their livelihood. In 1995, local fishermen occupied the Charles Darwin Station and threatened to kill tortoises and beat up staff, protesting a government ban on fishing for sea cucumbers and other creatures. The situation was defused by the Ecuadorian military and pressure from the United States.

The frigate bird, one of the most spectacular species in the Galápagos. Though they cannot land in water themselves, they harass other seabirds for their prey.

Invertebrates

Among the wide variety of anemones, chitons, corals, jellyfish, sponges, snails, sea slugs, shrimps, starfish, lobsters, sea urchins, sea cucumbers, barnacles and crabs, the most eye-catching is the bright red-topped, blue-bottomed **Sally lightfoot crab** (*Grapsus grapsus*), which can be seen scurrying over almost every rock in the archipelago. On beaches and in rock pools you can see many **ghost crabs** and **hermit crabs**. For divers, there's not as much living coral as in other top diving spots, like the Red Sea or the Maldives, but the abundance and variety of other marine life is stunning.

Plants

Far from being lush, tropical islands of coconut palms and ferns, like others in the Pacific, much of the Galápagos is dry, desert-like and covered with cactus. Formed from the tips of submerged volcanoes, and never joined to the mainland, it hosts a plant life which has developed according to the ability of seeds to survive winds and waves and the curious microclimates of the islands. Lack of suitable terrain and absence of pollinating insects limits the number of some plant species, such as orchids, of which there are only 11 species on the archipelago, compared with over 3,000 on the mainland. At the same time, many unique species flourish on the islands because they adapted to the harsh conditions. The **opuntia cactus**, for example, with its pretty yellow flowers, is unique to the archipelago and is also the most common cactus.

Including subspecies and varieties, some 900 plants have been recorded on the archipelago, of which a quarter are endemic, and another quarter introduced by man. For classification purposes, the archipelago is usually divided into seven vegetation zones.

The sea level **Coastal Zone** is home to salt-tolerant plants such as **mangroves** and **saltbush**. The **Arid Zone**, 80–120 m (270–400 ft) above sea level, hosts the ghostly and ubiquitous, gray-barked **palo santo tree**, which has leaves only in wet season, as well as plentiful **acacia**, various thorny plants and cacti. Slight rainfall in the **Transition Zone**, up to 100–200 m (330–660 ft) in elevation, makes for richer vegetation, including perennial herbs and the Zone's characteristic plant, the **pega pega**, or "stick stick" tree, so named because its leaves stick to your fingers.

During the dry season, from June to September, a thick fog, or garuha, creates a moist cloud forest in the **Scalesia Zone**, up to 500 m (1,667 ft), which is named after the ubiquitous and endemic **scalesia tree**. Growing to a height of 10 m (33 ft), this beautiful "sunflower" tree has white, daisy-like flowers and is usually covered with mosses, vines and bromeliads. Scalesias are also common in the **Brown Zone**, named after the color of the moss which forms on the tree's branches at altitudes of around 500 m (1,667 ft).

Above this level is the **Miconia Zone**, named after leafy **miconia bushes**, up to four meters (12 ft) tall, with pink or violet flowering heads. Vegetables, coffee and fruit are grown in this belt. At the top level, from about 650 m (2,167 ft) to the peaks of the island's volcanoes, the tallest being over 1,600 m (5,333 ft), is the **Pampa Zone**. Ferns, grasses and sedges grow in this high and misty climate but there are few trees except the giant **Galápagos fern tree**.

GALÁPAGOS TOURS

The best way to see the Galápagos is by boat, as Charles Darwin did. You sleep through the hours covering the considerable distances from island to island. Although expensive, most people book their tour of the Galápagos as a complete package with a travel agent in their home country. This usually includes international flights, hotels and transfers on the mainland, flights out to the Galápagos, and the complete cruise around the islands. Insurance, tips, entrance fee to the Galápagos National Park and docking fee aren't usually covered. The park entrance fee is currently US$80 per passenger, payable in cash at the airport, in either sucres or United States dollars. Credit cards and travelers' checks are not accepted. In addition, there is a municipal docking fee of US$12 at Baltra, or US$30 at San Cristóbal. Most packages fly you to the capital, Quito, and then on via Guayaquil to either Baltra or San Cristóbal where you embark immediately on your boat.

Boat tours are mostly a week long, but larger boats often offer three- to four-day cruises as well. Most people visit two visitors' sites a day, one in the morning and another in the afternoon, and return to the boat to eat, sleep and relax. Be aware that you will rarely be the only group at a particular site. Some believe three or four days is enough time to spend on a boat and see the islands and the wildlife. If you spend longer you will have a much deeper experience and discover the differences between the islands. Another plus is that you will encounter few other visitors on the more remote islands. Serious wildlife enthusiasts should consider going on a two-week tour to some of the even more-distant and less-visited islands, as well as the central sites.

It is also possible to make your own arrangements to visit the Galápagos. You can buy your flights yourself and book your cruise when you arrive in Quito, Guayaquil or Puerto Ayora. You can save money this way although in the high season (July, August, December, January and Easter Week) you risk not finding a vacancy on a cruise that suits you. If you have the time, a good plan is to make your way to Puerto Ayora outside the high season and shop around for a trip. This will give you a few days in Puerto Ayora, which itself is worthwhile and enjoyable. If you decide not to buy a cruise you can set up at Puerto Ayora or at Puerto Baquerizo Moreno on San Crist Ayo and take day trips to the nearer islands.

About one hundred vessels operate Galápagos cruises, ranging from simple, converted fishing boats to luxurious cruise ships. All rely on engine power although some also have sails. Which you choose depends on your budget and the style of trip you prefer. The large, comfortable cruise ships offer private bathrooms, bars and sundecks, and carry up to 100 passengers. The smaller boats vary greatly from fairly simple six-passenger vessels, to comfortable, modern yachts and launches carrying 12 to 16 passengers.

A guide licensed by the National Parks Service accompanies each cruise ship and, except in limited areas, no tourist is allowed

Carl Angermeyer, in his house on Santa Cruz Island, has probably lived in the Galápagos longer than any other islander.

on land in the park without a guide. A good guide, who knows the Galápagos and its wildlife and your language can make a big difference to your trip. Before booking a tour confirm that it will include a fully qualified guide who is fluent in the language of your choice. Guides are responsible for enforcing National Park rules, which stipulate among, other things, that visitors must stay on set trails and that no animals may be touched.

From your newspaper travel sections at home you can see how many tour operators offer Galápagos journeys. Prices can range from US$50 to over US$300 per day (excluding airfares) depending on the boat, facilities, season and how far in advance you reserve it. In general, the further you are from the islands when you buy a tour, the higher the cost, although with some of the most expensive cruises the cost will be the same in Quito, London or New York. Don't forget that the crew and the guides aren't paid well and are very dependent on tips. Each passenger is expected to pay about US$4 per day for the crew and US$5 per day for the guide. The following is a selection of operators in Ecuador based on experience or strong recommendations. Exclusion of any company doesn't imply poor service.

Kleintours ((02) 430345 or 461235 FAX (02) 442389 or 469285 E-MAIL kleintou @uio.satnet.net, Main office: Avenida Shyris 1000, Quito, Ecuador. One of the top operators in Ecuador, Kleintours' flagships are *Coral I* and *Coral II*, equipped to the highest standards. With room for only 20 passen-

gers, *Coral I* just has the edge over her sister ship, which takes 26 on board. Both ships serve excellent food and the guides are first class. One week per person in a standard cabin in high season costs: US$1,940.

Angermeyer's Enchanted Expeditions ℂ (02) 569960 FAX (02) 569956, Foch 726 and Juan Leon Mera, Quito, Ecuador. Its best boat, *Beluga*, a spacious and comfortable yacht, holds 16 passengers and has first class guides and food. One week in a standard cabin costs US$1,820 per person.

Metropolitan Touring ℂ (02) 464780 FAX (02) 464702, Avenida República de El Salvador 970, Quito, Ecuador. This company is one of the longest-running and reliable operators in Ecuador. Its luxury boats include *Santa Cruz, Isabela II* and *The Delphin*. The latter combines stays at the Delphin Hotel on Santa Cruz for passengers who aren't keen on spending nights at sea. Bookings for *Beagle III*, a former Darwin Research Station vessel, and a boat of choice for serious naturalists, can also be made through Metropolitan. Get in touch with Metropolitan Touring for their rates.

Quasar Nautica ℂ (02) 441550 FAX (02) 436625, Avenida Shyris 2447, Edificio Autocom, Quito, Ecuador, is a high-quality operator of sail and power yachts, arranging diving cruises. Prices on request.

Andes Discoveries ℂ (02) 236446 FAX (02) 506293, Paraguay 229 and Selva Negra, Quito, Ecuador, is recommended for various boats excursions.

TANSCORD ℂ (02) 467441 FAX (02) 467443 E-MAIL admin@transcor.ecx.ec, Avenida República de El Salvador 112 and Avenida de los Shyris, Edificio Onix, Of. 9C, Quito, Ecuador, or PO Box 17-21-1062, Quito, Ecuador, has a good reputation for Galápagos cruises, either with their boat *Reina Silvia* or through other well-tested operators. Contact: Brigitte Frank.

Safari Tours ℂ (02) 234799 FAX (02) 220426 E-MAIL sales@safari.com, Pasaje de Roca, off Calle Roca (between Amazonas and Juan Leon Mera), Quito, Ecuador, keeps a database of boats with current vacancies, and offers trips at wholesale price, plus a reservation fee. They are useful for last minute reservations.

Moonrise Travel Agency ℂ/FAX (05) 526403 or 526348, Avenida Charles Darwin (facing Banco Pacifico), Puerto Ayora, Galápagos Islands. They are an excellent agent for last minute reservations, and are as inexpensive as dealing with boat captains directly.

WHALE WATCHING

Whale watching is on the rise in the Galápagos waters, where several species of large whales can sometimes be seen. With the exception of the bottlenose dolphin, no species is predictable enough to be reliably sighted, but boats cruising between the islands encounter them occasionally. Whales avoid

The stark beauty and incredible wildlife of the Galápagos Islands make a cruise around the archipelago one of the world's better travel experiences.

boats that approach aggressively, and the most exciting encounters and opportunities to swim with them occur when the whales approach stationary boats themselves.

The most frequently-seen baleen whale is the 12x15-m (40x50-ft)-long Bryde's whale. The 18-m (60-ft) finback and the eight-meter (27-ft) minke whale have also been sighted, and there are occasional reports of 10-m (33-ft) humpback whales. Aside from baleen whales, the other most commonly sighted whales are 9- to 17-m (30- to 57- ft) sperm whales. Beaked whales and orcas (killer whales) are occasionally seen. Several species of dolphin live around the islands, but the only species consistently sociable with boats is the bottlenose dolphin. There's no point in approaching these dolphins; if they wish to swim with your boat, they will.

Galasam ☎ (02) 507080 or 507081 FAX (02) 567662 E-MAIL galapagos@ galasam. comec WEBSITE www.galasam.com.ec, Avenida 9 de Octubre 424, Edificio Gran Pasaje, Eleventh Floor, Guayaquil; in Quito ☎ (04) 306289 or 313724 FAX (04) 313351 or 562033, Calle Pinto No. 523 and Avenida Amazonas, operates many Galápagos tour boats and specializes in whale watches.

SCUBA DIVING

The waters around the Galápagos offer some of the world's best scuba diving. A rich variety of underwater environments and unpredictable conditions are constantly fascinating and exciting. Offshore pinnacle reefs on submerged volcanoes rise from deep surrounding water supporting rich sea life and big oceanic creatures. The Devil's Crown, a sunken volcano near Floreana Island, is a marine wonderland of sea lions, turtles, rays, morays, garden eels, whitetip sharks, hammerhead sharks and thousands of tropical fish. Hydrothermal vents in these submerged volcanic peaks heat the waters to temperatures as high as 30°C (86°F). Scientists are particularly interested in these places because of the creatures that have adapted to live in such conditions.

Though diving can be straightforward, strong currents, sometimes low visibility, large marine animals and cold water can be quite challenging. Although there are some good dive sites for beginners, the Galápagos are not the best place for divers. Drift dives are common. Even though the archipelago straddles the equatorial line, its waters are cooler than you might expect. Cold water currents and upwellings can bring water temperatures as low as 10°C (50°F), though the average is about 18°C (65°F) throughout most of the year. While a good wetsuit is adequate, dry suits provide more comfort underwater, although the dangers of over-

heating must be considered when air temperatures exceed 30°C (85°F).

Galápagos Sub-Aqua, on Avenida Charles Darwin at Puerto Ayora (E-MAIL subaqaua@ga.pro.ec) offers a full range of diving services, including introductory diving, full certificate courses, daily and live-aboard diving tours and full equipment rental. Prices from US$75 per day for introductory diving, with two boat dives, to first-class, one-week, live-aboard diving tours for up to US$1,560. **Scuba Iguana** E-MAIL jgallar @ga.pro.ec, based at Hotel Galápagos operates similar courses and dive trips. Both organizations are highly recommended. Many cruise boats also carry diving equipment on board.

When to Go

The high season in the Galápagos is mid-June to end-August, December to mid-January and around Easter Week. But these tourist periods are dictated more by vacation opportunities than by climate. In fact, the warmest months are December to April. If you like snorkeling or diving these two months are the most pleasant time of year to visit. The water is warm, the sea is calm and the air tends to be clear, even though this is theoretically the wet season. In May the sea is still calm, but getting cooler. By July the weather has become almost cold, and snorkeling isn't pleasant without a wetsuit. In August the sea tends to be rough and the weather becomes misty until October. The coldest month is September, when many boats stay in dock and many Galapagueños go on vacation. The weather in the Galápagos is just as fickle as it is in most other places in the world and you can be lucky or unlucky any time of year. In short, the Galápagos Islands are a year-round destination.

How to Get There

Most believe it's not worth trying to save money buying an inexpensive passage from Guayaquil. Cargo boats, military boats and expensive cruise ships make the crossing, but never on a schedule. If you have an aversion to flying, your best plan is to check with shipping agents in Guayaquil or go to the harbor and ask the port *capitano* if there's a boat about to head off to the islands. M/V *Piquero* leaves on 25th of each month, or thereabouts. More information on this tramp steamer can be obtained from Johnny Franco ☎ (04) 360779 FAX (04) 450441. The crossing takes three-and-a-half days and costs US$150, one way. Passengers are advised to bring their own rations.

The only airlines flying to the Galápagos are Ecuador's national carriers, TAME (Transportes Aeros Militares Equatorianos) and SAN-SAETA. TAME flies from Quito to Baltra airport via Guayaquil every day except Sundays in the low season. Flights leave Quito at 8:30 AM and stopover in Guayaquil before the 90-minute flight to the Galápagos. SAN-SAETA flights have a similar schedule with a stopover in Guayaquil, but their final destination is San Cristóbal. If you're joining a cruise, make sure you fly to the island from which your boat will depart.

The cost of a Quito-Galápagos-Quito ticket on either airline is US$378. In the low season (January 16 to June 14, and September 1 to November 30) it's US$323. You can also fly from Guayaquil at a reduced price or depart Quito and end your journey in Guayaquil. Prices are subject to change and are expected to go up by about 10% each year. Student discounts are available with an international Student ID card. Less expensive fares can be obtained in some countries if the Galápagos leg is added on to your ticket to Ecuador.

Flights to the islands are often overbooked, so you should arrive at the airport at least an hour before departure. On the other hand, if agents haven't sold all their seats, it could be possible to buy a ticket on the day of departure. Tuesdays are said to be best for same-day ticket purchases.

If you are on a tour, your boat's representative will meet you when you arrive at Baltra. He or she will then make sure you board your boat, either the port in Baltra or at Puerto Ayora. If you are traveling independently you must immediately buy a bus ticket from the counter inside the terminal. The bus will take you to the ferry to Santa Cruz. Another bus carries you on to Puerto Ayora. The whole complicated procedure takes about two hours and costs about US$4. On departure, the procedure is reversed, with buses leaving Puerto Ayora or from your hotel at 7:30 AM to enable you to catch flights from Baltra that leave about 11:30 AM. Arrangements on San Cristóbal are much simpler since the airport is a 10-minute walk from the town of Puerto Baquerizo Moreno. At either place, make sure you reconfirm your return ticket at least two days ahead.

Plant life on Floreana Island.

ECUADOR
AMAZON
EXPÉDITIONS

Travelers' Tips

CLIMATE

Given its location straddling the equator, one might expect Ecuador's climate to be constantly hot with no seasons. Up to a point this is true. The coast and the eastern rainforests of the Oriente are swelteringly hot throughout the year. But each of the four major geographical regions has its own climatic conditions with wet and a dry seasons. The higher you get the cooler it becomes, with the mountains getting very cold above 5,000 m (16,665 ft). The slopes of Mt. Cayambe, which lies on the equator, is the only place in the world where the latitude and the temperature are both 0°C (32°F).

The climate in Quito and the rest of the highlands is spring-like with pleasantly warm days around 20°C (68°F) throughout the year and slightly chilly nights. "Sometimes it's sunny and cloudy," it is said. "The rest of the time it's cloudy and sunny." Rainfall averages about 12 cm (47inches) each month except in the drier months of June to August. The western areas of the sierra are affected by weather patterns in the Amazon basin and these months tend to be wet. Around the third week in December there's usually a break of fine weather throughout the sierra, with little rain.

On the coast, daytime temperatures range from about 25°C (75°F) to 31°C (88°F) with humidity averaging 60%. From January to June, when rainfall is about 20 cm (79 inches) per month, there are regular heavy showers followed by clear skies. The rest of the year is dry, but cooler and often overcast. Water temperatures are higher during the rainy months.

Temperatures in the Galápagos Islands are similar to those on the coast, though the islands are cooler than the coast between August and November when a damp mist, the *garuha*, descends over the islands and temperatures drop to about 18°C (65°F). The wettest months on the islands are between January and April, though rain falls much less than on the mainland, and the sea is pleasantly warm.

The rainforests of the Oriente are always hot and usually wet. Daytime temperatures reach 33°C (91°F) and monthly rainfall averages about 35 cm (14 inches). June through August are the wettest and hottest months. It rains almost every day in the rainforest, usually in the afternoon. Humidity can exceed 70%.

Generally, Ecuador has a moderate, though variable and localized climate, so that at any time of year, some parts of the country will be enjoying good weather while somewhere else it will be raining. Sometimes it rains more in the dry season than it does in wet season.

Every few years the weather patterns are violently disrupted by the phenomenon of El Niño (baby boy), so named because warm currents come down from the north around Christmas time. When these waters are warmer or stay longer than usual there is increased rainfall, floods and even tidal waves. The 1982 and 1983 El Niño caused extensive destruction to the western lowlands and to the ecosystems of the Galápagos Islands.

WHEN TO GO

Any time of year is a good time to visit Ecuador, but for each region some months are better than others.

December to June are the best months for the Galápagos Islands because the weather is warm and the sea tends to be calm. Although this is wet season, skies are generally clear except during downpours. March and April are often the very best months.

PREVIOUS PAGES: Paddling through the backwaters LEFT in a dugout canoe, one of the great rainforest experiences. A Cuencan gentleman RIGHT. OPPOSITE: Catedral de la Immaculada in Cuenca, sporting its curvacious cupolas. ABOVE: Backstreets of a town in the western lowlands.

During the dry season in the Galápagos, from July to November, the weather tends towards overcast and the sea is just below pleasant swimming temperatures. The worst months can be August and September, when temperatures tend to be quite cool and waters rough. Because of overseas vacation periods, the busiest tourist seasons in the Galápagos are around Christmas and in July and August.

On the coast, the warm, but wetter months from January to April are popular with Ecuadorians and Colombians, who take vacations during this period. Many gringos visit the coast during their own peak vacation periods from June to August. For the Oriente, it's probably wise to avoid the wettest and hottest months from June to August. In the Sierra the climate is pleasant throughout the year.

If you want your visit to coincide with popular festivals, see FESTIVE FLINGS, page 35, in YOUR CHOICE. December is the best time for seeing bullfights in Quito.

VISAS

A passport valid for at least six months from your arrival date is all that is usually required to enter Ecuador. Citizens of some countries should obtain a visa in advance from their local Ecuadorian consulate. The list of these countries varies according to diplomatic relations, but at time of writing they include France, China, Guatemala, Cuba, Costa Rica, Vietnam, North and South Korea.

The normal tourist entry visa obtained from immigration on entry is good for 90 days. If you want to stay longer, check with your local Ecuadorian consulate before traveling. If you are only given one or two months on entry you will be able to extend your visa up to 90 days at the Immigration Office in Quito: Oficina de Migración, Amazonas 2639 and Republica, third floor, which is open from 8 AM to 12:30 PM on weekdays. Occasionally visitors are required to show evidence of financial independence when they arrive, either in the form of a return ticket and/or sufficient funds to support themselves during their stay at the rate of US$20 per day.

VACCINATIONS AND HEALTH

Check with your doctor or a travel clinic about vaccinations well before starting your journey. Several transmittable diseases and conditions occur in Ecuador, especially in rural areas. Vaccinations for yellow fever,

Hepatitis A, polio, rabies, tetanus and typhoid are usually recommended. The risk of cholera is low enough that vaccination isn't usually prescribed.

Most doctors also advise a course of malaria tablets if you will be on the coast or in the rainforest. If you are only going to the highlands you don't need to worry about malaria pills because malaria-carrying mosquitoes don't live above 2,500 m (8,330 ft). Mosquitoes aren't a problem on the Galápagos Islands, especially on a cruise.

The best precaution against malaria is to prevent mosquitoes from biting in the first place. When mosquitoes are about, particularly between dusk and dawn, wear long trousers, socks and a long-sleeved shirt. Apply repellent to exposed areas of skin, not forgetting the ears, and rub some in your hair. Sleep under a mosquito net if your room isn't sealed against mosquitoes.

Malaria is a serious illness and it isn't worth being casual about preventative precautions. On a recent trip down the coast together, a friend didn't bother much with repellent, nor was he taking anti-malaria pills. Overnight he became very ill with a high fever and had to be rushed to hospital, where he was put on an intravenous drip. If you develop a fever and flu-like symptoms after returning from a malarial region, you need to be aware of the possibility of a malaria infection and should see a doctor as soon as possible.

Contaminated food and water are another common source of disease in tropical countries. Drink only bottled water and make sure the seal has not been broken. Avoid drinks that come in little plastic bags. If you are going to be traveling around extensively, bring water-purifying iodine tablets in case bottled water isn't available. Avoid ice cubes, which are usually made from unpurified water, and use bottled water for brushing your teeth. Unless you are eating in a smart hotel, avoid salads and uncooked vegetables and confine yourself to peelable fruits, of which there are many in Ecuador. Make sure eggs are well cooked.

However careful you are, stomach upsets are a natural hazard of traveling; studies have shown that diarrhea occurs among 40% to 50% of overseas travelers. Come prepared with anti-diarrhea pills, such as Imodium or Pepto-Bismol, and toilet paper. If the nasties strike, rest plenty, drink plenty of liquids, such as herbal tea or soda water, and don't eat much, except yogurt and a some dry bread or toast. You should recover in a day or two.

Another health hazard of travel in Ecuador is heat exhaustion and sunburn. With a little common sense these conditions are easily avoided. Don't over exert yourself, drink plenty of fluids, stay in the shade and use sun block.

Many people, regardless of age or fitness, suffer from mild altitude or mountain sickness, even in Quito, at 2,850 m (9,500 ft), in the form of shortness of breath, headaches and general lassitude. This best way to avoid these symptoms is to drink plenty of water, take aspirin for the headache, moderate or eliminate alcohol and tobacco intake, breath deeply and slow down. You should acclimatize in two or three days. The traditional and effective Andean remedy for mountain sickness is to make a tea by boiling coca plant leaves (the basis of cocaine)

OPPOSITE: Like their former Spanish rulers, the Ecuadorians enjoy the thrill of bullfighting. ABOVE: Substantial fare at Latacunga market.

and drinking it through a straw. The leaves can be bought from the Indian ladies on the streets of the Old Town in Quito.

At higher altitudes climbers may suffer more acute symptoms such as loss of appetite, inability to sleep, rapid pulse and irregular breathing. In extreme cases thinking and judgment may become impaired and, very rarely, a potentially fatal complication called high altitude pulmonary edema, caused by fluid build-up in the lungs, can occur. Oxygen intake and descent to lower altitudes relieve the symptoms.

Wherever you are traveling, it is sensible to pack a small medical kit. If you are on medication, bring enough to last your stay. Bring bandages, gauze, tape, scissors, topical antibiotic ointment to prevent infection of minor wounds, and an anti-inflammatory drug such as aspirin. An antihistamine relieves itching from insect bites, while a steroid cream is helpful in treating skin rashes or relieving sunburn. Ask your doctor about antibiotics and also ask about medications for malaria, such as quinine sulfate or Fansidar.

Don't forget to bring enough strong sun block because the sun's rays are very powerful close at the equator. For the same reason it is also important to wear a good pair of sunglasses, especially in the mountains As for those stomach pills, don't leave home without them.

HOW TO GET THERE

Information about flights, fares and tours to Ecuador can be obtained from specialist South American travel operators in the United States and most European countries. Some of these operators also have information about specialist tours, such as adventure travel, climbing or bird watching.

The following operators are recommended in the United Kingdom:

Journey Latin America ☎ 0181 7478315 FAX 0181 7421312, 14–16 Devonshire Road, Chiswick, London W4 2HD deals in tickets and tours.

Hayes and Jarvis ☎ 0181-748-9976 Hayes House, 152 Kings Street, Hammersmith, London W6 OQU.

Worldwide Journeys and Expeditions ☎ 0171 381-8638, 8 Comeragh Road, London W14 9H.

Travel South America ☎ 01904 704443, The White House, Chantry Lane, Bishopthorpe, York YO2 1QF.

Penelope Kellie Worldwide Yacht Charter and Tours ☎ 01962 779317 FAX 01962 779458, Steeple Cottage, Easton, Winchester SO21 1HE.

Leading South American travel operators in the United States include:

Adventure Discoveries International ☎/FAX (615) 356-8731 E-MAIL Trekfun@aol.com, PO Box 92188, Nashville, TN 37209, USA.

Lost World Adventures ☎ 1 404 373-5820 FAX 1 404 377-1902 E-MAIL info@lostworldadventures.com, 220 Second Avenue, Decatur, GA 30030, USA.

Wilderness Travel ☎ (510) 558-2488 FAX (510) 558-2489, 1102 Ninth Street, Berkley, CA 94710, USA.

Wildland Adventures ☎ (206) 365-0686 FAX (206) 363-6615, 3516 NE 155th Street, Seattle, WA 98155, USA.

Information about travel in Ecuador can also be obtained from Ecuadorian embassies and consulates. These include:

In Canada ☎ (613) 563-8206 FAX (613) 235-5776

In France ☎ 01 45 61 10 21 FAX 01 42 89 22 09

In Germany ☎ 228 352544 FAX (02) 563697

In Great Britain ☎ 0171 584-1367 FAX 0171 823-9701

In Switzerland ☎ 131 351-1755 FAX 131 351-2771

In United States ☎ (202) 234-7200 FAX (202) 667-3482

Quito's Aeropuerto Mariscal Sucre is the gateway to Ecuador for almost all international travelers and tourists. See QUITO, page 66, for details of international airlines with service to Quito. Otherwise, visitors fly into the country's second international airport at Guayaquil, especially those going straight on to the Galápagos Islands. Few people arrive by boat these days unless they will be cruising in a yacht or working their passage on a cargo boat.

Backpackers traveling overland through South America enter Ecuador either from Columbia, crossing to Tulcán, or from Peru to Huaquillas or Macará. Minibuses, taxis and trucks run between border points for a small fee and the immigrations offices in both countries are open seven days a week during office hours. There are frequent buses to and from both sides of both borders (see page 256).

CAR RENTAL

Very few overseas visitors arrive in Ecuador by car though this may change when the coastal road from Colombia is finished. Many Colombians drive into Ecuador for their vacations, where they find prices much lower.

Some overseas visitors rent cars when they get to Ecuador and are prepared to put up with poor roads, bad signs and erratic driving. The big international car rental companies, such as Budget, Avis and Hertz, have offices in Quito and Guayaquil, and Hertz also has an office in Cuenca. Rental prices are no less than Europe and the United States though local Ecuadorian car rental companies are less expensive than the international ones.

A valid driver's license and a credit card is usually all that is required to rent a car, though I have heard that some companies insist on an international license. Look carefully at your rental agreement to see whether mileage is included and the amount of the insurance deductible.

EMBASSIES AND CONSULATES

If you get into serious trouble in Ecuador you will need your embassy or consulate. Also, if you are going to be in the country a while, or take part in adventurous activities, it's a good idea to register with your consulate and leave photocopies of your passport so they can issue you a new one quickly.

The following addresses of embassies in Quito may be of use:

American Embassy ✆ (02) 562890 FAX (02) 502052, Patria and 12 de Octubre.

British Embassy ✆ (02) 560670 FAX (02) 560730, González Suárez 111 and 12 de Octubre.

Canadian Embassy ✆ (02) 564795 FAX (02) 503108, Avenida 6 de Diciembre 2816 and James Orton.

German Embassy ✆ (02) 225660 FAX (02) 563697, Edificio Banco Consolidado, Sixth Floor, Patria and 9 de Octubre.

French Embassy, ✆ (02) 560789 FAX (02) 566424, General Plaza 107 and Patria.

Dutch Embassy ✆ (02) 567606, Edificio Banco BHU, 9 de Octubre and Orellana.

MONEY

In addition to keeping safe and healthy, handling money is a concern in a strange land. The best advice for Ecuador is to bring both United States dollars in cash and travelers' checks. You will have no difficulties in changing these into sucres in most towns. In remote areas, however, make sure you have enough local currency. Cash machines are becoming increasingly common in the big cities, so if you have a cash card and money in your bank back home, you will be able to withdraw sucres in Ecuador. This is usually the easiest way to change money.

The exchange rate between the United States dollar and other hard currencies with the sucre is very variable. In 1988 the dollar was worth about 500 sucres but nine years later, in 1997, it was worth seven times that amount: 3,500 sucres. Note that the better hotels, restaurants and shops accept United States dollars. Also note that the better hotels add 10% tax and 10% service charge to your bill.

SECURITY

Although Ecuador is considered to be the safest South American country for traveling it is important to exercise caution and watch your valuables at all times. Snatch thieves operating in crowded streets and markets are the most common criminals. Often they work in pairs, one of which distracts you, while the other relieves you of your bag, your camera and your watch. If a woman carrying a baby trips up in front of you in a market, watch your back. Other scams include contrived fights and pretend drunks.

In one classic scam, "Misdirected Man" gets on a bus carrying lots of bags and looking all confused. He sits next to you, claiming it's his seat. Then he realizes he's on the wrong bus. He jumps up and off the bus in hurry, taking his and one of your bags with him.

Also watch out for people who claim to be plain-clothes policemen. This is often just an excuse for some form of extortion. If they ask you to get in a car because they want your help in investigating a crime, or they claim you've been seen talking to drug dealers, do not do so in any circumstances. Instead, insist that they go with you on foot to the police station. Chances are they are hassling you, hoping you'll give them some money to go away.

Although they are generally safe and honest, you might encounter a troublesome taxi driver. A friend of mine was driven to remote spot by a taxi driver and threatened with a knife. He stunned the driver with a karate chop to the neck. He dragged the driver out of the taxi, and then drove the cab back to central Quito. Similar stories don't usually have such an ending. Taking taxis late at night, especially if you are alone and have had a few drinks, can be hazardous. For safety, pick up a cab from a stand outside one of the better hotels. If you don't like the look of a driver don't get in the cab.

Common sense is your best weapon in any city. The first rule is to avoid dangerous neighborhoods, especially with valuables. In Quito, the narrow market street of Ipiales near the Church of San Francisco in the Old Town is notorious for its pickpockets, as is 24 de Mayo for general vice and danger. The roads leading up to the Virgin Statue on the hill known as El Panecillo (Little Bread Roll) in the old town is known for assault and robbery. The Terminal Terrestre bus station is a hangout for petty thieves. And stay out of all city parks after dark, especially Carolina and Ejido.

Always carry a copy of your passport. Police sometimes make spot identification checks.

GETTING AROUND

Unless you are on an organized tour where transport is arranged, you will almost certainly use buses to get around. Squashed in a little seat in a crowded bus, on a dangerous mountain road, with soft porn on the video and a driver who seems to be falling asleep might not be everybody's idea of fun. But you have to get used to it: traveling by bus to remote areas is the price of enjoying Ecuador to its fullest.

There are a number of private bus companies and you will soon find that some are better than others. Recommended companies include **Reina del Camino** (Queen of the Road), which has a good safety record and fast buses; **Coaltur**, good for service from Quito to Guayaquil and the coast; **Pan-American** (especially for night buses); and **Manglaralto** for coastal services. **Trans Loja** has the worst safety record in Ecuador. Instead use **Cooperativo Viajeros** for journeys between Cuenca and Loja.

A word of warning about taking buses, especially the smaller ones in Quito: they are often so crowded that if you get stuck in the back you won't be able to get out when you want to. And the driver will not wait as you push your way to the door.

As an alternative to buses, some intrepid souls bring bikes to Ecuador. Cyclists enjoy biking in the mountains though the coastal areas are said to be rather uninteresting. Mountain bikers from all over the country bring their bikes to Jefferson in Quito, the best bicycle mechanic in Ecuador, at Bici Sport on Avenida 6 de Diciembre, out past the stadium in Quito.

Finding Your Way

Ecuadorian addresses refer to the nearest intersection. For example the main EMETEL office in Quito new town is given as Avenida 10 de Agosto and (y) Avenida Cristóbal Colón, which means that it is on or near the intersection between these two streets.

Street numbers are sometimes included in the address, as in Amazonas 1646 and Orellana for the British Council. Sometimes there are a number of streets with the same name in an address, which it makes it difficult to find the location on a map. Often only the last name is given, without the first name, so that a street given as Carrión could be Baltazar Carrión, Eudoro Carrión, Jerónimo Carrión, José Carrión, Manuel Carrión, Martín Carrión or Miguel Carrión.

The best way of finding your way around Quito is to buy the pocket-sized Quito book of street maps by Nelson Gómez called *Guia Informativa de Quito*. It has an A–Z index of street names referenced to excellent maps.

The best general map of the country is the **Map of Ecuador** (No. 278) 1:1,000,000, published by International Travel Maps, 345 West Broadway, Vancouver, BC, Canada. These maps are available from better map sellers overseas, some bookshops in Quito and from the South America Explorers Club (see page 70).

ACCOMMODATION

There is accommodation in Ecuador to suit all pockets, from the true budget traveler to the most prosperous vacationer. Obviously the less expensive the lodging (and there are some very inexpensive places) the less likely a reservation and many of these places don't even own a phone, let alone a fax machine. Don't despair. Except over public holidays, chances are that even these more upmarket hostelries will have a bed or two.

RESTAURANTS

Unless you're planning dinner for a dozen, or you want a table in the most elite of restaurants, and you speak fluent Spanish, you wouldn't consider phoning for a reservation. Besides, many of the best and most interesting places, won't have a number to offer you. In Ecuador, you take our recommendations, or follow your nose and choose a spot that looks popular. If you have to wait, grab a beer and enjoy the atmosphere.

COMMUNICATIONS

Fifty years ago writer Christopher Isherwood described the Ecuadorian telephone

system as "about as reliable as roulette." Remarkably the system isn't much better today. If you are staying at an expensive hotel you should have no problem making international calls, though the calls are heavily surcharged.

Otherwise you have to go to the local office of the national telephone company, EMETEL. The system is that you line up to give the number you want to call to an official behind a desk, stating how long you want to speak. They give you a piece of paper with the price of the telephone call, which you pay

OPPOSITE: Quito residents on Avenida Amazonas. ABOVE: The ubiquitous bus connects some of the remote villages. This one goes to Guamote, near Ríobamba.

to another official. You then wait until an operator gets around to dialing your number. You are then directed to a telephone cubicle. When the operator hears your overseas number ringing he or she will alert you to pick up the telephone in the cubicle.

If the call is answered at the other end, that's fine: you can speak for the amount of time you've paid for. If you speak for longer than the pre-paid time, your call will be cut off mid-sentence. But if there is no answer, you have to line up again to get your money back. And if you want to try another number or the same number again, you have to repeat the process. When dealing with the EMETEL officials it helps if you speak some Spanish.

The system seems to vary from EMETEL office to office. Some offices accept phone cards or calling cards, some charge extra for them, and some will not accept them at all. Calls within Ecuador can be made through an operator, or you can buy tokens for direct dialing. There are few public phones in the cities, though some shops will allow you to make local calls. Most EMETEL offices in the big cities have facilities for sending and receiving faxes. They are generally open from 8 AM to 10 PM, seven days a week.

Mail and small parcels (up to two kilograms or five pounds) can be sent from any post office, though it's advisable to check that your stamps are properly postmarked since officials have been known to steam off unmarked stamps. Bigger parcels should be send from the post offices at Ulloa and Daválos in Quito.

You can receive *post restante* mail at Lista de Correos, Correos Central, Quito. Your mail will be filed under whichever name is printed in capitals. American Express customers can also receive mail care of American Express, Apartado 2605, Quito. The office is in the Ecuadorian Tours building on Amazonas 339.

TOURIST INFORMATION

The CETUR tourist offices aren't particularly helpful for individual travelers. This organization's role seems to be keeping an eye on Ecuadorian tourism in general rather than answering individual tourists' specific needs. You are more likely to get better and more relevant information from private tour companies. Fellow travelers are also good sources of information, and comment books, at hostels, cafés and restaurant often have valuable tips as well as hilarious stories. Another good source of travel tips are the trip reports filed by members of the South America Explorers Club in Quito (see page 70). The staff of the club is well-informed about most aspects of Ecuador.

ETIQUETTE

Ecuadorians are generally polite and courteous people and they appreciate these qualities in others. They are also curious about visitors' views about their country, and even though they might modestly demur, they are delighted to hear praise of its finer aspects. Some Ecuadorians feel that their country is rather small and remote and are interested in news and views from the wider world.

Hand shaking is an important part of the social ritual. Shake hands when you meet somebody for the first time or when you meet an old friend. Shake hands again when you say good-bye. A greetings kiss is usually a single peck on the right cheek.

Ecuadorians are proud of their families and will be interested in yours. Family talk and family photos are always a good conversational starting point. If you are invited to an Ecuadorian house a small gift will be appreciated.

Ecuadorians tend to dress smartly and believed that how well you dress is a measure of how importantly you are treating the occasion. Try to wear a suit when meeting with government officials.

A LITTLE LANGUAGE

A little Spanish goes a long way in Ecuador, even if it's just a few words. The next to last syllable in a word is always stressed, except for words ending in "r," "l" and "z" when the last syllable is stressed. For exceptional cases an accent is written over the vowel in the stressed syllable, as in *delegación* for delegation.

GREETINGS

Hola Hello (note the "h" is always mute)
Adiós Goodbye, though *Hasta luego* (see you later) and *Ciao* are less formal and often used.
Buenos dias Good morning (used from midnight to midday)
Buenas tardes Good afternoon (from midday to 6 PM)
Buenas noches Good evening/night (from 6 PM to midnight)
¿Cómo está? How are you? (formal)
¿Cómo estás? How are you? (informal)
Muy bien, gracias Very well, thank you
Yo me llamo… My name is
¿Como se llama Usted? What is your name?
Mucho gusto conocerlo Pleased to meet you.
¿Puede Usted ayudarme? Can you help me?
¡Ayúdarme! Help!
Por favor Please
Gracias Thank you
De nada It's nothing, you're welcome
Con mucho gusto It's a pleasure
¿De dónde es usted? Where do you come from?
¿Habla inglés? Do you speak English?
No comprendo I don't understand
No hablo español I don't speak Spanish
Lo siento I'm sorry
Puede repetir mas despacio por favor Please repeat more slowly
Perdone Excuse me
¿Como? How, come again
¿Dónde está/están…? Where is/are…?

SOME USEFUL WORDS

Sí Yes
No No
Bueno Good
Malo Bad
Grande Big
Pequeño Small
Caliente Hot
Frio Cold
Bien Well
Bastante Enough
Izquierda (ees-key-here-dah) Left
Derecha Right
Todo recto Straight ahead
Cerca Near
Lejos (leh-hohs) Far
Muy Very
Más More
Menos Less
Arriba Up
Abajo Down

A pickup truck at Calderón, a village well-known for making decorations out of bread dough.

Servicios toilet
¿Dónde? Where?
¿Qué? What?
¿Cuándo? When?
¿Por qué? Why?
Aqui Here
Allí There
Hoy Today
Abierto Open
Cerrado Closed
Mañana Tomorrow
La Mañana Morning
Entrada Entrance
Salida Exit
Banco Bank
Aeropuerto Airport
Ciudad City
Pueblo Town or village

HOTEL BASICS

Una Habitación Room
Habitación individual Single room
Habitación doble Double room
¿Hay una habitación libre? Do you have a room?
Cabaña Cabin
Con dos camas With two beds
Con baño With bath
Ducha Shower
Abanico Fan
Aire acondicionado Air-conditioned
Llave Key

RESTAURANT BASICS

Comedor Informal local restaurant
Chifa Chinese restaurant
Cantina Canteen, drinking establishment
Barra Bar
Borracho/a Drunk
Una mesa A table
Camarero/a Waiter/waitress
La cerveza Beer
El vino blanco White wine ("v" is pronounced "b")
El vino tinto Red wine
Un vaso A glass
Una botella (boh-tey-yah) A bottle
El té Tea
El café Coffee
Con leche With milk
El azúcar Sugar
El Agua mineral Mineral water
Sin gas/con gas Still/sparkling
La carta Menu
¿Que va tomar? What will you eat?
Buen provecho Have a good meal
El desayuno Breakfast
La comida/el almuerzo Lunch
La cena Dinner
Un cuchillo A knife
Un tenedor A fork
Una cuchara A spoon
El plato del dia Dish of the day
La sopa Soup
El pan Bread
Las tostadas Toast
La mantequilla Butter
El pollo Chicken
Los mariscos Seafood
Las gambas Prawns
El pescado Fish
Ceviche Fish or shellfish marinated in lemon juice and herbs
La carne Meat
La ternera Beef
El chorizo Sausage
Herbido Boiled
Al horno baked
Asado/ornado Roast
Frito Fried
El huevo (oo-eh-voh) Egg
Soy vegetariano/a I'm a vegetarian
La menestra Vegetable stew
Las patatas Potatoes
Arroz Rice
La cebolla Onion
La sal Salt
La salsa Sauce
El postre Dessert
El Queso Cheese
La Fruta Fruit
La Manzana Apple
El Helado ice cream
La cuenta por favor The bill, please

SHOPPING BASICS

Supermacado Supermarket
Tienda Shop, store
¿Que desea? What would you like?
Quiero queso I want some cheese
Aqui tiene Here it is
Tambien galletas Also some biscuits
¿Algo mas? Anything more?

Nada mas No more
¿Cuanto es? How much is (the bill)?

Numbers

0 *cero*
1 *uno*
2 *dos*
3 *tres*
4 *cuatro*
5 *cinco*
6 *seis*
7 *siete*
8 *ocho*
9 *nueve*
10 *diez*
11 *once*
12 *doce*
13 *trece*
14 *catorce*
15 *quince*
16 *dieciseis*
17 *diecisiete*
18 *dieciocho*
19 *diecinueve*
20 *veinte*
21 *veintiuno*
22 *veintidós*
30 *trienta*
40 *cuarenta*
50 *cincuenta*
60 *sesenta*
70 *setenta*
80 *ochenta*
90 *noventa*
100 *cien*
101 *ciento uno*
102 *ciento dos*
200 *doscientos*
300 *trescientos*
400 *cuatrocientos*
500 *quinientos*
600 *seiscientos*
700 *setecientos*
800 *ochocientos*
900 *novecientos*
1,000 *mil*
100,000 *cien mil*
1,000,000 *un millón*

Time

Un minuto One minute
Una hora One hour
Qué hora es? What time is it?
Son las tres It is three o'clock
Mediodía Noon
Medianoche Midnight
Domingo Sunday
Lunes Monday
Martes Tuesday
Miércoles Wednesday

Jueves Thursday
Viernes Friday
Sábado Saturday
Enero January
Febrero February
Marzo March
Abril April
Mayo May
Junio June
Julio July
Agosto August
Septiembre September
Octubre October
Noviembre November
Diciembre December

ABOVE: Graffiti is just about everywhere in most Ecuadorian cities.

Recommended Reading

ANGERMEYER, JOHANNA, *My Father's Island*, Penguin Books, London, 1989.

BOX, BEN (editor), *The South American Handbook*, Footprint Handbooks, Bath, UK, 1996.

CONSTANT, PIERRE, *The Galápagos Islands*, Odyssey, Hong Kong, 1995.

CUVI, PABLO, *Travels along the Coast*, Dinediciones, Quito, 1996.

DESMOND, ADRIAN, and MOORE, JAMES, *Darwin*, Michael Joseph Ltd., London, 1991.

DAVIES, DAVID, *The Centenarians of the Andes*, UK, 1995.

DESCOLA, PHILIPPE, *The Spears of Twilight: Life and Death in the Amazon Jungle*, Harper Collins, 1996.

ELIADE, MIRCEA, *Shamanism: Archaic Techniques of Ecstasy*, Penguin Books, London, 1989.

GOMEZ, NELSON, *Guia Informativa de Quito*, authorized by Instituto Geográfico Militar, Quito, 1996.

GOMEZ, NELSON, *The Pocket Guide to Ecuador*, Quito.

HARNER, MICHAEL, J., *The Jivaro; People of the Sacred Waterfall*, University of California Press Ltd., 1984.

HARRIS, MICHAEL, *A Field Guide to the Birds of the Galápagos*, Collins, UK, 1992.

HEMMING, JOHN, *The Conquest of the Incas*, Penguin, London, 1987.

HICKMAN, JOHN, *The Enchanted Islands; The Galápagos Discovered*, Anthony Nelson, Oswestry, England, 1985, and Ediciones Libri Mundi, Quito, 1991.

HILTY, STEVEN L., and BROWN, WILLIAM, *A Guide to the Birds of Colombia*, Princeton University Press, USA, 1986.

KANE, JOE, *Savages*, Alfred A. Knopf, Inc., New York, 1995, and Pan Books, London, 1997.

MEISCH, LYNN, *Otavalo: Weaving, Costume and the Market*, Libri Mundi, Quito, 1987.

MILLER, TOM, *The Panama Hat Trail: A Journey from South America*, Abacus, 1988.

MOOREHEAD, ALAN, *Darwin and The Beagle*, Harper & Row, 1969 and Penguin 1971.

PERROTTET, TONY (editor), *Insight Guides: Ecuador*, APA Publications, Hong Kong, 1996.

POOLE, RICHARD, *The Inca Smiled: The Growing Pains of an Aid Worker in Ecuador*, Oxford One World, 1993.

RACHOWIECKI, ROB, *Ecuador & The Galápagos Islands*, Lonely Planet Publications, Victoria, Australia, 1997.

RACHOWIECKI, ROB, et al., *Climbing & Hiking in Ecuador*, Bradt Publication, UK, Fourth Edition, 1997.

SNAILHAM, RICHARD, *Sangay Survived: The Story of the Ecuadorian Volcano Disaster*, Hutchinson, London, 1978.

THOMSEN, MORITZ, *Living Poor*, Eland, London, 1989.

TREHERNE, JOHN, *The Galápagos Affair*, Jonathan Cape, London, 1983.

UNTERMAN, KATHERINE R. (editor), *Let's Go: The Budget Guide to Ecuador & the Galápagos Islands*, St. Martin's Press, New York, 1997.

WEINER, JONATHAN, *The Beak of the Finch*, Jonathan Cape Ltd, London, 1994, and Vintage, London, 1995.

WESCHE, ROLF, et al., *The Ecotourist's Guide to the Ecuadorian Amazon, Napo Province*, Cepeige, Quito, 1995.

WHITE, MICHAEL, and GRIBBIN, JOHN, *Darwin: A Life in Science*, Simon & Schuster, London, 1995.

WHYMPER, EDWARD, *Travels Amongst the Great Andes of the Equator*, originally published in 1891, reprinted by Peregrine Books, UK, 1990.

Quick Reference A–Z Guide to Places and Topics of Interest with Listed Accommodation, Restaurants and Useful Telephone Numbers

C

Q